Best Sports Stories 1989

Edited and Published by

The Sporting News

Editor/Best Sports Stories 1989
DAVE SLOAN

President and Chief Executive Officer
RICHARD WATERS

Editor
TOM BARNIDGE

Director of Books and Periodicals
RON SMITH

Published in the United States by THE SPORTING NEWS Publishing Co., 1212 North Lindbergh Boulevard, St. Louis, Missouri 63132.

Library of Congress Catalog Card Number: 45-35124

ISSN: 0067-6292
ISBN: 0-89204-333-4
10 9 8 7 6 5 4 3 2 1

First Edition

KENNEDY

Table of Contents

The Prize-Winning Stories

Other Stories

The Prize-Winning Photographs

Other Photographs

The Prize-Winning Color Photograph
Land of the Giants

by Dave Einsel of the Houston Chronicle. The winning color photograph, which appears on the back cover, shows National Football League referee Jerry Markbreit wading heroically into a tugging match between Houston's William Fuller and Denver's Ken Lanier (76). This photograph is funny and flawlessly composed, a winning formula in anybody's book. Copyright © 1988, the Houston Chronicle.

PREFACE

California, home to more Americans than any other state, was the unqualified leader in 1988 sports championships. Baseball, basketball, football—three of the four major sports champions were based on the West Coast.

The Los Angeles Dodgers, heavy underdogs after finishing 17 games behind San Francisco in the National League's 1987 West Division race, overcame huge odds to win their fifth World Series championship since moving west from Brooklyn in 1958. The Dodgers stole the Los Angeles spotlight from the National Basketball Association's Lakers, who a few months earlier had become the first NBA team in 19 years to successfully defend a league crown. The state's third title was produced by the National Football League's San Francisco 49ers, who defeated the Cincinnati Bengals, 20-16, in Super Bowl XXIII.

Although California could not lay claim to the National Hockey League's finest team—that distinction belonged to Edmonton for the fourth time in five years—it became the new home of the game's greatest player.

In one of the biggest trades in the history of professional sports, the league-champion Oilers traded eight-time Most Valuable Player Wayne Gretzky to the Los Angeles Kings in August in a blockbuster deal that included four other players, three first-round draft choices and more than $10 million.

The biggest sports events of the year, however, were staged in foreign countries. The Olympic spotlight focused on Calgary, Alberta, for the 1988 Winter Games and then moved to Seoul, South Korea, for the wild and action-packed Summer Games. There was controversy, such as the banishment of Canadian sprinter Ben Johnson for drug use, and there was joy. Americans such as Jackie Joyner-Kersee, Florence Griffith-Joyner, Matt Biondi, Janet Evans, Greg Louganis, Bonnie Blair and Brian Boitano captured the hearts of Americans with their medal-winning performances.

Wherever the action, *they* were there. "They" refers to the men and women who put as much effort into their pursuit of the perfect story or picture as athletes put into their search for excellence. The competition is fierce and the results gratifying. Those who chronicled the 1988 sports world for newspapers and magazines throughout the country continued to move toward the lofty goal of perfection, taking their readers behind the scenes for insight and perspective on the personalities and events that made the year memorable.

The Sporting News is proud to present a small sprinkling of those memories in the 45th edition of *Best Sports Stories*, the anthology that honors the year's top writers and photographers. TSN is editing and publishing its seventh edition of the anthology, which traces its roots to 1944 and the efforts of Irving Marsh and Edward Ehre. The contest to select winners and contributors attracted hundreds of newspaper and magazine entries. It was open to writers and photographers throughout the country and accepted only stories and pictures that were published in 1988. Serving as judges for the seventh straight year was a panel of five professors from the University of Missouri, home of one of the world's most-respected journalism education programs. They are:

Brian Brooks, associate professor of journalism at the University of Missouri and coordinator of the school's editing programs.

George Kennedy, associate dean of the University of Missouri School of Journalism.

Bill Kuykendall, associate professor and director of the University of Missouri photojournalism sequence and director of the International Pictures of the Year competition.

Daryl Moen, professor of journalism and director of the School of Journalism's Professional Programs.

Byron Scott, Meredith professor of journalism and director of the University of Missouri's service journalism program.

Those five judges can attest to the agonizing problems that arise when you sort through hundreds of creative, well-written stories in search of the *four* that deserve special recognition. Likewise, the selection process for *three* pictures. But, after painstakingly considering the merits of each entry, the judges chose the following winners, each of whom receives a $500 prize:

WRITING

Reporting	Eric Sondheimer, Doug Cress and Beth Barrett	Los Angeles Daily News
Feature	Sam Heys	Atlanta Journal-Constitution
Magazine	Howard Sinker	Minnesota Monthly
Commentary	Ron Borges	Boston Globe

PHOTOGRAPHY

Color	Dave Einsel	Houston Chronicle
B&W Action	Bernard Brault	La Presse
B&W Feature	Jerry Lodriguss	Philadelphia Inquirer

It also was difficult to weed the selection list to the choice stories that would appear in this book. By no means are the stories and photos that follow the winning selections losers. They are, rather, a tribute to the sports journalism profession, which seems to get stronger every year. All of the *Best Sports Stories* contributors are providing an entertaining look at the 1988 sports year, as seen through the eyes and lenses of those who were there.

Best Feature Story

Hills of Coal,
Feats of Clay

HIGH SCHOOL BASKETBALL

By *SAM HEYS*

From the Atlanta Journal-Constitution
Copyright © 1988, the Atlanta Journal-Constitution

The Farmer brothers learned their basketball on the side of a mountain. On a dusty, rocky patch of earth sprinkled with small black chunks of coal. Their shots were shadowed by an ugly, barren 40-foot-high cliff, left behind decades ago by a coal company that did a little strip mining and moved on.

Such "high walls" dot the landscape of eastern Kentucky, creating beneath them bits of flatland rarely big enough for a factory, but always big enough for basketball.

Richie and Russ Farmer played their basketball whenever they could: early summer mornings, days the wind gusted relentlessly through the mountains, by the light of the moon. They now play it for the vindication of Clay County.

For a county long on illiteracy and hard times and short on quality of life and high school graduates, the Farmer brothers and three other mountain boys are dishing out a little poetic justice. "Everybody thinks people from the mountains are dumb hicks, that we can't do anything," said Richie Farmer in thick mountain English. "But we can play basketball."

Indeed. Only one of its five starters is at least six feet tall—and he's only 6-foot-1—yet Clay County High School is ranked among the top 10 high school teams in America. For two years, they have been the best team in Kentucky, one of America's foremost hoops states, and their leader, Richie Farmer, is a lock to become Mr. Basketball in Kentucky at season's end.

But what the Farmers and their friends have done transcends county lines. They have uplifted an entire region: the mountains of eastern Kentucky, a pocket of isolation with little to cheer about.

Even its basketball, long the pride of the mountains, had hit hard times.

When Clay County won the state championship last year, it became the first mountain team to do so in 31 years. It did it by winning the Sweet Sixteen state tournament, which annually throws both large and small schools—Clay County has a senior class of 220—into a battle royal for the kingdom of Kentucky basketball.

Clay County coach Bobby Keith, an old mountain boy himself, put it in perspective at that time: "Sometimes people in the mountains have it a little bit harder than other people, and sometimes it's kind of hard to find enough things to be proud of. But this should take care of that for a while."

The Tigers are expected to give the mountains a second dose of pride this month by becoming the first team in 17 years to win back-to-back Sweet Sixteen titles. They had won 38 straight games against Kentucky teams going into the district tournament, and if they win this week's Region 13 tournament, they will enter the state tournament at Louisville on March 16 as the team to beat. They have been ranked No. 1 in Kentucky since November and are essentially the same team that won the state last year.

They are more than a team from the mountains, however; they are a mountain team. "When you talk about being a mountain team, people think of a team that tries to outhustle the other team," said Richie Farmer, "although they might be as talented."

"We want to win it for all the 5-10 and 5-11 guys that their high school coaches said were too small to play," said Keith after winning the state championship last year. "We want to prove them wrong."

The four players who have been the core of both this year's and last year's teams—the Farmers, Kevin Jackson and Russell Chadwell—are all 5-foot-11.

"Last year, the other teams looked at us and just laughed," said Chadwell, an 18-year-old senior who precedes each home game by throwing down a variety of slam dunks in pregame warm-ups.

Richie Farmer, 18, is Clay County's leader. He averages 27 points per game—his brother, a junior, averages 17—and played in his first Sweet Sixteen as an eighth grader. He has a 3.8 grade-point average and is a mature, nearly flawless floor leader.

Unlike Richie Farmer, who is being courted by countless colleges, Jackson, 18, has been promised a miner's job by a Clay County coal company when he graduates this spring. One of 10 children, Jackson has handled the family farm since his father was disabled. He married a high school sophomore last summer and now tends his own farm also.

Stanley Abner, a 54-year-old coal miner's son who teaches algebra and tends the scorebook and public address system at Clay County games, understands clearly what the Farmers, Jackson, Chadwell and 6-foot-1 junior Eugene Rawlings—the other starter on the 14-player roster—are accomplishing. "This just shows us what we can accomplish if we take the talent God gave us and use it," he said. "These guys are nothing but a bunch of overachievers. And Bobby Keith is the epitome of the work ethic."

Keith's favorite restaurant, Bob and Skyler's Steak House, opens at 4:30 every morning. "We miss a lot of business because we don't open any earlier," said owner Skyler Garrison. "Then they say we're sorry and won't work." The work ethic? When Wal-Mart opened in the county seat of Manchester 4½ years ago with 76 jobs, there were more than 800 applications the first day.

Clay County's unemployment rate is listed at 14 percent but most county officials put it between 30 and 35 percent. "That's about 20 percent who've never worked and there's no record on," said County Judge Executive Carl "Crawdad" Sizemore, one of a myriad of Sizemores whose political fiefdom is Clay County.

The walls of Sizemore's office on Courthouse Hill, above downtown Manchester, are decked with pictures of previous Clay County basketball teams. He talks quickly about the Sunday last March when the Tigers paraded home with the state championship. Cars lined both sides of the Daniel Boone Parkway for the 12 miles from the county line into Manchester. "I was amazed at how they lined up out of those creeks and hollows, people who may have never come to a game," he said.

Charles Marcum, who lives in the hollow below the Farmers, has missed only two of the 25 games Clay County has played in Kentucky this season. He has followed the Tigers around the state despite having to rise each morning at 3:30 for the 1½-hour trip to his job in a Harlan County coal mine. Because there is little coal mining in Clay County, now Marcum accepts his daily three-hour round trip over winding roads—as well as the three months he was out of work last year—stoically. Seeing his alma mater vanquish all obstacles on the basketball court makes his own hurdles easier to bear. "To me, this is the best thing ever to happen to Clay County, other than coal," said Marcum, 28.

Clay County is a slave to coal. The doorway to the high school gym is the escape hatch for a people who relish seeing the world shrunk to a hardwood rectangle less than 90 feet long and 50 feet wide. There, no one beats Clay County.

Off the court, Clay County has taken a beating of late:

• Just two years ago, Clay County was ranked 119th out of 120 Kentucky counties in quality of life. The ratings, compiled by an Eastern Kentucky University professor, were computed from education levels, average income, crime rate and farmland value.

• The county's biggest factory, Mid-South Electrics Inc., with more than 300 employers, was destroyed by fire 2½ years ago. Its owners are rebuilding it in neighboring Jackson County, the only county Clay topped in "quality of life."

• The Hardly Able Coal Co. has been dragged through the courts and national news media throughout the 1980s. The Manchester-based strip-mining operation—which pumped $600,000 per month into the local economy annually and had 125 employees—is bankrupt because of the more than $500,000 it has received in federal fines for mining violations.

• The county has received statewide publicity as a marijuana-growing hotbed. County officials readily admit marijuana is Clay County's No. 1 cash crop.

• A legacy of violence has shrouded the county since its leading families got into a nine-year, murderous shooting feud at the turn of the century.

Family lines still run deep in Clay County. Keith believes 99 percent of the people living in the county were born there. In 18 years as coach, he has had only two players who were not sons of natives. And they were brothers.

Four of Keith's first six players are the sons of former Clay County High School players. They grew up playing basketball with their fathers, coming to Clay County games and dreaming of being a Tiger. "They want to be better than their daddies," said Keith, 47.

When Keith went to a county elementary school last spring to show off the 5½-foot-high state championship trophy, a first grader approached him. "He said, 'When I get as big as that trophy, I'm going to play for you,' " Keith said.

Clay County's nine elementary schools—with names such as Horse Creek, Goose Rock and Burning Springs—run through the eighth grade and usually draw a couple of hundred fans to their basketball games. The countywide tournament fills the 2,500-seat high school gymnasium.

"They get to relating to these kids, and they get attached to them," said Skyler Garrison, who coached the Tigers in the 1960s and is one of the co-owners of the embattled Hardly Able Coal Co. His restaurant is the site of a daily, impromptu round-table basketball discussion. Old men sip coffee and compare Richie Farmer to the best guard ever to emerge from the mountains: Jerry West of West Virginia.

It was 60 years ago this season that basketball became a lifeline to the mountains of Kentucky, as the rest of the state and then America learned of the Carr Creek community of Knott County. About 200 people lived there, and 15 of them went to the high school that was perched on the side of a mountain. The basketball team had neither uniforms nor a gym. It practiced outside and traveled to its games by a mule-drawn log wagon or by foot.

In the finals of the 1928 state tournament, Carr Creek battled Ashland through four overtimes, finally losing 13-11. The Creekers went on to a national tournament in Chicago, where they became the darlings of the fans. They won two games and headed home. The mountains stood a little taller upon their return.

Finally, eastern Kentucky had a court upon which it could compete with the outside world. Mountain schools were poor and tiny, but basketball required little money, not much land and few players. By the 1940s, mountain schools were dominating Kentucky basketball.

Keith was born in 1940. "I was one of those little boys who dribbled a ball down a dirt road and dreamed of being a Tiger," said Keith.

He grew up to be a Tiger. At 6-foot-3, he was a fiercely competitive basketball player. He went on to play at junior college, where he was valedictorian, and then moved on to Union College in Barbourville, Ky., where he again was valedictorian.

Keith's six brothers and sisters all left the mountains to find adequate work. "So many of our good people have had to leave," he said. "These are the best people in the world. They want to stay, but there are no jobs for them and no chance for them to succeed."

Keith did what he always dreamed of doing. He went back to Manchester to coach basketball. In 1970, after eight years as an assistant coach, he was given a chance to prove his theory that "when these people are given an opportunity, they usually excel."

They have proved him right, winning more than 500 games for him, going to the Sweet Sixteen 11 times and giving Clay County the best winning percentage in Kentucky—85 percent—during his 18 seasons as coach.

Behind Keith's occasional backwoods expressions—he said he was glad to win the state title because "these things are harder to come by than chicken teeth"—is a shrewd coaching mind. He knows his opponents like a book and can work referees like a pump. His commitment to his players is unflagging; he has gotten scholarships, usually to small Kentucky schools, for all but three of the seniors who have played for him the last 17 years.

Keith underwent quadruple bypass surgery in August and has since lost 50 pounds, but his sideline intensity has not diminished. He teaches four consumer math classes a day—students call him "Bobby"—and owns Manchester's most popular men's clothing store. He admits to similarities between his Tigers and the small-town high school that won the 1954 Indiana state basketball championship and was immortalized in the 1986 movie "Hoosiers."

"We were both from rural areas, we were both small physically and we both beat big teams from a metro area," he said.

After winning state titles in 1954, '55 and '56, teams from Kentucky's three mountain regions went 29 years before making it to the state finals again in 1985, when Clay County lost to Hopkinsville 65-64. During the quarter-century before Clay County won the '87 state title, mountain teams were eliminated in the first round of the tournament 70 percent of the time.

The mountains' state title drought started in 1957, the year high school athletic competition was integrated in Kentucky. Predominantly black teams from Louisville dominated the Sweet Sixteen during the 1960s and 1970s, with Louisville teams winning eight state titles during one 10-year period.

Fittingly, Clay County had to beat a Louisville team to win the Sweet Sixteen last year at Rupp Arena in Lexington. The Tigers defeated Ballard High School 76-73 in overtime despite being soundly out-rebounded. Ballard's starters included two 6-foot-6 players, one 6-foot-5 and another 6-foot-3. "I'd rather play the big ones than the little ones," said Chadwell, he of the extraordinary leaping ability. "It just seems like you accomplish more."

The Tigers had won by 20 in the Sweet Sixteen semifinals against a Madison Central team with a lineup of players 6-8, 6-5, 6-4 and 6-5. In the quarterfinals, Clay County played before 24,041 people, the largest crowd ever to watch a high school game in the United States.

The Tigers were 35-3 last year and finished the regular season this year at 27-1. Their lone loss was in a December holiday tournament to Eau Claire High School of Columbia, S.C., the top-ranked team in South Carolina. Eau Claire started two 6-foot-9 players and another who was 6-foot-7, but the team still only beat Clay County 79-77.

In one incredible, 24-hour period in January—during the Louisville Invitational Tournament—the Tigers defeated the No. 2, 3 and 5 teams in Kentucky. "There's a great deal of pride in the mountains and there's not many things we can say we rank at the top of Kentucky in," said Keith. "But we do in basketball."

Judge's Comments

The best journalism always has been that which helps us understand the human condition. The best sports writers always have known that. From Damon Runyon to Red Smith to Thomas Boswell, the finest writers of each generation have gone beyond recounting games and anointing heroes to explore the themes of life that often seem distilled in the heat of athletic competition.

The best sports writing, like the best of all journalism, probes beneath the surface of the moment to lay bear the causes of defeat, the costs of victory, the connections between people and between events.

This year's winner in the feature story category, "Hills of Coal, Feats of Clay" by Sam Heys of the *Atlanta Journal-Constitution*, is the tale of a remarkable basketball team and much more. The Clay County Tigers of Manchester, Ky., are a championship team, certainly, but they are more importantly a source of pride to a region without much to be proud of. They are heroes, certainly, but they are more importantly symbols of hope and of victory against long odds.

Heys understands the role the Tigers play in their coal-country culture. He helps us understand it, too. And he makes us care about both the team and the culture.

After introducing the brothers who are the heart of the team, Richie and Russ Farmer, Heys tells us just why this is a story worth reading:

For a county long on illiteracy and hard times and short on quality of life and high school graduates, the Farmer brothers and three other mountain boys are dishing out a little poetic justice. "Everybody thinks people from the mountains are dumb hicks, that we can't do anything," said Richie Farmer in thick mountain English. "But we can play basketball."

That's a paragraph to make Red Smith proud.

There are other images equally telling. Heys introduces us, for example, to a typical fan, miner Charles Marcum. *"To me this is the best thing ever to happen to Clay County, other than coal,"* said Marcum, 28. We learn that Clay County ranks 119th of 120 Kentucky counties in quality of life; that its leading employer, the aptly named Hardly Able Coal Co., is bankrupt, that its most important cash crop is marijuana.

And, from Tigers Coach Bobby Keith, *"an old mountain boy himself,"* we learn what this story and this team are really all about. *"There's a great deal of pride in the mountains and there's not many things we can say we rank at the top of Kentucky in,"* said Keith. *"But we do in basketball."*

Best Commentary Story

The Boxing Degeneration

BOXING

By *RON BORGES*

From the Boston Globe
Copyright © 1988, the Boston Globe

If heroes are a measure of our society, then the events of recent weeks should tell us we are clearly on the slide.

About 25 years ago, a man named Sonny Liston ruled boxing, and everyone feared and disliked him. He was a glowering man who looked the way you remembered evil from children's ghost stories. He was the embodiment of everything our nation did not stand for.

Stories circulated that he was a leg-breaker for the Mob when not breaking heads in a boxing ring, and even after he won the heavyweight championship of the world by twice destroying a gentle flower named Floyd Patterson, it could not legitimize him in the eyes of the public.

It was feared that he was unbeatable, and lengthy was the debate on whether he was bad for boxing, but there was never much question about what American society thought of him. He was bad for it. Period.

No one asked him to sell a product. Instead, everyone waited impatiently for him to be beaten. He was not a hero for our day or for our country. He made us uncomfortable.

Before Liston, there were legendary champions, like Joe Louis, who fought first for his race and later for his country and won both battles with dignity. That is not to say that bad men did not win world championships, for boxing is often a bad man's business, but those bad men did not become our heroes. In the public eye, they did not become Joe Louises.

When Liston finally went down, it was to a brash young man who brought humor back to boxing. Cassius Clay was Joy and Laughter as well as Destruction. He was Brains over Brawn, but more important, he was the nice kid from Louisville with the big mouth over the hard man from the streets who skipped rope to the mournful sounds of "Night Train."

Today there seems to be a new Sonny Liston afoot, a leg-breaker from New York named Mike Tyson who has taken the joy from the sport and replaced it with vile epithets on national television, fearsome punches in the ring and utter disrespect for the people who helped him and the opponents who stand before him.

Mike Tyson is the product of streets in which terror rules, in which being smart means that your con is better or your gun is bigger than anyone else's. He is the product of a place where the biggest man in the street sells dope and 12-year-old kids carry Uzis instead of books and make $200 deliveries of small packages of junk.

In consort, that environment has made Mike Tyson a fighting machine, a boy unchallengeable by men. Sadly, it has also made him an American celebrity for the '80s, celebrity long ago having replaced heroism as the goal of a money-infatuated society.

Twenty-five years ago, America cowered from Sonny Liston, closing its petals to him the way a flower closes to the darkness; today, people run to stand in Mike Tyson's shadow and shower him with money.

"I don't need anyone," Tyson said last week. "All I have to do is win. As long as I win, I'm fine."

That is a sad comment on what America has become these past eight years, but what is sadder still is that Mike Tyson is correct.

He can hit his wife, as his sister-in-law insists he did. He can punch his fist through the wall and throw the television across the room when he is frustrated, as he admits he has done. He can sue to break a contract with his manager signed only months ago and serve the man with papers minutes before the heavyweight championship bout, as he did Monday night. He can turn his back on everyone who ever worked to free him from reform school and the sentence life had become. He can ask why his late manager, Jim Jacobs, would leave his share of the action to his wife rather than give it back to Tyson.

He can, he believes, do and say whatever he wants and still America will call to him. Sadly, it seems he is right.

Last Monday night, the hero should have been Michael Spinks, a kind man who has survived a ghetto upbringing in the worst project in American history and came out of it with love for his brother, wayward Leon; love for his family, including a sister who lives with him; love and loyalty for those who have helped him most, like his manager, Butch Lewis, and love for his seven-year-old daughter, who has lived with her grandmother since the death of Spinks' wife five years ago.

But Spinks was beaten to a pulp by Tyson in 91 seconds, the fourth-fastest knockout in heavyweight championship history, and he quickly became the butt of far too many ringside jokes. What apparently matters in America is victory. And, of course, the money it brings.

While Spinks lay senseless on the canvas, Tyson turned to Lewis at ringside and dragged his gloved fist across his throat. *Slit.* It was typically unkind, unamusing, unfeeling.

The crowd cheered.

They neither cheered nor saw the moment when Michael Spinks finally left the ring 15 minutes later, his brother Leon in tears, the two who have survived so much locked arm in arm.

"I did my best," Michael said.

"I know, I know," Leon replied as the tears rolled down his cheek and dripped down on his brother's shoulder.

"It's really all right," Michael said, the fallen man trying to sooth his brother. "I tried my best."

Only minutes after the Spinks brothers disappeared, a fan sat down at ringside and told a newspaperman, "That was a disgrace. The guy went down as soon as he was hit. Spinks is a disgrace. But that Tyson. He's really something."

There is something wrong there; something has gone out of focus in America when it idolizes such a man.

Twenty-five years ago, Sonny Liston did not sell Diet Pepsi or anything else. Last week, Mike Tyson received $4 million to do just that. One wonders if those Pepsi executives in their boardroom high above the streets of New York that spawned Tyson and that un-doubtedly will produce more beaten and angry young men like him, recall what their spokesman said not so many months ago.

"When I fight someone, I want to break his will," Tyson said. "I want to take his manhood. I want to rip out his heart and show it to him. My manager tells me not to say those things, but that's the way I feel. People say that's primitive, that I'm an animal. But then they pay $500 to see it. There's so much hypocrisy in the world.

"I never liked sports. Sports are only social events. What I do is an obsession. If I wasn't in boxing, I'd be breaking the law. That's my nature."

Welcome to the Pepsi Generation.

If one night one of those Pepsi executives finds himself facing the 12-year-old who one day will beat Mike Tyson, waiting for him with a grin and a pistol, he should give him his wallet very quickly.

And he should think for a minute about his spokesman . . . his hero . . . and where he's taking us.

Judge's Comments

Like Muhammad Ali, Ron Borges combines power and style. The result is a commentary that is a knockout.

Readers don't have to wonder where Borges stands or where he is headed. In the opening paragraph, he announces a thesis, then marches off in purposeful cadence.

He does it with style. His images start the videotape in your mind's eye rolling: *"Twenty-five years ago, America cowered from Sonny Liston, closing its petals to him the way a flower closes to the darkness; today, people run to stand in Mike Tyson's shadow and shower him with money."*

He marshals facts, uses context, relies on the declarative sentence and writes clearly but not simply. He uses literary devices to help explain and convince. This is learned commentary that informs and entertains.

Best Action Photo
Speedboat Breakup

by Bernard Brault of La Presse newspaper. This dramatic, tack-sharp picture of a driver being thrown from his speedboat as it breaks apart during action in the 50th Valleyfield (Quebec) Regatta is an example of first-class racing photography. Brault's photo demonstrates exceptional skill in long-lens handling and solid darkroom technique. The driver was only slightly injured in the July 10 accident. Copyright © 1988, Bernard Brault, La Presse.

Best Feature Photo
Victory Ride

by Jerry Lodriguss of the Philadelphia Inquirer. This photographer
showed his versatility by submitting a number of top-notch photographs from the Summer Olympic Games in Seoul, South Korea,
as well as interesting photos from such sports as baseball, basketball, boxing, football and track. This intimate shot of United
States sprinter Florence Griffith-Joyner following her second
world-record run in the 200-meter dash is a moving portrait of the
athlete and her ecstatic husband, Al Joyner. Copyright © 1988,
Philadelphia Inquirer.

Best Reporting Story

Recruiting of L.A. Prep Star Probed

COLLEGE BASKETBALL

By *ERIC SONDHEIMER, DOUG CRESS* and *BETH BARRETT*

From the Los Angeles Daily News
Copyright © 1988, the Los Angeles Daily News

A package shipped from the University of Kentucky to the father of a Los Angeles high school basketball star contained $1,000 in cash when it accidentally opened in the Los Angeles office of a delivery service, several of the firm's employees told the Daily News.

The National Collegiate Athletic Association, which regulates college athletic and recruitment programs, is investigating, a spokesman said Wednesday.

The player signed a letter of intent Nov. 11 to accept a basketball scholarship to the university, which was reprimanded last month by the NCAA for minor violations after a lengthy investigation of charges that substantial payments were made to other players.

The player, his father and university officials denied any knowledge of the money.

As one of the top high school basketball players in California, Chris Mills of Fairfax High School was heavily recruited by universities across the nation. The 6-foot-7-inch Mills was the Los Angeles City 4-A player of the year in 1987. This season he scored an average of 28.3 points a game.

An investigator for the NCAA was in Los Angeles Monday, Tuesday and Wednesday to determine whether a violation had occurred. The official, Charles Smrt, declined to discuss the substance of the case.

Late Wednesday, University of Kentucky president David P. Roselle issued a statement saying the university began an investigation after receiving a call last Friday from a Daily News reporter.

"Within a day we confirmed enough of the information given to us by the reporter to be seriously concerned," Roselle said.

"It is our intention to find out what happened, to report everything we find to the NCAA and to take full responsibility for whatever is proved to have occurred."

A shipment record obtained by the Daily News showed that the package was sent March 30 via Emery Worldwide air freight by Kentucky assistant basketball coach Dwane Casey to Claud Mills, father of the high school star.

Casey, interviewed in person in Pittsburgh before and after a national high school all-star game last Friday, said he did not put any money into the package.

"We don't recruit that way," Casey said. "But I have never, ever put any money in a package. That accusation is ridiculous."

Claud Mills, who confirmed he had been interviewed by the NCAA, said no money was in the package when he received it. However, he acknowledged having a conversation with an employee at Emery in which he was told a package containing cash was addressed to him and was awaiting delivery.

He said the caller from Emery gave this information: "Are you looking for a package from Emery? Well, I have a thousand dollars for you."

Chris Mills said after the all-star basketball game in Pittsburgh that he knew nothing about any money from the university.

Officials at Kentucky denied any wrongdoing.

"I can promise you it didn't occur," said Kentucky head basketball coach Eddie Sutton. "I feel very confident in my assistant coaches. I don't believe it. I think I know my assistant coaches well enough."

NCAA officials said serious, but unspecified, penalties could be imposed against the University of Kentucky if the charge in the Mills' case is substantiated.

"It's called improper inducement," David Berst, NCAA director of enforcement, said in a telephone interview from NCAA headquarters in Mission, Kan. "Cash inducement isn't the sort of thing you need a handbook to figure out if it's a violation."

On March 4, the NCAA said it failed to uncover any proof of wrongdoing after investigating charges the University of Kentucky had violated several NCAA rules, including cash payments to other players.

In a series of interviews in the last week, employees of Emery Worldwide told the Daily News that they noticed cash when a package broke open during handling late last month at their Los Angeles shipment center.

A computerized shipment record obtained by the Daily News listed Kentucky assistant coach Casey as the sender and Claud Mills as the addressee of a package handled by Emery on March 31.

Casey said the package he sent contained Claud Mills' videotape of his son playing basketball and was used to help determine whether to ask the high school star to sign a letter of intent to attend Kentucky on scholarship.

Eric Osborn, the Emery employee who found an opened package when it arrived in Los Angeles, said he looked inside and saw money sticking out of a videocassette box.

His supervisor, Paul Perry, said he called over several employees as witnesses and counted out the $1,000 in $50 bills and then had the package sealed by security personnel for delivery.

"I'm just the one who happened to see it because it popped open," Perry said. "It popped open, the driver happened to have it in his hand, you could see it plain as day. There was twenty $50 bills slipped inside the sleeve."

Deliveryman David Jones said Perry told him the package contained money in addition to the videotape. He said he did not see the cash because the package was sealed when it was given to him for delivery.

Emery's dispatcher Richard Flanders said Jones was directed to take the package containing the money to the Mills apartment in the Fairfax area. Jones said he made the delivery.

Claud Mills acknowledged that he received a videotape from Casey on March 31. He said he talked by telephone that morning with a man who identified himself as an Emery employee and was told there was a package containing $1,000 addressed to him.

Claud Mills said Chris Mills signed for the package and that when he got home he found the videotape but no cash, in the opened packet.

"I didn't receive no money from Dwane Casey," Claud Mills said. "Nobody from Kentucky gave me no money. They sent me a tape, but I don't know nothing about no money."

Chris Mills said he knows nothing about $1,000 in a package addressed to his father.

Pat Bertrand, public relations manager for Emery Worldwide at the corporate headquarters in Wilton, Conn., said last week that company policy requires a report be filled out every time a package comes open during shipment.

Perry said that Emery security men arrived and filled out a report on the opened package and the money.

"We called security, they came downstairs, took it, did a report on it . . . I counted it again, I put the money back in the slot, I took some brown tape, sealed it good, gave it to the (driver), and told him to deliver it," Perry said.

Chuck Bullerman, a manager of the security firm contracted by Emery, denied that he or anyone from his department had filled out a report.

"As far as we're concerned, there is no problem. Unless the consignee fills out a complaint, we don't get involved. As far as we're concerned the package was delivered to the consignee without problems," Bullerman said.

When informed that Perry had said Bullerman had filed a report, Bullerman referred further questions to Perry and declined to account for the contradiction.

Casey, the assistant coach, said shipping videotapes of high school stars by Emery is a routine practice to review the athletes' progress and determine whether to recruit them. He acknowledged sending the March 31 package to Claud Mills as well as several others.

"I have sent packages and tapes to Claud," Casey said. "We do that all the time with recruits. We send tapes of (Kentucky) games so they can see the style of game we play, and they send tapes of their high school games so we can see them play."

Perry, the Emery supervisor, said he counted the money in front of other employees because it is against company policy to accept currency, precious stones or guns for shipment.

He said that driver David Jones had problems finding the Fairfax area address on the package, prompting Emery to call Claud Mills for an address clarification.

"Yes, the street address was wrong," he said. "We had Orange Drive, and it was Orange Grove. That's what the driver told me on the phone. He said 'Paul, I don't want to deliver this. I don't want the guy beating me up,' or whatever the case may be.

"But then we called him (Mills) up and he said 'No, I live on Orange Grove.' That was the right address and he (Jones) went over and delivered it," Perry said. "We delivered it to Orange Grove."

Richard Flanders, the Emery dispatcher, said he discussed the package with the person who was listed as the addressee, Claud Mills.

"It was the same name on the paper work," Flanders said. "I told the guy on the phone, 'The driver is coming to you. He needs an apartment number.'

"The customer was freaking out because he said we had no right to look into his package," Flanders said. "But they had stuffed a video into the shipping envelope. It was too small (and) it forced open the package, exposing the money."

Claud Mills said his son, a two-time Parade All-America, picked the University of Kentucky because of Coach Sutton, and the style of play used by the team.

"Every school that came around to talk to Chris, we talked to them," he added. "Nobody offered Chris a thing. I'll take a lie-detector test. All we talked about was tuition, loans, and the money he'd receive from month-to-month legally."

Claud Mills said an NCAA investigator had questioned him earlier about a car he bought for his son. He said he paid $6,800 for the car, a 1984 Datsun 300ZX, with the proceeds of a lawsuit.

"I bought that car for Chris; he's my son," Mills said. "That car had 80,000 miles on it and the guy from the NCAA said '——, I came all the way out here because rumors were saying Chris is driving an '88.' "

"The NCAA said rumors had gotten out that Chris had a brand new '88 and the guy came out to verify it, and he looked at it, we ran it through the DMV to prove it," he said. "Now how am I supposed to sell Chris—if he could have gone to any college in the country—for a $6,000 car."

He acknowledged receiving the package from Emery, but denied there was any money in it.

"When I got the envelope, there was a tape in it," he said. "I don't even know if the envelope was opened because when I got back home my son gave it to me. He said 'Emery came with the envelope' and I said 'Where's my other tape?' and he said, 'They only sent one tape.'

"Every tape that I have is very important to me over the years," Claud Mills said. "I sacrificed a lot to do it, but as far as Dwane Casey and any thousand dollars, I didn't see any thousand dollars."

Judge's Comments

Few stories of 1988 had the impact of this one, which led to a major scandal involving the University of Kentucky's vaunted basketball program.

A package sent by Kentucky assistant coach Dwane Casey to Claud Mills, father of 6-foot-7 prize recruit Chris Mills, apparently came open in transit, revealing $1,000 in cash. The implication, of course, was that Kentucky was trying to buy Mills' services.

The *Daily News* handled the story well. It got interviews with Kentucky officials and NCAA investigators, leaving little for others to follow. The story is a thorough job of reporting a story of major national significance.

Also notable is the clear, concise writing style. There are no wasted words in this effort.

Best Magazine Story

The Elements of Baseball

BASEBALL

By *HOWARD SINKER*

From Minnesota Monthly
Copyright © 1988, Howard Sinker

To love the game is to appreciate it at its most basic level. We may be obsessed with the ornaments of baseball—the subtle flinch that sends a runner home on a balk at a critical juncture, a bunt sign missed or ignored, a stolen base that starts with a flash of cleats and ends in a plume of clay. But in the end, the game is as simple as three of the hardest things in the world: hitting, pitching, and catching a ball.

How come Gary Gaetti hit 31 home runs last season for the Minnesota Twins and Greg Gagne hit only 10? Why was Frank Viola the ace of the pitching staff and Dan Schatzeder just another lefthanded journeyman? What's the secret that allows 245-pound Kent Hrbek to play first base with a nimbleness that's lacking in most of his major league peers?

What are their elements of style?

The reasons for their success can't often be explained in the confines of a newspaper's sports section. I know that from spending four years writing about the successes and failures of the Minnesota Twins. The give-and-take of a clubhouse interview, the informal banter around the batting cage, and other rituals for talking baseball are hardly venues of depth.

So much happens during a season—especially a successful one in which a team, say, manages to win the World Series—that the skills required of a major league player can be overlooked. Fans heard often in 1987 about Viola's mastery of the changeup, an off-speed pitch that renders an unsuspecting batter helpless. Most of us, however, would be hard-pressed to explain precisely why it helped him so much.

The winter months provided time for reflection. On a couple of nights when the air was especially frosty, three of the Twins' best players tried to explain the secrets of their success. It wasn't always easy. Gaetti, Viola, and Hrbek have all played baseball almost since they were old enough to run, and it is sometimes hard for them to separate acquired skills from natural gifts.

They tried hard. They did pretty well.

GARY GAETTI ON HITTING

The best part of baseball is making contact, hitting the ball hard, getting it good. There's very little feeling to it, actually. You know how it is when you hit the ball off the end of the bat, and it hurts? Hit the ball the way you're supposed to, and you hardly feel a thing. It's almost like swinging and missing. It happens so fast that you can't break it down. You just know you made good contact. I don't like to put a percentage on how often I do it, but maybe it's two-and-a-half times out of 10. It's something I don't really keep track of. Hitting is hard. You take what you can get.

I think about hitting more when I'm struggling. I think everyone thinks about it more when they're not doing as well, for a lot of reasons. You're thinking about trying to get back to what you do when you're going good. You try to analyze what isn't working right for you. There are a lot of different ways to talk about hitting: the strategy of hitting, the fundamentals of hitting, the pleasure of hitting. I think fundamentals—talking about fundamentals—are very important because you just have to do certain things right. Not everybody has the same strategy. Everybody has their own style. But within that style, everybody has to do certain things the same way to get the right results. When I'm in a slump, the biggest thing I have to do is approach hitting with an open mind. If I don't have an open mind, I'm just going to frustrate myself. It helps to analyze films, but you actually have to go out and do it.

At the plate, I don't think. I just react. When I'm hitting well, I don't have to worry about fundamentals. My swing is right, and I can concentrate on the strategy of hitting the ball. It feels like I'm getting a good look at the ball all the way from the pitcher's hand into the hitting area. The feeling comes and goes. You change ballparks, you face different pitchers, maybe you don't feel physically alert. It could be a number of things that send you into a slump. I don't know if I believe in biorhythms, but I know there are times when my concentration isn't what it should be. You can't have 100 percent concentration for each pitch of every at-bat, even though you need 100 percent concentration to hit. When you don't have it, it can be very irritating. It can be embarrassing. It's just not a good feeling.

Hitting the two home runs in the first game of the playoffs, those were fun. I had a real good idea of what I wanted to do and how to approach Doyle (Alexander, the Detroit pitcher). And it worked. I had my strategy where I wanted it, but basically I just reacted to what he threw because I was seeing the ball well. That was something I'd never done against him. I'd never had the concentration against him that I needed. I felt like before the game I prepared myself well, and, for once, I saw him throw the ball. I wanted to be very patient against him and make sure I got a decent pitch to hit, and not swing at the pitch if I didn't see it well out of his hand. I did that by watching really closely from the on-deck circle, watching where he was releasing the ball from. I also went up there with the idea that I wanted to hit the ball where it was pitched. It sounds simple. When I'm in the on-deck circle, I'm just watching the pitcher. Swinging the bat isn't important because you've taken batting practice, and you should be ready to hit. When I take swings in the on-deck circle, it's usually because I'm not feeling right.

I've tried to describe hitting a home run before. It's a feeling of power, I guess. I guess it's kind of like—I don't want to sound too stupid saying something like this—but it's like I just performed the greatest feat in baseball by hitting a home run. Some home runs are more significant than others. Like the grand slam homer in the sixth game of the World Series was probably bigger for Kent Hrbek than any other homer, and you could tell by the way he went around the bases. I don't try to show off or anything. I just take a leisurely jog if I know it's a homer. I try not to make a big show out of it, like some people do. I don't ever do that. I run at what I think is a nice, easy pace without dragging it out. The best part is feeling the contact; the second-best part is hearing the crowd yelling when they finally realize it went out. I can feel it about a second or two before they can see it. It's funny when you hear them screaming in the stands when you know the ball's not going to come close. It think I'm hoping for them to use their reaction to blow the ball out of the park.

Hitting for power is all technique, all fundamentals. Like when we work out and bench press or do those things, I can't say that I'm much stronger than some other guys. I'll use (Twins media relations assistant) Remzi Kiratli as an example. He can bench press much more weight than I can because of his technique in weightlifting. He's not that much stronger than me; I'm not that much stronger than him. But my technique in hitting a baseball has to be that much better than his. Technique is a very subtle thing, but it's something I can notice. Greg Gagne is a great example. If he would drive the ball more often, he would have a quicker bat and generate more power on contact. There are some really good pictures that I saw of him and me at the same point on our home run swings. Gagne has good power, but because of his technique, his bat speed isn't always what it should be. Once you get to a certain point, it's hard to tell someone how to make an adjustment. I know how I hit. But to tell someone else how to hit, how to tell their body to do something, you just can't do it. The best you can do most of the time is make analogies. Like if you're going to use an ax to chop down a tree, there's only one way to use the ax. If you roll your wrist, the blade isn't going to hit the tree right.

I wish I could watch some guys hit more often. Usually I'm watching from third base and don't get a good look. I love watching Wally Joyner because he's so effortless and natural-looking. I used to watch Kent, but he's doing some weird stuff now. I love to watch Kirby Puckett hit. Believe it or not, I don't like to watch Wade Boggs. I don't like his style. I see so much more in him as a hitter than what he tries to do. He hits a lot of singles. I'd love to see him swing from the ass more often, try to really smash the ball. With the pitches he gets to hit, I think he'd be great at it. I don't really like to watch Don Mattingly. I just don't. He's pretty unorthodox.

If you'd asked two years ago about the best hitter I've seen, I would have said Hrbek. Then Kirby Puckett came on the scene. I've never seen anyone hit like Puckett. They talk about Paul Molitor being good and Boggs being good, but Puckett is just a hitting machine. That's all. His mechanics are great, his fundamentals are consistent. You take thousands of swings in the course of a season. In 600 at-bats, he puts more good swings on pitches than anyone except Boggs. They're two different kinds of hitters, but Puckett appeals to me more than Boggs because he swings hard all the time. Where am I? It depends on how you want to look at it. Overall, I've got to say somewhere in the middle. I'm trying to be honest. I'm better in some situations than others. I can't say I'm as good as those guys, but I do some things better. I probably pull the ball better than anyone, but that doesn't always work. If you're grading on bat speed, I'll be right there at the top with anybody. If you measure on consistency, I wouldn't be. I'd be down in the middle of the pack.

FRANK VIOLA ON PITCHING

I get the most satisfaction out of a good fastball—a good 86- or 87- or 88-mile-per-hour fastball that I can throw when I know I feel good. I can throw it to a spot sometimes, and there's nothing a batter can do about it, because he knows I've made a damn good pitch. It's fun to set up that pitch. When I use my changeup like I'm supposed to, the fastball looks like it's 92 or 93. That's fun to do, and it's fun to watch. I like going right after the hitter, but I also like to know exactly where the pitch is going to be. I feel like I do that maybe once every five or six starts. That's fun, but the pitchers who succeed are the ones who win the rest of the time, when they don't have their best stuff. That's when pitching is a total battle. I'm not going to let on when I don't have my best stuff, because you show a batter that you're a little scared, and they have the advantage. A sign of that is when you fall behind in the count again and again.

I've worked on my changeup more than anything else I've ever had to do in my life. Conquering that pitch is so important to me. I still really haven't gotten to the point of totally conquering it. But when I got to the point where I knew I could throw the changeup at any time, it was the greatest feeling in the world. I got to the point, I think, at spring training last year, where I could throw it when I was behind 2-and-0, 3-and-1. Fastball situations. I'd always had doubts about the pitch. "What if I get it up and they crush it?" I finally just said: To hell with it; let's see if it works. I was fortunate. It worked. Hard work paid off. To me, that's the whole game.

I know that I'm in control of a game when I'm getting the seventh, eighth, and ninth guys in their lineup. When I don't do that, that's when I get into the most trouble. The most unlikely guys are the ones who hit home runs off me, like in the fourth game of the World Series when Tom Lawless hit that three-run homer and really broke our backs. Mike Gallego, Dave Van Gorder, Fred Manrique: Guys who never hit home runs hit them off me. Garth Iorg has hurt me in the past, Tim Foli when he was with the Angels, Wayne Tolleson when he was with the White Sox. Butch Wynegar. I think it was Bert Blyleven who told me that Gaylord Perry approached the game by saying he was going to throw his best stuff against those guys to show there's no way they belong on the same field with him. You work so hard to get other hitters out that it's like a major letdown when they hit you. When you face a guy a few times and you get him out with fastballs, you think it's going to work again and again. But when you have a three- or four-pitch repertoire like I do, you've got to mix it up. It doesn't matter who the batter is. You're going to get hurt if you keep throwing him the same pitch.

I usually think more during my warmup pitches than I do when I'm facing the batter. That's how it is when I'm the most successful. My best success comes when I know exactly what I'm going to do on the mound, and I'm not thinking about it too much. The flow of the game should dictate what I'm going to do. I don't know if the statistics will verify it or not, but until I had that winning streak at the Dome last year, I always felt I had greater success on the road. It was knowing that the Twins weren't a successful road team, and I think I had more of a tendency to get into the flow of the game a lot earlier.

My game has improved ever since I discarded the slider. That was the one pitch that hurt me more than anything. I have a fastball and a slow curve that are really at extremes, and with my curve getting better, the need for a slider wasn't that great anymore. The slider is the most mistake-prone pitch that you can throw, in my opinion. If it doesn't work right, it's a flat pitch, and a major league hitter can get it because it comes in seven or eight miles per hour slower than a fastball and doesn't have the break of a curve. I haven't thrown it much since the All-Star break in '86. When I feel like I'm pitching well, the slider is the one pitch I can go a whole game without using. I might use it on an 0-and-2 pitch when I want to throw the ball down and in, when I know I don't have to throw a strike.

My pitching gets altered a lot depending on the flow of the game. That's where a catcher is important. I might think my fastball is pretty good, and he'll say it's coming in straight as an arrow. That's why the rapport between pitcher and catcher is so important. I feel most comfortable calling my own game. If I'm going to make a mistake, I want to make a mistake on a decision that I make—not a decision the catcher makes. That bothers me. I hever want to let on that the catcher might be calling pitches that I don't want to throw. I don't shake off the signs. I just keep staring in, so the batter doesn't know I'm really shaking them off. It's hard for a catcher because he's got so many different pitchers to work with. I'm a lefty, so what do you expect? I'm supposed to be hard to figure out.

There are times when I just don't have anything. You can't tell before the game, but it's obvious when you're a couple of batters into their lineup. You can't let up, or you're truly dead. Sometimes I'll get by because maybe it looks like I'm working my tail off, and they can't take advantage of me. Sometimes I'll just hope that whoever comes in after me doesn't have the same stuff I had. Sometimes you just get lucky. There was a game last August against Oakland when Dave Stewart (a 20-game winner) and I put on the most disgusting pitching performance ever. It was a shabby, ugly game to watch if you like pitching, and I was the one lucky to come away with the victory. We had pitched against each other the weekend before, a real good game, and then we pitched like hell. It's happened to me before when I've pitched against the same team twice in a row. Pitchers sometimes go out there thinking about trying to better themselves when they don't really have to. That's thinking too much. It happened in Game 4 of the World Series, and it almost happened in Game 7, but I finally adjusted. They got four hits in the second inning of Game 7 on changeups. (Roy) Smalley and Tim Laudner came up to me after the inning and told me to think about what I was doing. I wasn't going after them with my best pitch, the fastball. They told me to use my fastball like I'm supposed to use it. I started to, and the whole game changed. They were swinging at pitches up over their heads. I established my fastball, and then I could use my changeup. It's incredible how the game can change, depending on what the pitcher does.

A pitcher's arm hurts quite often. It's not so much hurt as discomfort. You know it's a normal thing, and it's going to go away in a couple of days. There are times when I've had a strained muscle in my shoulder, and that takes a little getting used to. That's something you can pitch with. You just have to do your exercises and make sure the trainer gets to work on it. Knock on wood, nothing really terrible has happened. You see so many stories about pitchers. One day the arm is great, the next day it's dead. I can't worry about that. If it's going to happen, it's going to happen. It does provide some motivation. You start taking things easy, and all of a sudden you're dead.

Your arm goes, or something happens that might lead to your arm going. You get paid damn good money to play a kid's game. It shouldn't be tough to take care of yourself.

KENT HRBEK ON FIELDING

I like the action at first base. I always enjoyed playing shortstop and pitching when I was in Little League. I don't really think about it much, but I'd like to play another position in the majors sometime just to see how I would do. Me and Gary Gaetti have talked about switching positions for a game—he'd play first, I'd play third—but I kind of doubt it. I take ground balls at third base during batting practice, but it'll be a cold day in hell before I get to play there in a game, that's for sure.

I started playing first base in the summer of 1975. I was in ninth grade, and they moved me over from shortstop because they had a shortstop who was a year older than I was, and he was better. They needed a first baseman. They moved me over, and I've been there ever since. I remember the day they moved me over, they put shin guards on me and threw balls in the dirt so I would learn to pick them out. I adapted to it. I think there are some skills involved from when I played hockey. That has to be part of the reason why I could adapt. You try to make saves in hockey, to keep the puck from going in the net. That's the way I look at my defense: Don't let the ball go by me. That's what I'm hoping for. Sometimes I'm out there imagining myself as the goalie.

I like the idea of making a great play to save the game, or whatever. It's pretty much the same thing as getting a key hit, even though people might not recognize it. The one that's going to be talked about for a long time is the one against Detroit in the playoffs when I was lying on my stomach and caught the throw from Gary. Then you also think of the play in St. Louis where the ball hit the edge of the dirt, and I booted it. They got something started because of that. It was key, the turning point. Little things like that can start something—and they can stop something from getting started. On the one with Gary, I knew he had a tough play because it was tough for him just to get to the ball. I just laid myself out and got it. The ball found my glove. I didn't find the ball. It was one of those "Close your eyes and see if the ball's going to be there" plays. You just watch the ball as long as you can and know the ball is going to be somewhere near you.

There are actually times when I close my eyes and catch the ball. A lot of guys won't admit it, but I'll tell you that I've done it. It's skill, really, because you have to realize where you think the ball's going to be. I have a clue. I know how much is on the ball, what kind of surface we're on: all the variables that you have to figure in. Hey, we had to have some luck to win the World Series, too. It wasn't all skill.

It's funny. Dwight Evans (of the Red Sox) told me last year

when he was moved over to first base from the outfield that anyone can play first base, but you have to work at it to be a good one. They stick a lot of the older players over there, guys who've moved from the outfield, because they're trying to hide them. I mean, sure, you can play first base, and you try to catch the ball. But a lot of games are won or lost over there. I work on a lot of little things that help get guys out. Sure, anybody can catch the ball if you throw it at them. But it's also how you set yourself up for double play balls: whether you want to be throwing inside the runner or outside the runner, whether you're going to make a stretch or a quick pickup off the bag—a whole bunch of variables.

I can still do the splits, but now I only do them when I have to. I used to do that a lot more when I was younger, and I was still learning about defense. That's how I used to stretch for the ball all the time because it was a natural thing. I learned that you can usually wait on the ball and pick it out of the dirt, and there are other times when you just can't stretch. I want the ball to come in from waist high to the letters, but I tell guys they can throw it anywhere as long as they don't throw it over my head, because then I know I can't get it. In the dirt I can still get it. I tell them just to keep it in the vicinity, and we'll be OK. I've gotten to know the way that everybody throws. Like Gaetti has always gone through times when he's a very erratic thrower. So I'm always expecting a bad throw from him. Greg Gagne very rarely makes a bad throw. If he or Steve Lombardozzi makes a bad throw, I'm not expecting it as much as when Gary's throwing. It's part of preparing. It takes a good half-year to learn a fielder. Like Al Newman. I'm still not really trained into how he throws the ball. Lenny Faedo (a shortstop from 1980-84) always scared me. He had a great arm, and every time he threw the ball it was bone-bruise time. The ball always came over twice as hard as from anyone else. That's how it felt. I might get one or two a week that hurt. It's usually on a throw where I don't know if I'm going to get it out of the dirt or with a stretch until it's too late. You get caught, and the ball comes in right on the bone where the finger connects to the hand. I usually catch the ball way up in the webbing of the glove. Usually.

I barely stick my hand in the glove. Actually, my whole palm is hanging out. I've always done it that way. I've seen other guys do something like that, but not with their hand hanging out as far as mine. It's just comfortable for me. Nobody's ever said anything. Maybe if I couldn't catch the ball or play the position, somebody would. I like to watch Don Mattingly. He can really play. He definitely can pick it. I think if I'm not the best, I'm right up there with him—me and Mattingly.

It's bothered me that I was second in Rookie of the Year (in 1982), it bothered me when I was second for the MVP (1984), and it's bothered me that I haven't won a Gold Glove. The individual stuff is great, but I'll take the World Series ring. You can stick the honors on the wall, but you enjoy that by yourself. I'd still like to have one Gold Glove, just to say that I won it. It's a pretty trophy. That and being the stolen base leader would make me the complete ballplayer. Think I have a chance?

I talk to players all the time at first base, and most of the time it's not about baseball. Everything else, from A to Z. There are a lot of guys who want to talk and some who don't. Mike Heath comes to mind as someone who's really funny. Jim Presley is funny because he never says a damn word. He just kind of looks at me like he wants me to shut up. He's never told me to. I'm not going to bug somebody, and I'm not talking to distract anybody. I just like to strike up conversations. When I was younger I didn't talk much because I didn't want to step on any toes. I remember my first game when Reggie Jackson said congratulations and asked me how I pronounced my name. Other first basemen? George Brett likes to talk. Greg Walker talks a lot, but that's because I know him. Eddie Murray is always yacking. Wally Joyner talks a bit, surprisingly. He doesn't seem like the type. Alvin Davis doesn't say much.

Hitting requires more concentration, because in the field you can just go about your work with your natural instincts. You have to set yourself up for an at-bat. In the field, the first thing I do is look for where my wife is sitting and where my mom is sitting. Otherwise I just check out my territory, make sure it's pebble-free, just move around and get comfortable. I have to make some sort of move when the ball is hit anyplace. The only time I don't get involved is when there's a strikeout. First base keeps me from having to sit and watch. That's OK. I was the first baseman on the world championship team. I'll take that.

Judge's Comments

The lead sentence tells it all: *"To love the game is to appreciate it at its most basic level."* This is what's behind the appreciation of most sports and, in this article about our "national pastime," what this prize-winner banks on for its appeal. But it goes beyond that, to the humans who play the game well enough to have "made the bigs."

"On a couple of nights when the air was especially frosty," writer Howard Sinker sat down with three members of the Minnesota Twins and got some relaxed, first-person observations. There are times when home-run hitter Gary Gaetti just can't concentrate at the plate; when star pitcher Frank Viola thinks too much and decides *"To hell with it; let's see if it works;"* and—get this one—Gold Glove first baseman Kent Hrbek shuts his eyes as he fields a difficult hop.

Those are real people out there, not baseball-card cutouts. Sinker does a good job of helping us share their joys and their anxieties by letting them speak in their own words. Who else but players themselves would contend that Wade Boggs doesn't swing hard enough, that .150 hitters give them more trouble than .300 sluggers, or that they're always expecting a really bad throw from the third baseman?

This article even survived the supreme test: It appeared in a non-sports magazine and was read by people who don't necessarily like the game. We all like to read about the human side of heroes.

Steroids: The Deadly Obsession

GENERAL

By *FRED MANN*

From the Wichita Eagle-Beacon
Copyright © 1988, the Wichita Eagle-Beacon

Every so often Bob Hazelton catches a glimpse of himself in the mirrors that line the walls of the Atilis Gym and lowers his head in his hands as if to avoid the man who stares back. There isn't much of him left after more than a decade of steroid abuse. Surgeons took his legs away piece by piece over the last two years. They started below the knees and kept cutting their way up—first the left leg, then the right—until only a few inches remained of either limb.

Hazelton, once a world-ranked heavyweight fighter based in Wichita, watched himself disappear like a cartoon character being erased by the artist.

Some days he can force a laugh about it, but not today. It is gray outside the gym, Christmas is coming, and he is a long way from his wife and sons in Haysville.

So he sits and broods and tries to prepare himself mentally for another workout. He stares out at the wintry sky, stares down at his hands, scarred and broken from the ring, and stares at the soap opera on the small television set behind the gymnasium counter. But he cannot put this off forever. He must go to work to keep in shape.

Finally, Hazelton tells his daughter, Cyndy, 21, that he is ready. He will start with curls.

Cyndy wheels him over to a bench, and Hazelton pushes himself onto it, wriggling until he has worked his way down the bench far enough to lie on his back.

Cyndy picks up a broad leather belt to strap her father down. She passes it over his stomach and beneath the bench, then cinches it tight, tighter, tighter still, until Hazelton grunts.

It takes three people to enable Hazelton to perform this basic exercise. Mark Ermigiotti, who works at the gym, places a 60-pound dumbbell on the right side of Hazelton's chest while Doug Kuraceba, a buddy, places another dumbbell on the left side. Hazelton grips the weights and Cyndy straddles his waist to steady him. Ermigiotti and Kuraceba step back on either side to spot for him.

Hazelton lies still for a moment, sucking in air, then extends the weights out to the sides. He curls them to his chest, extends them again, and repeats . . . three times, four times . . . his triceps leaping and writhing, his forearms trembling. Five, six. . . .

His torso shifts to the left side of the bench and strains against the leather belt. Cyndy squeezes her legs tighter to keep her father from slipping further. Seven, eight. . . . Hazelton's neck glows, and the veins swell like hoses. A tremor shivers up the nape of his neck stirring the tendrils of his blond rat-tail now damp with perspiration.

Eight. . . .

He does another rep, then he must quit.

He nods and relaxes his body while Ermigiotti and Kuraceba move to his sides to take the weights from his hands.

It has been a heroic effort. Hazelton lies still for a moment, then tries to raise himself. Cyndy slides her hip between his stumps to give him something to push against, then takes one of his hands and pulls him up.

He slumps at the end of the bench, and drops his head in his hands, his shoulders rising and falling as he re-fills his lungs.

His heart is not in this anymore. Lifting used to be an obsession for him. Even after his ring career. More so then. He wanted to build a massive, perfectly sculpted body, like the men in the pictures that cover the gym walls—Arnold Schwarzenegger, Franco Columbo, all the gods of "body beautiful" who used to pump iron right here at Atilis.

★   ★   ★

But now he lifts only to keep himself strong in case he has to go back into the hospital for more cutting on his stumps, or more treatment for infections or heart problems. In addition to costing him his legs, steroids also scarred his heart, and, at age 42, Hazelton has had two heart attacks.

Mirrors are unforgiving. The man who looks at Bob Hazelton from the wall of Atilis is a man Hazelton is still trying to know and understand.

He used to be a 6-foot-5½ blond-haired, blue-eyed Adonis, the 15th-ranked heavyweight fighter in the world in 1978.

Today, he is 4-foot-2, and trapped in a wheelchair, the bones in his stumps rendered too soft by steroids to be fitted with prosthetic legs.

"It's sickening," Hazelton says. "I heard when you got old you shrink, but this is ridiculous."

He does not have to search far for somebody to blame for what happened to him, and he blames him every day. He did it to himself.

And he is unsparing in his self-flagellation.

Hazelton cast himself as the central figure in a modern sports tragedy: Trying to make his body perfect, he destroyed it.

"I consider myself the dumbest person in the world," Bob Hazelton says.

It started in 1971. His goal when he began taking steroids, or "juicing," was to fill out his large frame and gain size and power for his boxing career.

Hazelton fought professionally for 10 years, starting in California, moving to New Mexico, finally to Wichita, where he settled down in the late 1970s.

He fought some name fighters in his time—George Foreman, Bob Foster, Lucien Rodriguez. Three times he was scheduled to fight Duane Bobick, and had he defeated Bobick, there are those who thought he would have been one step away from a championship bout with Larry Holmes. But the fight never came off.

Hazelton's last fight in Wichita was May 12, 1979, against Rodriguez, the No. 2-ranked European heavyweight, and Hazelton put up a weak battle. He was TKO'd in the third. The reason he lost, he now says, is that he went into the fight with a painful groin infection that was caused by steroids.

Hazelton learned about the importance of weight from George Foreman. He had fought the future champ in 1969. Foreman was just starting out after winning the gold medal in the 1968 Olympics and was being prepped for a run at the title. Hazelton, white, blond, handsome with five pro fights on his resume—all KO victories—was being prepped as a stepping stone.

The fight was held in Las Vegas on Dec. 6, 1969, and it did not last long. Foreman cut the inside of Hazelton's mouth so badly that the fight had to be stopped in the first round.

"After Foreman, I was totally confused," Hazelton says. "I felt I embarrassed myself. I wasn't that good a fighter to fight someone like that."

He had weighed only 194 pounds for the fight. Foreman had 30 pounds on him.

So Hazelton hit the juice. He took small amounts of steroids at first, maybe a single injection a year, under a doctor's care, he says.

He knew nothing about the harm steroids could do to his body, and if the doctor knew, he never told Hazelton.

"I never heard anything bad about steroids until '81, after the first blood clot," Hazelton says.

Steroids are a synthetic form of testosterone, the male sex hormone, and are prescribed by doctors for such therapeutic uses as the treatment of anemia. But athletes who take them without medical supervision generally exceed recommended dosages, and run the risk of serious side effects such as sterility, abnormal liver function, high blood pressure or cardiovascular disease.

Testosterone naturally produces conditions that lead to hardening of the arteries, and steroids speed the process. It increases the ratio of "bad" cholesterol (low-density lipoproteins) to "good" cholesterol (high density lipoproteins) about fourfold. "Bad" cholesterol clings to the interior walls of the arteries, eventually clogging them and restricting blood flow.

Hazelton says his arteries eventually narrowed to the size of a pinhole.

Clots formed in the left leg and doctors performed bypass operations on it, taking other veins and using them to re-direct blood flow around the blockages.

Dr. Romulo Magsalin, who started treating Hazelton in 1985 when the site of one bypass operation failed to heal, said chronic steroid use was the most probable cause of the damage to Hazelton's arteries. Specialists in Wichita had the same opinion, Magsalin said.

Hazelton has no doubt. "What people don't know," he says, "is when you take steroids, it doesn't mean it's going to hit you now, or in a year. It's the type of problem you can never get rid of."

Hazelton was on and off the juice most of his boxing career. After it ended, he needed an outlet for his competitive drive, so he hit the weights even harder to pump up his body. It was the Charles Atlas dream. He wanted to be big, as big as he could be, bigger than his friends who lifted beside him in the gyms of Wichita.

By 1985, Hazelton says, he was spending $200 to $300 a week on steroids, primarily deca-durabolin, one of the most potent. He bought them on the black market that thrives in weight-lifting circles. At his peak, he took 800 to 1,400 milligrams a week orally or by injection.

Magsalin says patients who are given steroids for therapeutic purposes normally take 5 to 10 milligrams a day orally, and 50 to 100 milligrams over several weeks by injection. "People engaged in body building easily exceed one hundred times the normal therapeutic dose," he says.

Hazelton far exceeded even that.

He was a juice junkie.

By 1986, Hazelton had blown himself up to 312 pounds, Magsalin said.

Hazelton's wife, Liz, knew instinctively that steroids were harmful, and urged him to stop. She hated the way they affected her husband emotionally. She had married him in 1982, finding him charming and charismatic. But when he took steroids, she says, he would erupt with unpredictable flashes of temper.

He did not hurt her, but living with him was difficult for her and her children—two sons by a previous marriage.

"I was always angry when he was doing steroids," she says. "I don't feel it was fair to him, or to ourselves. It is hard to put up with his emotional swings. There's two different sides; the person you know and love, and the person who comes out after taking steroids.

"It was like Jekyll and Hyde. They're not even conscious of it. It's a split-second thing. The littlest thing aggravates it.''

★   ★   ★

Liz Hazelton did not care how big her husband's body was but he was obsessed by it. "At one time he was phenomenally big, and he still didn't think he was big enough," Liz says.

By 1986, bypass operations on the left leg no longer solved the problems. Doctors tried a triple bypass, but within three weeks the new vein was clotted, Hazelton says.

"The leg was starting to blow up bad," he says. "I couldn't walk 100 yards. It was so big I couldn't get a pair of jeans on."

"His calf would look like an elephant's leg," Liz says. "Then he had open ulcers on his ankle and foot. His leg was dead."

"I felt this thing was going to be the destruction of me," Hazelton says. "They couldn't get rid of it."

And yet he continued to take steroids.

"I knew steroids caused it," Hazelton says, "but I didn't want to face the facts.

"Gangrene was starting to set in my left leg. It was breaking down so bad there were holes in my leg. The skin was so dry and dead it would just split.

"I went to Florida to visit my mother 'cause the leg was so bad. My mother was very upset I was in so much pain. I went to a doctor, and he said, 'You got a choice: You got two months to live, or the leg has got to come off now.' "

On Nov. 11, Hazelton's 40th birthday, his left leg was removed below the knee.

He tried to look as if he were handling it, but he wasn't. "I was suppressing all my feelings so people wouldn't think I was weak. All I could think of was: "How they gonna look at me?'

"I thought I was the most terrible looking thing in the world."

And then, in September 1987, he started taking steroids again.

"I figured there wasn't much left but what there was left I wanted it to look good," he said.

"I thought it was impossible. These steroids could not be doing all this. I was still coming into the gym for workouts. I don't think I was trying to prove I was no less a man, but being competitive around my friends, I think I had to maintain some type of image.

"I felt I could get as big as I was with two legs. And maybe people would look at me up here," Hazelton says, nodding at his chest, "not down there."

Says Liz: "All he had left was his body. After he lost his left leg, he especially just had his body. To him, building up his body was everything."

Hazelton remembers his return to steroids with bitter self-disgust.

"I was doing everything for Robert Hazelton, nothing for anyone else. I figured if I was going to die, enjoy life. Some doctor thought it would be OK (to take steroids) if I took blood thinner. That's crap.

"I kept working out, kept trying to prove to myself I was still something."

Three weeks after he went back on steroids, his right leg started to hurt.

"But it was a pain I hadn't had before—from the kneecap down to the foot. It got to a point where I couldn't even turn my foot without doing it with my hands. Pain medication couldn't touch it. At midnight one night, I went to the emergency room. They found an occlusion (blockage) in it.

"I had self-destructed again."

Surgeons at St. Joseph Medical Center in Wichita performed a bypass, he says, but the pain returned in a week, more intense than before. The pain left him rigid. He slept an hour a night, he says. He spent most of the dark hours clutching the rail of his bed and twisting his body as if trying to get away from the pain.

"The pain was so bad I couldn't even talk," Hazelton says. "I told myself, 'I'm just completely destroyed now.' "

Two days later, the right leg was taken off below the knee.

Three days later, the stump became infected. They had to cut again. And again.

"I don't remember how many times they amputated," Hazelton says. "I remember three times in one week."

His stay in St. Joseph lasted three months, he says. He finally got out on Christmas Eve last year.

But there were more amputations ahead.

Three more inches came off the left leg, two off the right.

"I got maybe six inches left on one side, maybe eight on the other side," Hazelton says. "That's it."

He has been in and out of hospitals for cleaning and draining infections. The nerves in his stumps had been cut on so much that they became swollen, and in September a nerve block was performed to deaden his right stump.

"It's a never-ending battle," Hazelton says. "The thing that kept me strong was I found the Lord. People don't like to talk about it. I can't figure out anything else to say.

"I should have died in St. Joseph last year, but God and my wife gave me strength to go on."

Hazelton gives speeches to high school students, warning about drugs and steroids. He has given clinics in Florida and Philadelphia, where he has been visiting Cyndy. He will talk to any group that will listen. Recently he was honored by a fitness magazine for speaking out against steroids, he says. Someday, he would like a job counseling kids.

But he still has to figure out the man in the mirror.

He is starting to like him better. He likes him better than the guy who used to fight.

Hazelton never liked boxing, he says, never liked climbing into a ring to hurt somebody. "That wasn't me. I really wasn't happy."

He only started boxing as a kid for self-defense. His dream was to play professional football. His parents had separated when he was 17, and it tore him up. Boxing helped him escape. Once he got a career going, he was caught up in the fast life and tried to live up to his image of a professional athlete, he says.

The guy in the wheelchair is nicer, he says, more real, not such a phony, closer to the Bob Hazelton of his youth.

But for 40 years he had two strong, active legs, and a body he worshiped and spent most of his time developing and pampering.

And now . . . "I'm not handling this very well," he says. "People think I am 'cause God gave me the gift to smile in the daytime.

"It's hard sometimes. I'm only human. . . . I don't know. Some people wanted me to accept this a lot quicker than I have. It's just not that easy."

Cyndy, a daughter from a previous marriage, had never seen her father until he came for his recent visit. Hazelton was nervous about her reaction to his physical condition, but she accepted him instantly and left her job as a receptionist to be with him and help him through the day.

It was a gratifying lesson for Hazelton to learn, even if it was sad to learn it so late:

"I found out when all this was over people still cared about me whether I was strong or weak," Hazelton says. "They didn't care what I was as long as I was alive.

"Being off steroids, it's a relief. By working out and eating right and just being more accepting of life the way it is, I'm all right.

"But I hope it's not too late."

Sherrill Paid 'Hush Money'

COLLEGE FOOTBALL

By *DOUG BEDELL*

From the Dallas Morning News
Copyright © 1988, the Dallas Morning News

Even as an NCAA investigation into irregularities in the Texas A & M football program wound down earlier this year, Coach Jackie Sherrill continued cash payments to a former player who said the money was to ensure his silence about rules violations.

Former Aggie fullback George Smith said Sherrill paid him $4,400 in a series of cash and money order transactions that date back to November 1986. Smith termed the payments "hush money."

Sherrill refused to comment on Smith's allegations until after the Aggies finish their football season next month. However, A & M president William H. Mobley and vice president Robert Smith, interviewed by *The Dallas Morning News* Thursday, said the university had notified the NCAA that it had received allegations of additional rules violations. Mobley, meanwhile, said he has ordered an internal investigation to be headed by Robert Smith, the official in charge of finance and administration.

"Based on our further discussions this morning and information you have available," Mobley said, "without question we'll proceed expeditiously and bring to bear investigative resources we need to seek to establish the validity of the issues on whether or not there are violations of NCAA rules or whether or not there are other institutional issues involved."

Mobley was named president of the university in August.

George Smith, a Georgia high school All-America when Sherrill recruited him in 1982, said he received $500 in cash on Sept. 13—four days after Aggie officials announced at a news conference that the National Collegiate Athletic Association had levied major sanctions against the university's football program.

That payment, one of three Smith claims to have received since June 6, was sent to Smith's Atlanta home in an overnight express envelope. The envelope bore the return address of Bob Matey, a member of Sherrill's support staff.

Two other overnight express envelopes bore the return names and addresses of A&M receivers coach George Pugh and a Matey associate who is not employed by the athletic department.

The News obtained all three envelopes from Smith. One, which was dated Sept. 26 and contained five $100 bills, was opened in Atlanta in the presence of a *News* reporter.

Later, in more than eight hours of tape-recorded interviews, Smith told *The News* that Sherrill and his staff provided about $10,000 in money, extra benefits and airline tickets. Smith joined the Aggies in the summer of 1982 and quit the team in early 1984 to transfer to Clemson University.

On Wednesday, Robert Smith said that Sherrill did not deny sending money to George Smith, but maintained that he was being coerced.

Texas A&M was assessed a two-year probation in September by the NCAA, which substantiated numerous violations of regulations that govern extra benefits to student-athletes. The Aggies also were barred from postseason play this season.

George Smith, one of the most highly recruited high school players in the country in 1982, said Thursday that he had been contacted Wednesday night at his Atlanta home by coach Pugh's wife. As a result of that conversation, Smith said, he would refuse to stand by the statements he made in the tape-recorded newspaper interviews. Before those interviews, Smith signed a notarized, sworn statement that he would "be truthful in the information he provides."

A&M vice president Robert Smith, no relation to the former fullback, said George Smith had contacted him early Thursday, only a short time before A&M officials were to meet a reporter and editor from *The News.* George Smith refused to say what his conversation with university officials entailed.

"If I say it didn't happen, nothing happened," George Smith said Thursday. George Smith said that Pugh, a longtime Sherrill assistant who recruited him, was being unfairly singled out by Sherrill as the allegations unfolded.

★   ★   ★

Controversy has dogged George Smith's collegiate athletic career. In 1982, four All-America selection committees, including the *Parade* All-American Team, named George Smith to their first squads. Most recruiting services ranked him as first or second in the state of Georgia. And Sherrill, entering the first year of his employment as A&M's head coach and athletic director, engaged in a bitter war for the 6-foot, 226-pound fullback's commitment.

At first, Smith said he bowed to family and community pressure to sign a letter of intent with Georgia. Then, at Sherrill's urging,

Smith said he gave the NCAA information implicating a Bulldog assistant coach in improper recruiting activities.

As a result, Smith's commitment to Georgia was nullified, the school was assessed a one-year probation and the assistant coach was fired.

Smith then signed with A&M. Throughout the process, Smith claims he was never offered any improper inducements by Sherrill or Pugh, the A&M assistant coach who headed Aggie recruiting in the Southeast.

But in interviews with *The News*, the ex-player did recall that Sherrill had pledged to "take care of me" and provide a good-paying job working around the head coach's College Station home.

"I said, 'Well, coach, how will I get home in the winter months or for the Christmas breaks and things of that nature?' " Smith recalled. "He said: 'We can get you a summer job. That's not against the rules. Also I have work that I need done around my house. We can work that out. And I can pay you what I want to pay you. . . .'

"Once he told me he was going to take care of me and I wouldn't have to worry about nothing, I said, 'OK. I'm coming to school here.' "

Smith said Sherrill ultimately paid him hundreds of dollars for minor yard work—an apparent violation of NCAA extra benefits regulations.

In other apparent violations of NCAA rules, Smith claimed:

• Sherrill and Pugh routinely paid for round-trip plane flights between College Station and Atlanta.

• The head coach/athletic director also arranged for Smith to receive credit for a physical education course he did not attend during the summer prior to Smith's official enrollment at A&M.

• Sherrill was aware that Smith and other players were scalping their complimentary tickets to alumni at inflated prices. Smith claims a Sherrill assistant set up those transactions.

★   ★   ★

Smith's recollections reveal an apparent systematic disregard for NCAA regulations. From the final days of Smith's high school career in 1982 through the most recent shipment of "hush money" in September, the A&M program operated with duplicity, Smith said.

For example, as the Feb. 10, 1982, national signing day approached, Smith said he made up his mind to attend A&M based on the strong pitches from Sherrill and Pugh.

However, Smith said, when family members and prominent Georgia boosters began pressing the star fullback to change his mind, Sherrill and Pugh attempted to arrange an improper transaction.

At their suggestion, Smith was to meet the night of Feb. 9, 1982, with Sherrill, Pugh and former Pitt All-America linebacker Hugh Green at a local fast food restaurant.

"We were going to go out and maybe have a drink or something and I was going to sign with A & M the night before (the official date) . . . ," Smith said. "I wasn't supposed to tell anybody I signed with them Tuesday night. That was the agreement."

The A & M letter of intent, Smith said, was to have been post-dated, in violation of NCAA rules. Smith said his secret liaison with the A & M contingent was thwarted when the grandmother with whom he was living refused to allow him out of the house.

And, instead, Smith wound up signing with Georgia the following afternoon.

Sherrill and Pugh, Smith said, were incensed. In fact, both became embroiled in a shouting match at Coffee County High School as Smith announced he was going to Georgia.

Smith's high school coach, Bonwell Royal, gave this version to the local press: "He (Sherrill) looked terrible, like this whole thing had really ripped him. He pointed his finger at me and said, 'George Smith will never play a down at Georgia.' He said he wouldn't stand to have a player bought out from under him, that he'd go to the NCAA."

By the time the NCAA's investigation was complete, Smith had been branded *persona non grata* in his home state. Newspapers called him a "turncoat." Neighbors sneered.

And Sherrill, according to Smith, came to the rescue.

Within two days of his release from Georgia and signing with A & M, Smith was on his way to College Station. At that time, according to the Official Airline Guide, a one-way plane ticket from Atlanta to Houston cost about $200.

"My mom had to scrape the money up," Smith said. "She went around and borrowed money so I could fly out. But they (Sherrill and Pugh) gave me the money to reimburse her, and I sent the money back."

Such payments of plane fares for student-athletes and prospective recruits are prohibited for all but official, sanctioned visits to NCAA institutions. Smith already had taken his paid visit to College Station.

In fact, Smith said, Sherrill and Pugh would arrange for reimbursement of air fare for every trip home Smith took for the next two years.

All told, Smith estimates he made that round-trip journey at least nine times. According to the airline guide figures, those tickets would have cost about $3,600.

To obscure the transactions from the NCAA, Smith said he often was instructed to have his uncle charge the tickets on a personal American Express card. The amount of the ticket was then sent from College Station directly to the uncle in cash or money order, Smith said.

Plane tickets were not the only perk for Smith. First, in apparent violation of NCAA rules, Smith said Sherrill provided him with money to pay for room and board at the athletic dormitory the summer before official enrollment. That cash was paid Smith in addition to a salary for construction work during the first half of the summer of 1982, Smith said.

"It was somewhere between $700 and $800 . . . ," Smith said. "I kept my money that I made from construction, and they gave me the money to pay (associate athletic director for finance) Wally Groff for staying in the dormitory, eating in the cafeteria."

Next, during the second half of the 1982 summer, Sherrill arranged for enrollment of Smith in a physical education class he would never attend.

"They said I had to take that course in order to stay in the dormitory, but I didn't pay for it," Smith said. "I think I was supposed to pay but I didn't. They paid for the class."

Financial aid to student-athletes before the date of official enrollment is expressly prohibited under NCAA guidelines.

★   ★   ★

As his first season approached, Smith said a member of Sherrill's staff informed him that an influential alumnus would be purchasing his four home-game complimentary tickets at an inflated price.

"He just told me, 'I got a guy that's gonna take care of your tickets and you just need to be patient. He'll come by and holler at you after the ball games. He'll be in the dressing room.' "

A man he knew only as "Bill from Lampasas" then regularly left $400 for Smith's four tickets to the season home contests.

Sherrill was aware of Smith's ticket dealings by Christmas in 1982, when the booster left $1,600 total for tickets and a bonus, Smith said.

When Smith returned from Christmas vacation, Sherrill confronted him. Apparently, Sherrill considered the alumni transactions too risky, Smith said.

"He came to me and told me that he didn't want me dealing with that guy any longer," Smith said. "He said, 'If you need anything you come to me from now on.' "

During the summer of 1983, Smith said he and Sherrill struck an agreement about obtaining cash for living expenses.

"I said, 'Well, coach, you know I'm going to need some clothing and I'm going to need some money for the season. What are we going to do about that?'

"He said, 'Well, I don't want you selling your tickets to anyone. What you do from now on is . . . you come to me and I'll let you go over to my house and work and earn it. Nobody told me how much I can pay you.' "

When Smith showed up to do yard work, he said, Sherrill simply asked him how much money he needed.

"I said, 'Well, I need $400.'

"He said, 'That's all you had to tell me. Remember this here: Don't ever tell me what you're going to do with the money. Just tell me how much you need.'

"And from then on I'd go and ask for $200, $300 or $400. And he'd give it to me."

During the school year, Smith said he would approach Sherrill for money in the athletic department offices. Often Sherrill would ask how much was needed, then tell Smith to wait outside his office for 20 minutes or so, Smith said.

"I'd come back in and Jackie would have the money," Smith said. "He'd say, 'Make sure you don't be flashing this and don't say anything about it.' "

But apparently Smith's teammates knew Sherrill was "taking care of" Smith.

"They'd see him coming in the cafeteria and they'd say, 'G! Here comes your dad. Better ask for your allowance,' " Smith said.

★   ★   ★

Prior to the 1984 season, Smith said he grew disenchanted with the Aggie program. Although he had averaged nearly five yards per carry during his freshman year, playing time diminished during his second season with the arrival of new recruits like running back Roger Vick and the return of previously injured stars like Tommy Sanders.

Smith said he told Sherrill he wanted to leave, and the head coach helped him transfer to South Carolina's Clemson University.

In fact, Smith said, Sherrill arranged for payment of Smith's plane ticket. The head coach even later sent along some spending money, Smith said.

In all, Smith estimated during his A & M playing days he received more than $10,000 worth of cash, extra benefits and plane tickets from Sherrill.

But the money did not stop with Smith's departure from College Station.

As the NCAA was gearing up its investigation into the Aggie program, Smith contacted Sherrill for more help. He had quit school and applied for early eligibility for the 1986 professional draft.

Smith said Sherrill sent him $800 on Nov. 18, 1986, to set up an apartment in New York City.

Then, after talks with Smith, Sherrill sent $500 on July 10, 1987, and again during January 1988.

As the NCAA moved toward conclusion of its inquiry, Smith was spending brief stints in the Tampa Bay Buccaneers training camp and with the United States Football League's Jacksonville Bulls. He then moved to Atlanta to find work. During that period, Sherrill sent three more overnight express mail deliveries of cash or money orders totaling $1,900.

The decision to expose Sherrill's misdeeds, Smith said, was made out of anger. Smith said he had expected Sherrill this year to provide about $3,000 in a lump sum for vocational school tuition. The money instead continued to come in small batches, Smith said.

"I wanted him to send me back to school," Smith said. "I wanted to finish up. That's what I really wanted. . . . He owes me a degree. I would never have left A & M if I hadn't gotten screwed by the coaching staff. So I got screwed out of graduating from here. . . .

"All this was done to keep me quiet for another couple of months."

A Chip of Pure Diamond

TRACK AND FIELD

By *DAVE DORR*

From the St. Louis Post-Dispatch
Copyright © 1988, the St. Louis Post-Dispatch

Piggott Avenue between 14th and 15th streets in East St. Louis was, in the summer of 1972, the soul of the south end of the city.

At the corner of 15th, across from Lincoln Park, sat a pool hall and a grocery. Next to the store on Piggott was a restaurant. Next to the restaurant was S&S Liquor, a tavern. At the end of the block, at 14th, there was shrimp for sale.

On a steamy summer night, Piggott could turn violent. The S&S —called "the cut rate" in street talk—drew from the entire south end. It was an escape for those in an impoverished existence that dragged on, day after hot day.

Some residents there were stone poor. They lived amid stripped, abandoned cars that sat rusting, streets that were strewn with litter, and vacant lots with weeds waist-high. Some nights, skirmishes, with shouting and cursing, spilled out of the "cut rate" and into the street.

But there was an unspoken grapevine law along Piggott that anyone wandering into any of the stores or the pool hall was not to bother the Joyner children—Alfrederick, Jackie, Angela and Debra.

The Joyner home at 1433 Piggott—across the street from the tavern—was cramped, with two grandparents, two parents, four youngsters, four small bedrooms, one bathroom, a kitchen and a living room somehow squeezed into it. The house was a frame with a roof, scarcely more than protection from the elements. Nonetheless, it served as a haven.

On the frigid nights of January and February, when the temperature would plunge below zero, the water pipes froze. A bucket full of lighted coals sometimes could unfreeze them. Or Alfred

Joyner, the children's father, would turn on the faucets and let the water run all night.

To the four Joyner children, playing Monopoly on the front porch on summer days, Piggott wasn't beset by problems. Piggott was a wide world, generating a life of its own, as seen through the eyes of a child. It was, in one respect, beautiful.

Alfred said of his four children: "They had more fun among themselves than with anyone else. They went everywhere together."

They were poor, but the Joyner children didn't know it.

"We tried to make hard times into good times," Alfred said. "We did try."

Alfrederick—who was known as Al—was 12 and Jackie 10 in the summer of '72. One of the games they played was for $5, a princely sum when you're 10, with Tyrone Cavitt, then the recreation supervisor at the Mary E. Brown Community Center at Lincoln Park.

"Five dollars says you can't beat 'ol Tyrone around the block," he'd say to the four Joyners, waving a bill tantalizingly in front of their faces. Off they'd go. Up Piggott. Then right on 14th to Trendley. East on Trendley to 15th. Shoot down 15th and take a sharp right on Piggott. Sometimes, Cavitt would turn around and backpedal, laughing with high-pitched glee as he teased them: "C'mon, c'mon— you sure are slow." What he really saw in Jackie was a young Wilma Rudolph, the gold-medal sprinter America produced in the 1960s.

When the group got to 1433 Piggott and stopped, gasping for breath, Jackie would hurry inside to fetch her mother, Mary Joyner. Or Mary might already be standing on the porch, hands on hips.

"Tyrone Cavitt," she'd say, feigning disgust, "what are you up to again?"

The Joyners absorbed values and standards from Piggott and the recreation center in Lincoln Park that they neither recognized nor understood at the time. In the years to come, Piggott would connect Al and Jackie, brother and sister of extraordinary gifts, to some of the world's great cities for international track and field meets: Moscow, Zurich, Rome, Los Angeles, Helsinki, Berlin, Seoul.

Last September in Rome, silhouetted in the lights of Stadio Olimpico as Jackie long jumped, it was evident how at age 25, her body had matured. Svelte and statuesque at 5 feet 10. Eight percent body fat. Smooth, dark brown skin concealing bundles of fast-twitch muscle fibers that give her sprinter's speed.

"A chip of the purest diamond," said Bob Forster, her physical therapist in Santa Monica, Calif., when he first examined her six years ago.

"I look at Jackie and Al and I see such specimens," Forster said. "Al is broad at the shoulders, narrow at the waist, almost zero body fat. But his legs are thin from the knee down. He has weaknesses. Jackie has no flaws physically. None.

"She stands alone among the 200 athletes I've come into contact with. If I had worked with 10,000, she'd probably be one in 10,000."

★   ★   ★

In January 1962, Evelyn Joyner stopped by to visit her son, Alfred, and his wife, Mary, who two months later would give birth to their second child.

Before Evelyn left the house, she patted Mary's stomach and nodded approvingly. "If it's a girl, she'll be the first Joyner girl," she said. "Name her after the first lady. Hear me, now?"

Mary was 19, Alfred was 17 and a junior at Lincoln High School. "Keep On Pushin' " by The Impressions was a song he knew by heart. It became his motto.

On the day Jackie was born, Alfred learned of it when he returned home from track practice. He was born in the house at 1433 Piggott. It belonged to his grandmother, Ollie Mae Johnson. To Alfred, she was "Grandmama." She nicknamed him, "Bubbles."

One day Ollie Mae said to Mary: "You and Bubbles have nothing to worry about. All I ask is that I be allowed to live and die in this house."

Observing his mother's wishes, Alfred's daughter was given the name of the first lady in the White House in 1962, Jacqueline Kennedy. Alfred skipped lunch at school the next day to see his baby at the hospital.

"She was so tiny she looked like she'd break in two," he recalled.

Alfred's wish was the same joy he felt had accompanied the birth of Alfrederick two years earlier. Alfred was 15 and Mary 16 when she found out she was pregnant with him. Alfred's mother confronted her son, crying.

"You're so young you've still got baby's milk on your breath," she said, angrily. "And you're bringing a child into this world? How you going to feed it? Clothe it?"

Al was born in January 1960. In October of that year, Alfred and Mary were married by a justice of the peace in Belleville.

"Mary and I were so in love," Alfred said. They kept the marriage secret from most of the family for months. Mary and her newborn son lived with her grandmother in another part of East St. Louis until 1962, when she joined her husband on Piggott.

His mother's words stung Alfred. Anxious to prove his manhood to himself and to his mother, Alfred walked into the St. Louis offices of an Army recruiter. The only jobs he held were shining shoes, mowing five yards regularly and protecting the cars of patrons at the pool hall who parked on Piggott. The Army guaranteed security. What better way could he improve his lot?

His mother provided the answer when he came home with the Army registration papers. She burned them in an ashtray with the admonishment: "You and your brother, Fred, are going to be the first Joyners to graduate. You're going to finish high school."

They did. Fred, a good athlete, graduated from Lincoln and attended Parsons College in Fairfield, Iowa. On Alfred's high school graduation day in 1963, Mary attended the ceremonies. Mary gave her husband a card and $10, telling him softly, "I'm sorry there isn't more."

His track coach, George Holliday, also gave him money. Alfred had fulfilled his mother's wish.

★   ★   ★

Years later, Jackie would be first—and a lady—in a manner that far exceeded what her grandmother Evelyn had in mind when she selected a name.

Not only is Jackie the first lady of East St. Louis, she is the first lady of track and field. Other firsts, equally as impressive:

• From 1977-79, at ages 15, 16 and 17, she won the Amateur Athletic Union national Junior Olympic pentathlon championship, becoming the first black to break through in an event dominated by white athletes.

The pentathlon comprised the 100-meter hurdles, long jump, shot put, high jump and 200-meter dash, conducted over two days. In 1980, the javelin and 800 were added, making the event the heptathlon. She won the national championship that year, too.

• On May 17, 1980, she became the first black to deliver the competitors' oath at the Illinois high school track and field championships.

• On Aug. 4, 1984, a brother and sister from Piggott Avenue completed a historic double at the Summer Olympic Games in Los Angeles. Al became the first American in 80 years to win the triple jump gold medal. Jackie, injured, finished second in the heptathlon. Her silver is the only Olympic medal won by an American woman in a multi-event.

It was a night of nights for East St. Louisans who watched the drama on television. Afterward, the streets were filled with people who wanted to share their pride. Cavitt, 42, and employed now by the St. Clair County Head Start program, remembers because he was one of them.

"Everybody wanted to talk about the Joyner kids," he said.

Cavitt understood why. The Joyners represented hope.

Holder of the heptathlon world record, Jackie is recognized as the foremost all-around female athlete of her time. The overriding question is whether she is the finest female athlete ever.

"Few men can compete with her," said Gary Kinder, a St. Louisan who will be the top-ranking U.S. decathlete at the Seoul Olympics that begin Saturday.

"She can be compared to (Jim) Thorpe and (Bob) Mathias," said Frank Zarnowski, a track-and-field historian considered the leading authority on the heptathlon and the decathlon, the 10-event men's competition.

Thorpe, an American Indian, won the pentathlon and decathlon at the 1912 Games in Stockholm, Sweden. His margin of victory in the decathlon was 688 points. Thorpe was forced to return his medals months later when he was declared a professional because he once played semi-professional baseball. Yet Thorpe still is considered the finest American athlete ever.

In 1952 Mathias won his second of two Olympic decathlon titles by 912 points, the largest margin ever.

Like Thorpe and Mathias in the decathlon, Jackie is separating herself more and more from the rest of the world in the heptathlon. She has six of the eight all-time best scores.

Based on this year's scores, Jackie goes into the Seoul heptathlon competition with an edge of 412 points over her closest pursuer, East Germany's Anke Behmer.

Zarnowski, dean of the graduate program in business at Mount St. Mary's College in Emmitsburg, Md., measured the quality of Jackie's world-record score of 7,215 against the decathlon. He came up with a score of 8,800 in her seven events vs. the 10 in the decathlon.

The numbers are meaningless unless you know that 8,800 is just 47 points shy of the world record held by Britain's Daley Thompson.

Mathias, now 57 and the president of American Kids Sports Association in Irvine, Calif., said Jackie is "so good in the individual events she wouldn't have to do the heptathlon. It's tough to do the multi-event. Anyone who can put it all together as she has is absolutely phenomenal."

No American woman owns an Olympic gold medal in multi-event competition, which was added to the Games in 1964. Jackie is the first American to hold a multi-event world record since Mildred "Babe" Didrikson Zaharias, generally acknowledged as the world's greatest all-round woman athlete. In the 1932 Olympics, Didrikson set a world record in winning the 80-meter hurdles and an Olympic record in winning the javelin. She placed second in the high jump but shared the world record.

★   ★   ★

Each of the Joyner siblings attended Lincoln High. Al later went to Tennessee State, transferring at the end of the first semester to Arkansas State. Debra followed him to Arkansas State on a volleyball scholarship. Angela attended Vocational Training Center in Centreville.

In 1980, Jackie exchanged the hardscrabble of East St. Louis for the clean-cut lines of UCLA and discovered the vistas of a brand new world—one full of wonder and promise. There are few weeds in glitzy Westwood, where the UCLA campus is situated. She also met a track coach at the school whom she would marry six years later. His name is Bob Kersee.

Last month, Joyner-Kersee recalled how this California panorama, half a world removed from Piggott Avenue, made a deep impression.

"I didn't realize we didn't have a lot until I went to UCLA," she said. "I knew I didn't enjoy wearing the same clothes back-to-back, but that was my mother's rule. I learned early you didn't have to keep up with the Joneses to be someone's friend."

Her father smiles. In his mind, Mary dressed her children old-fashioned. He bought their clothes until Jackie reached 14.

"I cared about clothes. I didn't want the kids to be laughed at," Alfred said. "I pampered Al because he was the only boy. I got him a leather coat once. I knew he wanted those things."

Today, the Joyner house on Piggott is a charred shell, ravaged by a fire two years ago. Faulty wiring in the house next door started a blaze that engulfed much of 1433 Piggott.

Jackie, to her dismay, carried the baggage of East St. Louis to her new world on the West Coast.

Calling her father in 1980, she asked: "Daddy, is it true East St. Louis leads the nation in murders? Are they picking on me?"

He said: "Don't you be shouldering guilt. You are a bright spot from East St. Louis. You are a seed that has blossomed."

Whereupon, in the next eight years, she has bloomed as grandly as if she was a single red rose that sprouted among the weeds on Piggott. She has fulfilled the prophecy of her mother, who wrote on the back of her first baby picture:

"A star is born."

The Queen Finally Falls

TENNIS

By *BUD COLLINS*

From the Boston Globe
Copyright © 1988, Bud Collins

She can't win the big one—nine times.

Will that be the knock on Marvelous Martina—that she was on the brink of a ninth Wimbledon title and a 48th straight match victory, and didn't make it?

"Eight is Enough" may have been a sitcom, but it might be her epitaph. She walked into the throne room of her palace for a ninth time on finals day, regally took a 7-5, 2-0 lead—and then the joint came tumbling down like a house of cards. When the rubble was cleared, the Queen of Diamonds lay lifeless, her glittering crown gone, and a 19-year-old Queen of Hearts held all the aces.

It was a royal flushing of one potentate yesterday on Centre Court. A six-card straight was old news, as a new majesty one was installed.

The Fall of the House of Navratilova was bound to happen, of course. Cleopatra, Catherine the Great, Queen Victoria all gave way to the clock. But while Stephanie Maria Graf transformed Martina's drive toward a historic pedestal into a demolition derby (5-7, 6-2, 6-1), there was still the memory of how, year after year, this woman had returned to the palace of tennis, and made her subjects bow respectfully.

She wasn't the most popular of champions at the Big W, but she was the best.

"What was I—a Martian?" she asked after the usual 15,000 onlookers Thursday had sided so vigorously with Chris Evert in their semifinal match. She probably didn't like it much when her pal, Chrissie, said, "Martina's fragile, beatable. I think Steffi will beat her."

So the prophecy of another fallen empress was fulfilled, and 82-year-old Helen Wills Moody could go to sleep last night knowing that her 50-year-old record of 50 successive match wins most likely was safe for at least another half-century, or at least until the second round of 1995 when 26-year-old Steffi Graf may register No. 51. We will still have to wait until 1997 to see Moody surpassed by Graf's ninth championship. If it comes to that.

Does that give you an idea of what it took and meant to maintain the Reign of Navratilova?

Granted, she hasn't been No. 1 in the hardhearted softwaring view of Medusa, the women's computer, for a year. But her stronghold was intact until yesterday. Win Wimbledon, and sneer at computers.

But now Steffi has pulled down her temple like a Samson in drag, turned Martina out to the wilderness inhabited by ex-champs, become the new sweetheart—the first since Evonne Goolagong in 1980, then Chris America in 1981, interrupted the reign of Navratilova.

Martina was never a sweetheart. She couldn't quite win for winning. Even in her death-rattling triumph over Evert in the semis, a last bright thrust at hanging on, strangely she was rapped by press and public. Wouldn't it have been noble, they said, if she'd given Evert the disputed last point? Evert's final shot was called out. There was some question. Since when does a pro contradict an official's verdict in a charitable gesture?

Somehow Martina got marked lousy for not doing so. It figured.

Her life never quite suited the opinion makers. She had too many hangers-on, she played too much like a man. Those were among the knocks, along with her refusal to play Olympic tennis for the USA. She was a prima donna, a head case. You heard all that and more. She was the tabloids' dream athlete.

Maybe she was just a frightened kid who had to flee her homeland in 1975 to pursue her ambition: to be the very best who ever lived at the game she loved. She found that professional sport was a shallow life where you were either overpraised or overlooked, but she kept on until she'd reached the goal and clutched the American fantasy of being rich and renowned.

Now she was out of the big job. Ex-Wimbledon queen. But not before she had set new standards of greatness, emblazoning arenas across the world, while living according to her own dictates. Maybe she was from Mars—otherworldly in presence and play, a woman apart.

Mars was the god of war. This lefthanded Martian—Martina—is a wonderful goddess who has come through so many wars, and won most of them.

That Rainy Day Feeling

by Christopher Smith of the Brantford (Ontario) Expositor. Members of the Delhi high school football team and a few loyal fans endure a heavy rain during action in a championship game. Copyright © 1988, The Expositor, Brantford.

Crash Landing

by free-lancer Bruce A. Bennett for the American Three-Quarter Midget Racing Association 1988 Yearbook. Everything goes topsy-turvy for driver Billy Courtwright and his Kindberg car during action in a 1988 three-quarter midget racing event. Courtwright escaped injury and even finished the race. Copyright © 1988, Bruce A. Bennett.

The Mourning Anchor

GENERAL

By *RICK REILLY*

From Sports Illustrated
Copyright © 1988, Linda R. Verigan
Director, Rights and Permissions

What is it the poet said? Like muffled drums, our hearts beat a funeral march to the grave. And so it is that Bryant Gumbel, a man who is nothing if not prepared, keeps a list of his pallbearers.

Who has been true? Who has transgressed? Though only 39, he has done it many times. Gumbel hates surprises. The list changes every few months or so. He keeps track.

"I don't want to wait until something happens to see who my friends are," says Gumbel. "Or maybe I just don't want to be the guy who, when he dies, they can't find six guys to carry his coffin. Maybe this is a way to be sure I have six."

There have been days when he has wondered. Gumbel has a couple of thousand acquaintances but very few friends. Not that he couldn't have more. It's his choice. "If I'm in a room with 100 people, will I be able to find one person I'd like to have dinner with?" he asks. "Probably not," he answers.

Forget that. There are times when friends visit the Gumbels and Bryant won't come out of the den. "I've long since stopped apologizing to company for his grumpiness and aloofness," says June, his wife of almost 15 years. "Sometimes he doesn't feel compelled to entertain. It doesn't bother me anymore."

Strange man. Stubborn man. A man who might have best described himself when he said, "It's not that I dislike many people. It's just that I don't like many people."

The problem with people is that they just aren't as good as a certain Chicago probate judge who has been dead for more than 16 years—Gumbel's father, Richard. People don't try as hard as he did; they don't work as hard, achieve as much, carry themselves as tall.

And who could be as heroic? Once, in the Philippines during World War II, Richard continued to march despite being obviously ill. The medic finally pulled him aside, sat him on a rock and took out his tonsils, then and there. And what did Sergeant Gumbel do? He got up and marched on. The man never let up. When he returned from the war, he put himself through Xavier University in New Orleans while working full-time to keep his family eating. He was senior-class president and yearbook editor. Then he put himself through Georgetown law school while working two jobs. He graduated second in his class.

Let's face it. Compared to Richard Gumbel, most people come off like Lumpy Rutherford. So Bryant finds it hard to be impressed; he finds himself getting let down a lot. He has more feuds than some people have friends: David Letterman, Connie Chung, Linda Ellerbee, Steve Garvey. It's not his fault. People aren't good enough. People aren't professional enough. People aren't true enough. And so he sits alone in the den of his 14-room home in Waccabuc, N.Y., making a list that weighs heavy on his mind. Who can be trusted to hold up one-sixth of his memory?

If you happen to be among the listed, consider yourself lucky. In Gumbel, you have a man of wit, style and grace. You have a man who, as anchor of NBC's *Today* show, is the only TV interviewer who might make Ted Koppel look over his shoulder. When the situation gets tense, Gumbel is a lock as the silkiest talent strapping on an earpiece.

You also have to have a friend you can take to any party, for there is no subject on which he is not conversant. You have the world's best Trivial Pursuit partner, a *Jeopardy!* fiend, one of the last of the Renaissance men. You also have the Beau Brummell of this age, an impeccable dresser, a man with more than 100 suits (18 of them made specially for the Olympics by award-winning designer Joseph Abboud), some with the tags still uncut, a man who wouldn't think of leaving the house without color-coordinated tie, cuff-links, underwear and socks.

You have a whiz in the kitchen, a connoisseur of champagne, a global citizen, a 12-handicap golfer, a father of two (daughter Jillian, 5, and son Bradley, 9) and a multimillionaire by virtue of a contract with NBC that pays him some $7 million over the next three years, enough to keep him up to his thorax in cuff links.

And that doesn't include the biggest prize of all: his job as host of the most expensive TV undertaking ever—NBC's coverage of the Seoul Olympics. Over the 16 days of the Games, Gumbel's image will be projected by more prime-time cathode rays than any network anchor's in history. The assignment is the fattest enchilada ever handed out by NBC, and the ultimate testament to Gumbel's talent is that no one has yet mentioned that it went to a black man.

★　　★　　★

It's 98 degrees in Chicago, and Rhea Gumbel, 68, has all the win-

dows open in her seventh-floor apartment. She has an air-condi-
tioner in the bedroom, but it's not enough to cool the whole apartment. She would go somewhere cooler if she had the energy or a car,
but she has neither. Sold the car. Too much trouble. So five mornings
a week, she takes the bus to her job as a city clerk. Plenty are the
days when she wishes she could afford to retire.

"Did you see what Oprah Winfrey bought her mother the other
day?" one of the other clerks asked Rhea recently. "A brand-new
beautiful mansion, that's what." Rhea knows what that woman
would *loooove* to say next: *And your son, the big-shot NBC man, host
of the "Today" show, what does he give you? You live in a lousy
apartment. You won't go out at night and get milk because you're
afraid of walking into the streets. What kind of fancy son is this you
have?*

Still, she would never ask him for money. For one thing, she's too
proud. For another, "It would hurt me like a knife if he said no.
Besides, if he wanted to do something for me, he'd go ahead and do it
on his own, wouldn't he?"

She knows what the trouble is. She has this one glaring fault.
She's not his father.

Judge Richard Gumbel was a big man, 6-foot-1, four inches
taller than his younger son, Bryant. Richard, the child of a New Orleans gambler, was "one of the most amazing men I've ever met,"
says Dr. Norman Francis, president of Xavier.

As a student, Richard was nearly straight A. As a leader, he was
the first black to hold office in a national Catholic student organization. As a father, he was both strict and kind. While rearing his four
children in the racially mixed neighborhood of Hyde Park, near the
University of Chicago, he not only wouldn't let them get away with
bad grammar, but he also wouldn't let their friends get away with it.
"He was very hard to impress," says Bryant's brother, Greg, 42, a
sportscaster with the Madison Square Garden Network and, starting
with football season, with CBS. "A C should have been a B, and a B
should have been an A, and if it *was* an A, why wasn't it an A before
this?"

Yet when the family went on a picnic, Richard would play pepper with his boys for two hours. Or they would go to the sandlot and
work on grounders for three. On summer days Bryant rarely missed
a Cub game at Wrigley Field and also saw plenty of the White Sox at
night at Comiskey Park. What a life. In his day, he not only caught
more than 100 batting practice balls and fouls, he wore them all out,
too.

Greg lost that boyhood idolization of his father in high school, but
Bryant never did. Greg was handsome and popular in high school;
Bryant wasn't. Because racial attitudes then favored lighter skin,
and his skin was the darkest of any in his family, including his cousins, Bryant felt ugly. Lacking social confidence, he stayed away
from the dances and the back row at the Bijou, and held close to his

hero. "I don't think I'll ever see a man as good," Bryant once said of his father.

When Gumbel set out for Bates College in Lewiston, Maine, in 1966, he was still not very sure of himself. After a small success in his social life during his freshman year at Bates, he wrote home: "For the first time since I've been here, I don't feel like a complete failure to myself or to you."

Gumbel may have even married to please his father. June Baranco, a student at LSU who would later become a Delta stewardess, came through Chicago to visit a friend for a few days in 1968. On one of those days, Gumbel's dad ended up taking June on a tour of Chicago. Richard liked her. In fact, Bryant told *McCall's,* ". . . at the very beginning he thought more of her than I did. But that fact was very important to me." They were married in 1973.

His first job after graduating from Bates, where he majored in Russian history and had a 2.6 average, was as a salesman for an individual paper manufacturer in Manhattan. Those were lonely times. He didn't like the job, and he wasn't much good at it, so he quit without telling his dad.

The last Christmas Eve his father was alive, in 1971, Bryant looked around his New York apartment and took stock. He had a mattress, an eight-inch black-and-white TV and a light bulb. Total. He went out, bought a Blimpie sandwich and called his parents, collect. Deck the Halls.

He finally took a job writing for a small monthly, *Black Sports,* and that was what he was doing on April 10, 1972, when a friend of the family called to tell Bryant his father had collapsed in his courtroom and died of a heart attack. Richard never saw Bryant on TV.

How long did it take him to get over that death? "You're assuming I am," says Gumbel.

And the truth is, he's not. As Greg has said, "Without sounding as if I don't miss (my father), I think it's fair to say Bryant misses him more. He suffers more. He gravitated tremendously to Dad. It's certainly nothing we've ever talked about, but I would say Bryant was probably my father's favorite."

This summer Bryant recalled the last time he saw his father. He was saying goodbye, and he had wanted to kiss him, but thought, "Nah, you're a man, now," and shook his dad's hand instead.

Ironically, a week after Richard's funeral, Bryant's career began to bloom. An acquaintance at KNBC in Los Angeles asked him to try out for the weekend sports anchor job. Gumbel flew in and was so good that the producer assumed Gumbel had memorized the audition script. Within a year, he was doing the weekday sports.

The world discovered Zero-Stumble Gumbel during the 1974 Oakland-Los Angeles World Series. He was doing a wrap-up for his own affiliate, using NBC cameras, and the network people watching were so impressed that they called him in. "Here comes this chubby guy with hair down to his shoulders," remembers the associate producer that day, Michael Weisman, now executive producer of NBC Sports. "He stands up and rolls it through in one take. *O.K., guys, see ya later.* We were dumbfounded. We had experienced network guys who would've taken two hours to do what he did in two minutes." In the truck, NBC Sports VP Chet Simmons was yelping, "Will someone please tell me: Who in the hell *is* that kid?"

The next year that kid was hired as cohost of NBC's wraparound show, *Grandstand,* paired first with Jack Buck and then with Lee Leonard, both of whom were phased out over the next few years. It wasn't their fault. Next to Gumbel, everybody else clunked like a dryer full of tennis shoes. When the show folded, Gumbel joined the first wave of ubiquitous sports anchors.

Before long, Gumbel was the rock of 30 Rock. Once, he was supposed to do an opener from the floor at an NCAA title game. What the producers didn't know was that the empty seats behind Gumbel at rehearsal would be filled that night by a very loud band. When the show went on, there was a trombone threatening to turn Gumbel's tympanum to Malt-O-Meal. He not only couldn't hear what his producers were saying from the truck, but he also couldn't hear what *he* was saying. Unruffled, he spun through his segment as though he were chatting over a backyard fence, finishing at the correct second, cueless. "He saved the telecast for us," says Weisman.

Today called in 1980, and Gumbel began doing three sport slots a week for the morning show, a role that escalated sharply in '82 when he beat out Phil Donahue and various others for one of the cohost jobs. *Today* was another triple-host circus, Gumbel along with Jane Pauley and Chris Wallace, but before long, those two were playing the Supremes to Gumbel's Diana Ross. Later that year Wallace was reassigned to Washington, Pauley became host 1A, and that kid was suddenly The Man.

The early years on *Today* were dicey—the show was still running a distant second in the ratings in the summer of 1983—but by '85 it had tied Good Morning America in the Nielsens, and last winter it held a comfortable lead. One big reason, says *Today* writer Merle Rubine, is that "Bryant just improved every day, absorbed new material every day, got better, smarter, wiser and more sophisticated as he went along." Says rival Harry Smith, co-anchor of *CBS This Morning,* "As a sports guy and a black guy, he came into all this guilty until proven innocent. Yet he sits there and proves himself day after day."

Gumbel will turn 40 during the Olympics, the Carnegie Hall of his career. He will be dissected daily by every newspaper critic with a TV in his den. What, him worry? "Look, if Michael the Archangel hosted these games, he'd be lucky to satisfy 50 percent of the people," Gumbel says.

Anti-Gumbelers say his microchip perfection will wear out its welcome the first week. *Hey Gladys, does this Gumbo guy ever screw up?* Is he ever at a loss for words? Can a man who knows everything ever be surprised? Jim McKay, the perennial Olympic host for ABC, may have slipped a bit, but he at least seems human; he at least seems thrilled.

Gumbel-maniacs think he'll be golden. Bob Costas, who will follow Gumbel each night as NBC's late-night Olympic anchor, says picking Gumbel was "a no-brainer. They needed somebody who had stature, who was tremendously facile and glib, who had supreme confidence in himself and wasn't likely to be rattled by anything. That's Gumbel."

What some people don't like about Gumbel is that he seems to *know* how good he is. Jim Lampley, the former ABC sportscaster now with KCBS in L.A., is impressed with Gumbel's ego, and Lampley is no wallflower himself. "Bryant makes me look humble," he says. "In Seoul, he'll make us all look humble."

Egocentric? OK, so Gumbel once said that Pauley, *Today* movie critic Gene Shalit and weatherman Willard Scott "never looked better" than with him on the show. And, OK, Gumbel doesn't read his mail or look at tapes of his performances or those of his competition. And, OK, Gumbel always has to have the last line and the last laugh. Even he admits, "I've always got a comeback." But what's he supposed to do, take dull pills? Does Paulina Porizkova walk around without makeup?

Says *Washington Post* TV critic Tom Shales, "To me, calling Gumbel 'cocky' sounds too much like 'uppity.' It sounds almost racist." And if there's one thing you can say about Gumbel, it's that he's so good, the question of race almost never comes up. In fact, the only racism he encounters comes from other blacks. "You're not black enough," they write. Gumbel doesn't listen. "It's like (Georgetown and Olympic basketball coach) John Thompson said to me once: He wanted to be free not only from what the whites expected of him but what the blacks expected of him as well."

Only one problem: How do you get free of what you expect of yourself?

★   ★   ★

"My mom sees her sons as baby boys," says Gumbel. "Well, I stopped being her baby boy a long time ago."

Rhea has noticed. When Bryant is in town, he stays at a hotel and takes her out for dinner. Greg was on hand for his younger sister Renee's wedding. Bryant? He was at Fergie's wedding in London. "Renee is still hurting from that," says Rhea. And his sister Rhonda? Her birthday is the same day as June's. "You'd think he couldn't help remember that birthday," Rhea says. "But he never does."

But all that is side hurt. The real hurt is Rhea's. She reads of Bryant speaking eloquently about her husband, but never about her. She was so "heartbroken" after one article that she wrote a letter to Bryant that was almost unreadable from the tear stains.

"OK, so I'm not a big shot," she says, reciting the letter from bitter memory. "I'm not a big person in the social life, not a cultural leader. But I brought you into this life, not him."

Bryant wrote back, "I'm not going to dignify some of your remarks. You wrote it when you were hurting."

Greg: "I think my father is probably bigger in death to Bryant than he was in life. With that constant, every-day comparison, there's no way she can measure up."

Bryant: "She probably doesn't think I'm as proud of her as I am. I just don't show it. I'm not good at showing a lot of things. . . . Besides, you've got to understand where most relationships are with me. If it's halfway decent, it's way up there with me. I guess she sees it as much less."

He's got that right.

Rhea: "I'm just trying to forget I have him."

Gumbel has a spare dark suit and tie hanging in his office in case the news is tragic and the suit he's wearing is too light for the occasion. He brings six golf shirts on a three-day golf trip just to make sure he looks perfect. Gumbel *never* loosens his tie or takes off his jacket, even in summer.

"Bryant is a perfectionist squared," says *Today* writer-producer Paul Brubaker. The reason is simple. If he knows that he "will never see someone as good" as his father, he knows that includes himself. Guilty as charged.

"In his best year, my dad didn't make what I do in a month," says Gumbel. "There's something profoundly wrong with that. My father did what he did better than I do what I do. What my father did required a lot more intelligence than what I do. He was smarter. He was more important to society. He had more worth." It is a constant process, Gumbel has said, "measuring myself against my father and always coming up short."

And so, to alleviate the guilt, to prove his worth, Gumbel works obsessively. He didn't become a lawyer as his father had hoped, so he'll be 10 times as good in television. His goal is to go into every interview unsurprisable. No answer can shock him because he knows all the answers. Gumbel sometimes stays over at his Manhattan townhouse, but when he sleeps at home in Westchester, he's up at 3:45 a.m., catches the limo at 4:30, arrives at Rockefeller Plaza at 5:30, studies notes for the day's show in his office until 6:15, goes to the studio to do his "sunrise tease" for *Today,* does the show until 9:00, tapes interviews and Olympic voice-overs or studies research on forthcoming guests until about noon, almost never breaks for lunch, studies and goes to meetings until about 4:00, reads research material for the show in the limousine on the way home, eats a quick dinner, then heads back to the den to finish studying from 7:30 to 11:00 and goes to bed by midnight. Gumbel might know more about Dan Quayle than Dan Quayle does. *Are you watching, Dad?*

Take the Olympics. He went on a coach-hopping tour, meeting with Olympic coaches from coast to coast. He personally edited scripts for more than 50 Olympic features and did the voice-overs himself. He took six weeks off to absorb eight network-prepared Olympic guides, each thicker than the Dallas Cowboys' playbook.

The remarkable thing is that he retains it all. He has a mind that would turn an IBM mainframe green. Without notice, Gumbel can tick off, to the day, how long he has been married, who started in 1963 on both sides of the line for the Chicago Bears, and the last five Speakers of the House.

It borders on the supernatural. Once, Gumbel was doing highlights on *NFL '81* when he was handed the news that the New York Yankees had just fired Gene Michael. He broke the story and then proceeded to reel off the last seven managers fired before Michael, with the year of each pink slip. "You will hear people say he's a son of a bitch," says *Today* writer/producer Allison Davis, "but you won't hear anybody say he's not a smart son of a bitch."

The only problem with perfection is that when you get there, there's nobody to talk to. "I have high expectations of people," he says. "When they achieve something, I say, 'So what?' "

People aren't good enough.

One morning, a presidential speech at the U.N. ended five minutes early. Connie Chung, the NBC newswoman, was anchoring the network desk with Gumbel. Producer Steve Friedman asked her off the air to remain on camera and help Gumbel kill time. She refused, saying she wasn't prepared. Gumbel killed the time himself, but he hasn't spoken to Chung since. "She acted in an unprofessional manner, so I disassociated myself from her," Gumbel says. "If it was an isolated incident, I'd forget about it. But it's not." Chung says she doesn't want to talk about it.

People aren't professional enough.

Once, during the taping of a prime-time *Today* special in Rockefeller Center's Channel Gardens, NBC late-night talk-show host David Letterman leaned out the seventh-story window and yelled through a bullhorn, "I am Larry Grossman, president of NBC News. And I'm not wearing pants!" While the *Today* show continued uninterrupted (Letterman was too far away for the microphones to pick up his voice), Gumbel was so angry that he has since refused to appear on Letterman's show—this despite the fact that *Today* show producer Friedman and Letterman's producer had discussed staging some kind of stunt. Doesn't matter. A professional wouldn't have done it, says Gumbel. Letterman says he doesn't want to talk about it. Gumbel says he doesn't want Letterman to grovel. "I just want him to pick up the phone," he says.

What? And ruin a good shtick? The Gumbel feud is an eephus pitch right in Letterman's wheelhouse. One night on his show Letterman said Gumbel was the kind of guy who would spend a weekend "alphabetizing his colognes." Then there was the night a huge marquee appeared behind Letterman's desk with the billing BRYANT! THE MUSICAL.

Gumbel, who refers to Letterman as "the ———," isn't laughing.

"It's this hip-sick-I'm-cool-you're-not kind of mocking humor that I don't think is particularly funny," he says of Letterman's show. "He's insecure and it shows. But since he's competing against test patterns, he looks terrific." So forget the nightly coast-to-coast bashing Gumbel is taking from Letterman; he'll hold out. "Bryant can hold a grudge for a long time," says Brubaker. "He doesn't worry about p.r."

People aren't true enough.

Gumbel is godfather to Steve Garvey's daughter Whitney, as Garvey is to Bradley Gumbel, yet now the relationship has chilled. Gumbel won't say what happened, only that "You're seeing the new Steve Garvey now . . . the one who had too much pressure to become STEVE in capital letters."

People don't try enough.

If there's one thing Gumbel can't stand it's somebody "mailing it in," giving a half-hearted effort. This includes everybody from interviewees ("If somebody wants to sit there and look like an ——, I'll let him look like an ———," Gumbel says) to interviewers ("Nancy Reagan is a wonderful interview as long as you stick to wonderful subjects," he says. "But get to something else and she's monosyllabic. So when I interview her, I come out looking like an ———. But when David Hartman interviewed her, writers said he was 'warm and endearing.' Give me a break.")

Sometimes, women aren't good enough.

Gumbel has a grudge against *New York Daily News* TV critic Kay Gardella. He once promised that if they ever showed up at the same press conference, he would walk out. Nor is he fond of former *Today* contributor Ellerbee, who claims he refused to introduce her *TGIF* pieces on the show. "He's never liked me," says Ellerbee. "He has a locker-room mentality when it comes to women. . . . I think I was too strong a woman for him."

Says Gumbel, who denies, by the way, that he refused to introduce her *TGIF* pieces: "It's nothing personal against her. She just thinks everything is done better by a woman."

Hmmmm. Sounds a little like Gumbel in heels. Pauley once called Gumbel's attitudes toward women, "Neanderthal." Truth is, Gumbel seems to be the anti-Alda. He likes all-male social clubs and eight-inch Cuban cigars. Like all good men, he believes that if talking won't settle an argument, a good punch will, which is exactly what he once threatened to do to Simmons during a contract negotiation. He hates "sensitive" movies—"You'll never get me to see *On Golden Pond* or *Julia* or *Tess*," he says—and Woody Allen's films, but he loves Schwarzenegger's. One emotional movie he says he likes is a man's flick, *Islands in the Stream,* Hemingway's story of a doomed artist. Every day, a march to the grave.

That's Gumbel. A Hemingway man. A man's man. Grace under pressure. Men being valiant to other men. "I'm the kind of guy who cries when guys truly hug after a very important touchdown," he says. He can be sheer ice in a tender moment—during their courtship he signed letters to his wife with "best wishes"—but when the team is at stake, when competition is at stake, he gets emotional. In 1980, when he was wrapping up a 90-minute special on the Moscow Olympics—the Games he was supposed to host for NBC but didn't because of the U.S. boycott—Gumbel became so choked up he almost couldn't finish. Talking about it still brings tears to his eyes. "It was just so very emotional because of what we missed," he says.

True sports between men on the field, he cherishes. For instance, he is reverential about golf, partly because it is "a control game"—you control your fate, your opponent doesn't—and partly because it is primarily a man's game.

"Playing golf with somebody is such a pure thing," he says. "Sex is a pure thing too, but the closest thing you do with a guy is play golf with him. Your emotions are exposed when you play golf: humility, pride, anger, it all comes out with each swing. You lay it all on the line."

He belongs to two country clubs, Burning Tree, the political heavyweight's course in Bethesda, Md., and Whippoorwill in Armonk, N.Y. He assumes that both clubs have the same number of black members: one. And by the way, one member who helped Gumbel become a member at Burning Tree was a certain gentleman, name of Bush—George, that is.

Can you imagine if his father could be with him now, just for one weekend? Gumbel does, all the time. They would catch a game from the box seats. Take him to the club, have breakfast, get a couple of caddies and play a Nassau with the VP.

"He never sat in box seats in his life. Or had a caddie or played at a private club," says Bryant. "It's just not fair. The only reason I have what I do now is because of what he did back then. You're supposed to work hard so you can enjoy it, but he never got to enjoy it."

And so, whenever Gumbel plays with a buddy and the buddy invites his father along, Bryant aches. "It's such a beautiful thing." Pause. "Maybe I elevate golf too much."

Or is it fathers?

★   ★   ★

Rhea Gumbel has folded her hands in her lap and is about to cry. "He's distanced himself not only from me, but from the whole family," she says. "You love him and raise him, but you'd never dream this would happen."

She stares at the television, the box where her son lives, and then rolls her eyes to the ceiling: "If his father were alive, this would never happen. If he, for one minute, thought that they weren't looking out for me...."

After a long pause, her visitor gets up to go. "What time is it?" she asks.

"Two o'clock."

"Good," she says.

"Why good?"

"Only eight more hours until I go to bed."

★   ★   ★

March to the grave. High above a checkerboard landscape, Gumbel reaches into the pocket of his first-class seat, pulls out his Filofax and draws out a yellowed piece of paper. The creases are so deep that the paper threatens to rip at the touch.

It is the eulogy from his father's funeral, the one Gumbel wrote and delivered that spring day in 1972. He keeps it with him always. It ends: *I say goodbye for those who knew him as "Your Honor." . . . I say goodbye for those who knew him as Dick or Richard and thereby shared in the joys which come of fine and rare friendship. I say goodbye for those who knew him as family. . . . I say goodbye for my dear mother who knew him as husband. . . . I say goodbye for Gregory, Rhonda, Renee and myself, who were lucky enough to call him father. . . . Goodbye, Daddy. We love you so very much. God has taken from us and unto himself, the finest man we'll ever know.*

He reads it once, cries a little, folds it up and puts it back in his Filofax.

You want pallbearers?

Bryant Gumbel is one still.

Ready Now Family's Rock

BASEBALL

By *BILL PLASCHKE*

From the Los Angeles Times
Copyright © 1988, the Los Angeles Times

They were married that summer on the only day Randy Ready didn't have a baseball game. It was El Paso, 1982. Ready was a 22-year-old infielder with a passion, and his girl Dorene was someone who understood.

The church was tiny, the congregation numbered two: a buddy and his girlfriend. They doubled as the best man and maid of honor. They kissed the bride. They threw the rice.

And then they pulled up in Ready's beige 1968 Nova, into the back climbed Randy and Dorene, and off they went into the West Texas night. If you are a minor league player with a game the next day, this is what is known as a honeymoon.

Their friends drove, Randy and Dorene swigged champagne, they told awful jokes and drank some more, and then somebody slipped a Frank Sinatra cassette into the tape deck. Then all together, they sang.

"Sang all of his old songs," recalled Ready. "You know, like that one, 'Fairy tales can come true, it can happen to you.' "

It is six years later. Ready is sitting in the quiet of a major league clubhouse, and softly, just for a second, he is humming that song. Then he suddenly stops, shaking out whatever it is that has been rolling around inside his head. Ready no longer wants to hear about fairy tales, occupied as he is with finishing a second consecutive season burdened by his reality. Baseball, you see, is no longer his work, but his escape. Baseball has become the *easiest* thing he does.

When he goes home after work, Dorene is not there. She lives a few miles down the highway in an extended care facility, helpless for more than two years, and perhaps indefinitely, because of a serious brain injury. Waiting for Ready are his three young children, help-less because of youth. Andrew is 5. Twins Colin and Jared are 3.

Ready comes home to where he must be the rock, the one with the will so strong that he is uneasy explaining it.

"You do," he says softly, "what you got to do."

On June 13, 1986, the day Ready played his first game as a Padre after being acquired from the Milwaukee Brewers, Dorene collapsed on the floor of their home in Tucson, Ariz. She was unconscious for 7-10 minutes. What happened to her brain during that period of no oxygen is known as cerebral anoxia.

That much was made public. He left his team and cancelled his season to care for her and their children.

What you might not have heard, because of his reluctance to dis-cuss the situation since then, is that Dorene never really woke up. Today she lives in a special home in Del Mar, unable to care for herself, unable to walk, with a voice that never rises above a whis-per. Ready lives a few miles away with sister Cindy, who helps him with the children.

On the field, much is made of his versatility—he is a second base-man, third baseman, left fielder. Yet that is nothing compared to his roles at home, where he is husband, father and mother.

As a husband, he visits Dorene every other day. He brings her home for things such as birthday parties. Her condition has im-proved only enough so that she can initiate five phrases. Ready keeps track. One is "I love you."

As a mother, he has done diapers, baby food, sloppy baths and messy breakfasts.

As a father, he does the disciplining. Only, this is one spanking where the pain is truly shared.

"To be spanking them and hear them shout, 'I want my mommy,' . . . that kills me," Ready said. "What can I tell them, that I want her, too?"

Then he comes to the ballpark. When the Padres finish next week in Houston, Ready will likely wind up batting around .260, with a handful of homers (he has six) and several dozen RBIs (he has 31). He will say he is disappointed.

Teammates will say that they are amazed.

"I don't know what's going on in that little man's head, but some-thing is definitely clicking that keeps him going," Tony Gwynn said. "That man is *tough*."

Last season, he rejoined the team for the first time after his wife's accident and hit .309 with a career-high 12 homers and 54 RBIs. Teammates were so impressed that several, despite having a batting champion and rookie of the year on the same club, quietly wanted him to be the team's most valuable player.

They continue to look at him with respect bordering on awe. Ready has come to represent the work ethic and comeback spirit of the 1988 comeback club as no other player has.

"He'll even joke about it—when he leaves the clubhouse he'll look over his shoulder and say, 'Well, I'm headed back to reality,' " Tim Flannery said. "I don't know how he gets by day to day. Honest, I don't."

Don't be silly. Ask him how he gets by, and he looks at you like you've just asked him how he puts on his socks. He just does.

"I guess if you got a problem, you confront it," Ready said. "You be realistic about it, you do what you can, then you rely on your faith for the rest.

"People keep telling me that my life has to get better. I have to believe them."

If the words sound careful, well, this is the first interview he has given on his off-the-field life in more than a year. Throughout the end of last season and this spring, he answered constant questions about his wife by running his finger across his throat. It meant you could ask him anything but that.

He doesn't want to be made a hero. He doesn't want to be made a martyr. All he wants is more starts than benchings, and a few pitchers who aren't afraid to elevate a fastball.

"I don't talk about it in the clubhouse, because I get *away* from it in the clubhouse," Ready said.

He agreed to this interview but asked that his privacy be respected with regard to certain details and that he and Cindy be the only ones interviewed. When a contact was made with Cindy, whom Ready only half-jokingly refers to as a saint, she politely declined to speak.

So why has Ready chosen to talk?

"I think he has finally dealt with it now," Flannery said. "It took him 1½ years, but he is finally getting on with his life. The wound never heals, but I think he understands it better now."

Ready does. And he doesn't.

Ready spoke evenly: "My wife suffered the most severe of head injuries, she needs maximum assistance at every level, it could be that way for the next 30 or 40 years. But meanwhile, my life and our children's lives goes on. I realize that's the way it has to be."

He paused.

"But then there are still times I get home and think about a normal life," he said. "I wonder, just what is a normal life?"

For him, and because of more than just what has happened in the past two years, it is a good question.

Normal began in Fremont, about 35 miles south of San Francisco, where his mother was a waitress and his father a carpenter. Their lack of money made Ready the answer to the following trivia questions:

• Who is the only Padre to have worked on the Alaska Pipeline? At age 15?

Ready joined his father in Alaska for three harsh summers, working 14 hours a day in wilderness camps with almost every penny going to his mother when he returned home in the fall.

One summer, he arrived in Fairbanks to discover his mandatory Alaska residency card had not yet been processed. He couldn't work until it was. With just a few dollars in his pocket, he spent the next week living in the front seat of an abandoned truck across from the union hall until the card arrived. He was 16.

"I guess I grew up kind of quick," he said.

• Who is the only Padre to have worked a graveyard shift at Winchell's doughnut shop? While still attending high school?

Ready did this to keep the family fed because, at age 16, his father died. Max Ready was planning to drive down from Alaska to take Randy and his brother to Hawaii for a vacation. At 4 a.m. the day before his trip, they received the phone call.

This is where he learned about grief and how something as simple as baseball can pull you out of that grief.

"I didn't want to grieve, so I played baseball, played all the time, and eventually it got better," Ready said. "Of course, some things, I don't know if you ever get over them.

"My dad was not a big guy, but he was scrappy, a perfectionist, never quit. Not a big guy, but tough."

It was only by acquiring these traits that Ready made it through his senior year at Kennedy High School. It was Winchell's from midnight to 8 a.m. School from 8 a.m. to 1 p.m. Baseball from 2:30 p.m. to 5 p.m. Dinner, bedtime, and then a few hours later, Winchell's again.

"It was in high school," Ready said, "that I learned how to take power naps."

After three good years at two colleges (Cal State-Hayward and Mesa College in Grand Junction, Colo.), the Milwaukee Brewers made him a fifth-round pick in the June 1980 draft. And he was stuck again. As a second baseman, he was stuck behind Jim Gantner. As a third baseman, behind Paul Molitor. He could play shortstop, too, but you've heard of Robin Yount.

In all, before being traded to the Padres, he spent parts of seven years with the Brewer organization and ended up with 120 big-league games.

The best that happened to Ready during those years? Happened in a Burger King.

It was the end of spring training, 1981, when the Brewer minor leaguers had just returned to their Roadway Inn in Phoenix. There were several pretty women by the pool, and most of the players rushed off the bus to gawk.

Not Ready, who by that time had seen too much of life to gawk. He walked over to the Burger King, where he was standing in line when one of the women, swim-suit-clad and soaking wet, appeared at his side.

"Didn't I see you by the pool?" he asked.

"What was your first clue?" Dorene said.

"Right then," Ready recalled, "I realized she was one of those tough girls. I liked that."

It was a perfect match. They were married a year later, had their first child Andrew a year after that and settled in to a life of defined roles.

"I played baseball, and she was the rock," Ready said.

It was Dorene who worked two jobs during the winters so he could be with the children.

It was Dorene who once convinced him to remain home with the kids a few extra days one winter instead of reporting to the Brewers training camp early. Good thing, because some of the Brewers who reported early were injured in a clubhouse explosion.

Finally, in one of her finer moments, Dorene insisted that Ready visit the Brewer bosses in the late spring of 1984 and demand to know if he had made the big-league team.

"She told me, 'I've got a family to run, I need to know,'" Ready recalled. He was so inspired that on the way to manager Rene Lachemann's office, he backed his car into the team bus.

"So I walked in to see Lach, and I asked, 'Am I on the team or not?'" he explained. "Lachemann told me I would have to ask the general manager (Harry Dalton). So I said, 'Get Harry in here.'

"Harry walks in and says, 'Congratulations.'"

Three months later, he was sent to Triple A, but he still hasn't forgotten the inspiration. He was finally able to pay back Dorene on June 12, 1986, when, after being sent down to Triple A for a second consecutive year, he received the phone call in Milwaukee that he was being traded to San Diego. It was a city near their home in Tucson, a city with sun, her dream city.

"San Diego, San Diego!" she screamed upon hearing the news. "We're going to San Diego!"

She was so excited that she woke up the children. The next day, a Friday, Ready flew to San Diego. She flew to Tucson with plans to join him in San Diego on Saturday.

Ready reported to San Diego Jack Murphy Stadium, and started at third base that night against Fernando Valenzuela of the Dodgers. In his first at-bat, he struck out on four pitches. He also botched a bunt.

He returned to the hotel that night wondering what else could go wrong. He called Dorene, they talked, they felt better. But an hour later, the phone rang from home, and it wasn't Dorene. It was a cousin. Dorene had been found on the floor, unconscious. It was a brain aneurysm. She had been rushed to a hospital in a coma. He had to get home.

It was too late for a flight, but he rushed to the San Diego airport anyway. There, in the longest night of his life, he waited.

"I was on the phone all night, trying to figure things out," Ready said. "I called one of my friends who started a prayer chain for me. I called anybody I could."

The first plane finally left around 7 a.m. He walked into Dorene's room at Tucson's El Dorado Hospital around 10:30 a.m.

"I looked at her all hooked up to everything . . . and I said 'Whoaaa,' " Ready recalled. "I could not believe my eyes. There was shock. There were tears. Everything."

A doctor summoned him out into the hall and asked him a question he had never heard anyone ask before, not even in the movies.

"He told me I had 48 hours to decide whether or not I wanted to terminate my wife," Ready recalled. "The man laid it right on the line."

Ready, a Christian, barely paused.

"I told him that's not my department," Ready said. "That's not my decision."

Three weeks later, after his wife had stabilized and his children were placed in the care of his mother-in-law, Ready returned to the Padres. They sent him to Triple-A Las Vegas on a rehabilitation option to find his swing. He played in 10 games, collecting at least one hit in each, and then the Stars traveled to play Tucson.

He stepped off the plane, drove to his home, walked in his front door, and couldn't believe it was the same house. In the eyes of his children he saw confusion, fear, uncertainty. Andrew, still two years old, was not getting to bed until midnight. Then he was waking up at 6 a.m., crying for his mother.

In the first game against Tucson that night, he didn't get a hit. And then he packed up his duffel bag, drove home again and didn't pick up another baseball for six months.

"I quit because I realized my wife was the rock, and the rock was gone, so I had to be the new rock," Ready said. "I had to be here with the children until we all knew what direction we were headed. I could not play baseball with all this other stuff happening."

In leaving the team, he ended one ritual but started another. He would tend to the children during the day, and then visit the health club at night, working out from 10:30 p.m. to midnight. By the time the following spring came around, he had never been readier for a season, and it showed. He ended it by hitting eight homers in his last 24 games despite a torn rib cage.

"With all he went through, his season was amazing," Flannery said.

This past winter, he went back to the same ritual, only it was more difficult. Dorene, after spending the season in an experimental treatment center in Bakersfield and then living with her mother, was moved back into his house.

"It was no problem, except in the morning," Ready said. "The morning is the piranha hour. All the kids—the little ankle-biters— wanting breakfast, while we have to give Dorene her shower, which takes two hours right there."

That's the Ready response to most of the things that have happened to him in the last two years—no problem. And he's genuinely feeling better about things now. Dorene is well cared for, even if it is costing him hundreds of dollars a month after insurance. His children are growing up nicely.

"Thanks a lot to my sister, the kids have manners," Ready said. "They know how to act in other people's houses. I'm proud of them."

He's proud of most everything except an occasional thought that's just about himself. It is a normal thought, a human thought, but Ready still doesn't quite believe that he is allowed to be human.

"It's a terrible thing to say," Ready said in a voice just above a whisper, "but it's harder this way than if Dorene had just died."

He scuffed at the clubhouse carpet and quickly changed gears.

"But you do what you've got to do."

Making a Killing

HORSE RACING

By MARK KRAM

From the Philadelphia Daily News
Copyright © 1988, the Philadelphia Daily News

A Ford sedan with New Jersey plates and a horse trailer hitched to the rear pulled off the Pennsylvania Turnpike into a dark and deserted rest area. Behind the wheel sat Dan Chansky, the owner of both a standardbred stable and a rap sheet that included a jail stretch for assaulting a cop. Seated on the passenger side was Pete Strautman, who was cradling a can of beer and who still could hear his wife scold: *"Pete, do you know what will happen if this ever gets out?"* Strautman had told her: *"Naaa. Nobody will ever know."*

Chansky and Strautman had departed Pocono Downs in Wilkes-Barre with the standardbred race horse Sonic Lord at 2 a.m. Sonic Lord had been entered there three weeks before and Chansky had been neither shocked nor disappointed when, at 7-1 odds, the animal broke stride and hobbled in eighth. Sonic Lord had a dropped suspensory, a sore ankle and earnings in 1981 of only $1,135. Chansky had purchased the horse at a sale in New York for $2,000 in June 1981, had him fraudulently insured for $12,500 in July, and now—34 days after he had acquired Sonic Lord—Dan Chansky and Pete Strautman planned to kill the horse and collect the insurance.

Chansky parked at a rest area "somewhere close to Valley Forge" and he and Strautman hurried out of the car. One of them carried two plastic garbage bags, the other a roll of duct tape. Inside the trailer, which was illuminated by a single white bulb, Strautman seized Sonic Lord and draped his head with the plastic bag. The head jerked to the side and Sonic Lord whinnied in panic. Strautman recalls that Chansky then wrapped a strip of tape around the neck of the horse—thus securing the bag and shutting off the flow of oxygen—and that he wrapped another strip around the tip of the nose. Sonic

Lord drew at the plastic for air, and with each aborted breath his confusion and fear heightened. Strautman wedged the plastic deep into the nostrils. Chansky stood to the side, and urged:

"Come on, Pete, get it over with."

Strautman held the plastic in place and remembers that a "gurgling sound" welled deep within Sonic Lord as the animal bucked and shuddered. Minutes passed—two or three—and the horse collapsed. Strautman tore off the plastic. Sonic Lord continued to draw shallow breaths as blood dripped from his nose and formed a pool on the trailer floor. The breathing continued and Strautman remembers that as he stood there—and peered into the contorted eyes of the animal—Strautman experienced an odd and unforgettable sensation. Strautman says now, "I could feel its life slip away."

Chansky shouted, "Pete, come on." Strautman climbed back in the car and the two drove home to New Jersey. Chansky filed a claim form with the American Livestock Insurance Company, stated that Sonic Lord had died of a "hyper seizure," and in due course received a check for $12,500. Enclosed in the envelope, stapled to the check, a letter from the insurance company said, "We are sorry for your loss." And Dan Chansky recalls:

"We laughed our asses off."

★   ★   ★

America will conduct its annual celebration of the race horse Saturday in Kentucky. Some of the top thoroughbreds in the United States will appear in front of a live crowd of 100,000 at Churchill Downs in Louisville for the 114th running of the Kentucky Derby. This is the polite side of the horse world, but there is another side—a desperate and forbidding one—and it is in these shadows that Dan Chansky and Pete Strautman committed their horrific deeds. Their story is a chilling one.

Sonic Lord was one of 10 standardbreds—trotters—and thoroughbreds Chansky and Strautman killed in order to defraud insurance agencies. Beginning in December 1975 and ending in November 1983, a period in which Chansky directed a wide range of other illegal activities, Chansky and Strautman suffocated horses with plastic garbage bags, broke the neck of another, and shot still others with guns and hunting arrows. Chansky is serving a 24½-year sentence for racketeering, theft, fraud and animal cruelty in Riverfront State Prison in Camden. Strautman, who cooperated in the prosecution of Chansky and who served six months of a 4½-year sentence for animal cruelty, is now out of jail and says at his farm in Freehold, N.J., "I am not a cruel person."

Chansky, 37, sits in a room at the prison and says of himself: "I will have to answer for my acts to a higher authority."

No central clearinghouse exists to quantify the extent of such acts, but an eight-week investigation by the *Daily News* revealed that it is both a widespread and alarming problem. In addition to interviewing Chansky on six occasions at the prison and Strautman at his farm, the paper reviewed close to 1,200 pages of Monmouth County grand jury documents that led to their indictments. The *Daily News* also interviewed a private investigator in South Carolina who specializes in equine fraud, state and federal law enforcement officials, and a dozen equine insurance executives in the United States and abroad. The investigation found:

• Fifty-seven horses killed in four states between 1982 and 1985 for the purpose of defrauding insurance companies. In addition to the 10 horses Chansky and Strautman were convicted of killing in New Jersey—part of a $226,000 insurance fraud—19 quarter horses were killed in Arkansas in a $97,250 scam; 17 quarter horses were killed in Texas to collect $780,000; and 11 standardbreds were killed in New York for $500,000 in fraudulent funds. William Graham, a private investigator from South Carolina, has handled "well over 100 equine fraud cases" and says quarter horses in parts of North Texas, Georgia and Oklahoma "have as much chance as a point man in Vietnam."

Eight of nine defendants were convicted in the Arkansas fraud and received prison sentences in 1986 as lengthy as 7½ years; six of 11 conspirators have been tried and convicted in Texas and have been sentenced to prison terms as lengthy as 25 years; and seven of eight defendants in the New York fraud received prison sentences in 1987 of no more than 90 days. U.S. attorney John Stevens, of Beaumont, Texas, who directed the prosecution of the Texas conspirators, claims convictions are difficult to secure in equine frauds because of the presence of circumstantial evidence.

"We can show a paper trail that would seem to indicate fraud," Stevens said, "But the question is—without a witness to the actual act—can we prove it in court?"

• Cruel and unspeakable methods. Horses have been suffocated with plastic bags and by their owners jamming pingpong balls into their nostrils. Other horses have been electrocuted, set afire, hit with cars or poisoned. One had its neck broken. In the Arkansas conspiracy, a highway accident was staged in which the horses were dropped from a cliff. Still another was killed when one of the conspirators jammed a coat hanger into its rectum and punctured its intestines.

Said Graham: "People who kill horses for profit make the Marquis de Sade look like a Sunday school teacher."

• Loopholes in the insurance system. "The system for insuring horses is ripe for abuse," Stevens said. This is due, in part, to lax underwriting practices and shifting equine values. Spokesmen for insurance companies claimed that between 25 and 50 percent of the horses insured in this country are insured at inflated values and that, like a building or automobile, a horse that carries inflated insurance can be in peril. Because equine policies are written for a year—and the horse values can fluctuate radically in that span—a percentage of overinsuring is accidental. However, there also is an unscrupulous element afoot, people who contrive false sales agreements in an effort to secure higher insurance. Horseman Cecil Jines, the convicted "ringleader" of the Arkansas fraud, recalled that he and his cohorts began killing horses for insurance proceeds because "we saw how easy it was."

Chansky concurs. "We would get a letter (from the insurance company) that said, 'We are sorry for your loss,' " he remembered. "We would laugh and say, 'Well, if they feel so sorry, we can give them something else to be sorry about.' "

Equine insurance adjusters speculate that between one and 10 percent of the claims submitted involve fraud. "That is only an educated guess," said Walt Knorpp, who owns an insurance agency in Clarendon, Texas. Knorpp placed the percentage as high as 26 percent in 1986—equine frauds peaked with the oil bust in the Southwest and the Tax Reform Act of 1986—but contends there has been a "gradual decline." Graham cites the prosecution of the Arkansas conspirators and others as an explanation for that decline.

"Getting rid of these people," Graham said, "is like getting rid of tooth decay."

Graham, who weighs 240 pounds and answers to the name of "The Fat Man," describes people who kill horses for profit as "devoid of conscience and driven by the pursuit of the almighty dollar." Graham did not participate in the investigation of Chansky, and the two never have met, but the investigator scowled and in a slow Southern drawl said, "I have been around bleeps like him my whole life."

Chansky is skeptical of Graham and doubtful that The Fat Man ever would have been able to build a strong case against him. Chansky says that while "Pete (Strautman) seemed to enjoy killing the horses," Chansky derived a "sense of power" from defrauding insurance companies. He likens the conspiracy he headed to a shark that eventually "bit itself in the tail" and "swallowed itself." Chansky adds that he and others became "consumed by greed."

"The bottom line," Chansky said, "was make what we could, when we could, and do it as quickly as we could."

★   ★   ★

Only a handful of the thousands of horses foaled each year ever possess a residual value in the breeding shed. The others are destined to be sold as plow horses or to be shipped, in the words of Pete Strautman, to "the Alpo Stables." Slaughterhouses will purchase a horse at public auction for $300, slaughter it, and sell the remains at substantial profit. The hides are sold to a tannery, the bones are sold for soap and the meat is sold and processed into pet food. Chansky had sold horses to slaughterhouses until it occurred to him that he could make much more insuring horses and killing them himself.

No one had to persuade Dan Chansky to exploit the system. He had done it before and says now that he had "little respect for the law." Born in the Fort Apache section of the South Bronx, and raised from age 13 in Jackson Township, N.J., he developed an affection for riding horses as a teen-ager and at age 17 discovered the world of harness racing. He found it captivating. He hoped to get a license to own and train standardbreds, but there would be an obstacle: He had been convicted of punching a Jackson Township police officer at age 23 and had been sentenced to a year in the Ocean County jail. The New Jersey State Racing Commission refused to issue Chansky a license.

Lack of proper certification did little to obstruct Chansky; while he could not train horses officially, he trained them unofficially and still purchased and sold them. The part-owner of C & D General Contracting, and then JDP Trucking with Strautman, Chansky had some money, but not enough to finance the horse racing operation he imagined for himself. Chansky purchased 10 standardbreds initially and says now, "I should have set my sights a little lower."

None of those 10 horses did well, and in order to finance his stable —if only to the point of breaking even—Chansky sold percentages of his horses to people who had enthusiasm but no knowledge of the sport. Strautman called them "suckers," and Chansky seemed to know where to find them. Chansky said he sold one-half of standardbred Formal Tyson to seven different people and retained 50 percent of the horse for himself. He only did that once, but it would be common for him to purchase a horse for $400 and sell it to "some poor schmuck" for $4,000.

Keeping a standardbred in training can cost $10,000 to $17,000 annually. "Neither of us should have been in horse racing at that level," recalls Strautman, who adds that it was the expense of caring for horses that led to the decision to kill them for the insurance proceeds. Chansky says the idea to kill the horses was "a group effort." Strautman disagrees and calls it "strictly a Chansky production." Strautman also says that Chansky helped him commit the killings, but Chansky denies participating in the actual acts. Chansky says he paid Strautman between $300 and $1,500 per job and adds it was "Pete all the way."

"Why else would I have paid him?" Chansky says.

Strautman shakes his head no and says, "He was there. He had to be. Knocking off a horse is no piece of cake."

Chansky disagrees. "Pete did it," he says. "He seemed to enjoy doing it. I remember this strange look would come over his face. He seemed to get a power surge from it."

Evidence produced for the Monmouth County grand jury would appear to corroborate Strautman. One of the convicted co-conspirators, Thomas Soffell, told investigators that Chansky had been an active participant in the demise of JDs Harold. Soffell told an investigator for the Monmouth County prosecutor that Chansky and Strautman loaded the animal on a trailer and "proceeded to place a large plastic bag" over its head. Soffell continued that "Mr. Strautman held the horse and Mr. Chansky secured the tape around the opening of the bag." Soffell added that Chansky suffocated the horse because it "was almost broken down" and that if he had sold it he would not have gotten his investment back.

Chansky claims the horses he and Strautman killed had either broken down or had no racing future. Citing a typical scenario, Chansky remembers he purchased standardbred Algors Tar Boy at the Old Glory Horse Sale at Yonkers Raceway in New York in April 1982 for $800 and passed his ownership to Barbara Engler in a "paper transfer" for $30,000. Chansky remembers that the horse had been a "big, mean" animal, virtually impossible to handle, and that he directed Engler to obtain $30,000 of insurance. Chansky called in Strautman, and not long after the insurance had been secured, the animal was killed.

"We had to give it the appearance of an accident," Chansky remembered. "We had to be inventive."

The 10 horses died in the following manners:

• Suffocation. Five of the 10 horses were suffocated with plastic garbage bags: standardbreds Sonic Lord, Sandman A, JDs Harold, Nu Shot and Happy Paradise.

"I remember we always used (a brand that advertised its extra toughness)," Strautman recalled. "We tried a cheaper brand, but they would always tear.

"I remember we would call a vet on the phone and say, 'Hey, Doc, we have a sick horse here,' and the doc would say, 'Bring it over to the office.' We would load the horse in the trailer, do what we had to do, and then, at the office, we would walk back to the trailer and pretend to discover that the horse had died. Me or Chansky would shout, 'Holy (bleep), Doc!' The cause of death would be recorded as a heart attack.

"We should have won an Academy Award."

• Neck breaking. Strautman says he broke the neck of one horse, My Golly Miss Molly. He remembers that he cornered her in a barn at Spruce Hill Farm in Freehold. "I grabbed it on top of the head with one hand and grabbed its nose with the other hand," Strautman recalled. "Then, I just twisted until I heard the neck pop."

Chansky recalls this episode well. "Pete just wanted to prove to himself that he could do it," Chansky said, and added that to make the death appear accidental, Strautman dragged the dead horse to a corner and jammed her head under the side of the shed.

• Shooting. Strautman says he led standardbred Pine Haven Boo to the pasture at his Freehold farm in December 1975 and from a distance of 30 feet shot the horse in the head with a 12-gauge shotgun. Strautman reported to the insurer that the horse had been killed by deer poachers. He recalls that it was far more difficult "bagging or strangling a horse than shooting it."

"Up close it gets kind of personal," Strautman said.

• Hunting arrows. Three of the 10 were shot at point-blank range in the chests with hunting arrows: standardbreds Algors Tar Boy and Carols Destiny, and thoroughbred Kingdom of Heaven. Chansky or Strautman—depending on whom is doing the retelling—would shoot the horse, withdraw the arrow, and replace it with a splintered piece of fence or a sassafras branch. Chansky recalls that he and Strautman killed Carols Destiny in August 1980 during a violent thunderstorm in order to fabricate a cause of death in which the frightened horse had been running from a bolt of lightning when she broke through a fence and impaled herself.

"Horses *are* afraid of lightning," Chansky said, "and accidents *do* happen."

Strautman prided himself on "doing the job right," and he still is disturbed at how he and Chansky botched the elimination of Algors Tar Boy. Chansky remembers Algors Tar Boy as a "big, mean horse" and that Strautman shot it in the chest with an arrow at a Millstone Township, N.J., farm in June 1982. Strautman replaced the arrow with the sharp end of a rake handle, and the horse, bleeding profusely, staggered off into the field. Chansky and Strautman returned the next day and were shocked to find the horse still alive in its stall and "waiting for its feed."

"The horse had a big heart," Chansky said.

Strautman had to "bag" Algors Tar Boy. He says now:

"I kind of feel sorry for that one, but we did the others as humanely as we could. People have to understand: Either we killed them or the slaughterhouse killed them. Either way, these horses were doomed to die."

★   ★   ★

The Fat Man leans back at his desk and taps some tobacco into his pipe. On the wall behind him is an oil painting of John Wayne peering from beneath the brim of his cowboy hat. The Fat Man identifies with Wayne, and as he sits in his office in Seneca, S.C.—a room cluttered with telephone directories, a weapon or two and a brochure from a Nevada whorehouse—Bill Graham lights his pipe and grows wistful.

"The horse is a friend to man," Graham says. "The horse helped build America. Horses are beautiful creatures."

The Fat Man seems to drift in thought, and then adds with a scowl: "Only a diabolical bleep would kill a horse."

The Fat Man, who drives a Camaro Iroc, quotes from Shakespeare and has a passion for Beethoven, is a former Marine, cop and college professor who has crisscrossed the United States in search of horse killers. Graham has a caseload sitting on his desk that is "as high as six copies of 'War and Peace'—unabridged"—and has encountered a wide spectrum of grotesque acts. Graham remembers one horseman who "hot-wired" his horse to death with an electrical current; another who suffocated his horse by jamming ping-pong balls into its nostrils, and still another who inflicted a horse with "a case of ballpeenitis."

"I had a woman who said her horse was frightened during a storm and was running around in the paddock when it sustained injuries to the head," the Fat Man drawls. "The horse had an abrasion on its head the size of, oh, a quarter, and it died. The woman tried to collect (the insurance), but it seemed strange: That old horse would have had to have been running 70 miles per hour to be injured like that."

Graham shakes his head and cackles with laughter. "I stopped over to see the woman at her office," he continues, "and I said, 'Ma'am, your horse died of *ballpeenitis.'* She said, 'What? I've been a horsewoman for 30 years and I never heard of *ballpeenitis.'* I said, 'Ma'am, *ballpeenitis* is no disease. Either you or your husband hit that horse in the head with a ballpeen hammer.'"

The Fat Man adds, "She dropped the claim."

Graham likes to say, "I do not adhere to the Marquess of Queensberry rules," and indeed he can be intimidating. Unlike a claims adjuster, whose main function is to negotiate settlements, Graham works at the request of insurance companies that suspect "something ugly afoot." His fees are high—between $350 and $1,000 per day—and his focus is directed: He will do *anything* to help save his client money. One adjuster who used Graham in the past says that while the Fat Man is effective, he also "walks a fine line between legal investigation and harassment." Graham likens himself to "The Four Horsemen of the Apocalypse" and describes his approach as such:

"Say there is a Mr. Jones. I will take Mr. Jones aside and I will tell him, 'Mr. Jones, we appear to have a serious problem with the circumstances surrounding the demise of your horse. Now, I want to be able to resolve this in a climate of reason and understanding. I would strongly recommend that you walk away from this claim. This offer is withdrawn as soon as I leave the room.'"

The Fat Man describes that as "the polite approach" and claims that it works in 80 percent of his cases. The other 20 percent hear this:

"Mr. Jones, do you like oral sex? I hope you do, sir, because there will be a ton of it in prison."

The insurance companies that hire Graham are apt to wince at his bold and colorful tactics; the threat of litigation stemming from a wrongful accusation is a continual concern. Graham shrugs and says, "I despise lawyers."

He is currently involved in an investigation in California and hopes to begin pursuing a case in Texas. Unlike the thoroughbred industry—a sport controlled by people of wealth and influence—"distinctly American breeds" such as standardbreds and quarter horses appear to Graham to attract a "blue-collar element" in large part responsible for equine fraud. Graham chuckles and says:

"I swear there is *nothing* funnier than standing there in a barn with a horseman who has tobacco juice running down the side of his face—and who is standing knee deep in bleep—and who is talking like he is the trainer of Man o' War."

The Fat Man roars with side-splitting laughter. "You would think the horse could talk and walk on water," he says.

Graham is of the considered opinion that insurance companies are in part to blame for the fraud cases that have erupted. Citing the difficulties of establishing the precise value of a horse—and the absence of a central clearinghouse for checking the character of potential clients—The Fat Man claims the insurance companies have to start "keeping their eyes open more." He says that while the problem has "slowed some," the professional horse killer is still a problem.

"The SOBs are still out there," Graham says. "He is a person who knows enough not to kill a human, but he will damn sure kill a horse."

The Fat Man puffs a cloud of smoke in the air and adds: "There is a special place in hell for people who kill horses."

★   ★   ★

Pete Strautman leans into the refrigerator, pulls out a can of beer, and says, "Neither of us were choirboys."

He sits at the kitchen table of a cluttered farmhouse in Freehold and remembers how he and Chansky would be off driving somewhere and how Chansky would concoct "a hundred different scams." Strautman had been a roofer, and still is, and remembers how he and Chansky got to know one another at a New Jersey construction site in 1971. The two became friends.

"I would say we were close," says Strautman, 41. "Put it this way: If there happened to be a $10,000 contract out on my head, and I had no place to run and no place to hide, I would have handed Chansky a piece and said, 'Here, Danny, do the job, collect the 10 grand.' "

Chansky would tell people, in an effort to intimidate them, that Strautman had been "shot in the head in Vietnam and is a little whacko." Strautman claims he never has been shot in the head, but he had been a sergeant in Vietnam and remembers that he had a "little loan operation" there on the side. He charged 40 percent interest but explains: "It was a high-risk area." Strautman laughs at that and adds that it always had been a dream of his to be a soldier of fortune and "kill Cubans in South America."

"I would enjoy something like that," Strautman says. "But Chansky is wrong. I never enjoyed the horses. I just did it."

Strautman is a broad-shouldered, powerful man. His blue T-shirt carries the insignia of a place called the "Boot Hill Saloon" and stretches across a sharply defined chest. Born in Germany and then raised on farms in the United States, Strautman can remember his father taking a knife and, with a sudden turn of his hand, slitting the throat of a pet pig. Strautman also remembers how at the age of 12 he encountered an abandoned kitten on the side of the road. He cradled it in his hands, looked down at it, and squeezed. "Am I such a bad person for killing the kitten," Strautman says, "or is the bad person the one who left the poor little animal on the side of the road?"

Strautman finishes his can of beer, stands to get another, and adds, "People call me 'The Horse Hit Man,' but those are the same people who will go to the grocery store and buy a can of Alpo for their little pink poodles. I am not proud of (killing horses), but believe me, it would have been done without me. I decided, 'If I can make a thousand, why not?' "

Investigators for the Monmouth County prosecutor pursued Chansky and his cohort for three years. Their investigation began in 1980 when one of Chansky's co-conspirators illegally cashed two stock checks from the brokerage account of one John Irwin—who subsequently died—and alleged that Irwin himself had used the funds to purchase a horse from Chansky. The investigation expanded from there. Monmouth County prosecutor John Kaye identified Chansky as the "ringleader" of a conspiracy in which $226,000 of fraudulent insurance proceeds had been collected from 13 companies for dead horses, burned automobiles and sunken boats. Strautman received a plea-bargain arrangement from the state and was especially helpful to them in the prosecution of Chansky. The Monmouth County grand jury cited Chansky in 98 counts of a 101-count indictment in 1983. He pleaded guilty in January 1985 and entered prison that April.

Chansky is of the continued belief that neither the prosecutor nor the "esteemed Mr. Graham" could have proven that Chansky caused the deaths of the horses without the cooperation of Strautman. Claiming Strautman "was like a brother to me," Chansky shakes his head at the thought of "Pete sitting here with the prosecutor sipping coffee and spilling his guts." Chansky says the prosecutor could have "speculated" that Chansky had killed the horses, but adds, "Pete sealed it."

"How else could they have proved it?" Chansky asks. "Say a horse died of lead poisoning. Unless the prosecutor has a witness step forward, there is no way on this earth he can prove that I actually killed the horse."

Circumstantial evidence and the threat of legal action has helped hinder the prosecution of equine fraud. Insurance companies are reluctant to pursue suspicious claims, in part due to the cost of an investigation. Terry McVey, president of Equine Adjusters in Lexington, Ky., claims he has witnessed suspicious equine deaths that left him with a "sick feeling in the pit of my stomach," but adds that none of those suspected frauds would have been financially worthwhile to pursue.

"The people who do this seem to know that the smaller the claim is, the less apt the insurer is to pursue it," McVey said.

People such as McVey and Walt Knorpp contend that equine underwriters have begun to do a better job of substantiating the value of horses and evaluating the character of prospective clients. That, according to both, has closed some of the loopholes that exist, but neither are confident that "moral risk" will disappear entirely. Neither is Strautman.

"As long as there are horses," Strautman says, "and there are people to insure them, there will always be someone out there looking for the edge."

Strautman still speaks to Chansky occasionally. Chansky calls him collect from prison. Strautman accepts the charges but doubts that he and Chansky ever will be close friends again.

"Not like before," Strautman says. "I know Chansky is a liar and a thief."

Strautman opens another can of beer and asks:

"Can you do something for me, next time you see Chansky? Tell him he still owes me a thousand dollars. Tell him that, will you?"

★   ★   ★

Chansky is seated across a small table in a small room the prison sets aside for interviews. He laughs and shakes his head. "Pete said that?" he says. "He sends me away for 24½ years and I owe him a thousand dollars. Great."

Chansky is dressed in blue denim pants and a plain white shirt stretched tight across his bulging stomach. He weighs upwards of 250 pounds but claims he has dropped 40 pounds since entering prison. He also has taken some college correspondence courses and a Bible class in which he has received certificates for such courses as "Your New Life With Jesus" and "The Church." Chansky tells people he is a "better person" now and that, while he believes he "should have gone to prison," he also believes that others belong there with him. That Strautman received such a light sentence angers him.

"Dan Chansky belongs here, but there are people who belong here with him," Chansky says. "There are people who should be in here, like me, sitting in the lunchroom and hoping for parole."

Unlike Strautman, who has received some threatening calls from "some animal lover" in the wake of his conviction, Chansky has had few problems in prison. In the beginning, while at Trenton State Prison, one of the guards had heard of the horse deaths and began to follow Chansky down corridors, clicking his heels on the tile floor. The guard would even neigh like a horse. Chansky says that one time he turned around, reached inside his shirt and pulled out a plastic garbage bag. "I still have one of these," Chansky told the guard.

"He left me alone after that," Chansky says.

The door to the room opened at the conclusion of the interview and a guard entered. Chansky stood to leave, to return to a cell that approximates the size of a barn stall. Chansky says he contemplates that irony frequently, and adds, in a somber voice, that God would judge the acts he committed. Chansky considers that and adds with a grim chuckle: "I just hope God is not a horse."

Champion of the Counting House

PRO FOOTBALL

By *TOM FITZPATRICK*

From New Times
Copyright © 1988, New Times, Inc.

You're Bill Bidwill, the man they derisively refer to as "Dollar Bill." You have been in Arizona a pitiably short time and already everything has turned lousy for your inept team of losers and malcontents.

Something happened opening night, in your own ballpark, that told the story. You should have been able to stand in triumph that night before a crowd hungry for a pro football team of its very own.

It had been that way in Tampa, Seattle, New Orleans and even Indianapolis run by Bob Irsay, the grotesque clown who fled Baltimore under cover of darkness.

But it wasn't that way for you. They jumped to their feet and booed you with the almost palpable venom reserved for true villains of the counting house like George Steinbrenner.

How could you arouse such a reaction in six short months when it took Steinbrenner a full 15 years in a sophisticated city like New York?

If the distance from the grandstands to the field hadn't been so imposing on opening night, they might have done worse.

Perhaps reality boiled over and scalded the crowd to action in the instant it saw you attempt to take a bow on the playing field before the game.

Previously, the fans had humiliated themselves by getting down on their knees to buy the tickets you priced high enough to defy the imagination.

They thought they were buying into a dream in which they were going to their very own Monday Night Football game with the legendary Dallas Cowboys on the opposite side of the field.

But it all turned to dross when they had to leave their offices by two in the afternoon to get a parking place for a game that started in the bright sunshine for the convenience of the television people on the East Coast.

★   ★   ★

Maybe these fans who early on had connived to buy tickets suddenly realized the joke was really on them. They have already seen enough of your inept team to realize the Cardinals are not often going to be on the long end of the score.

But your gladiators will be champions in the counting house. Did it ever occur to you that your strategy of creating instant egregious wealth could do something even more significant? Single-handedly, you, Bill Bidwill, could be the catalyst that turns the country against the National Football League. The greed is too evident; it is rotting in the sun and fouling the atmosphere like a beached shark. The sick effort to get it all too fast is too evident to conceal anymore.

No wonder your first home game was witnessed from 50-yard-line seats by Nelson and Bunker Hunt, the men who tried to corner the world silver market.

Your presence on the Arizona State campus has tipped the scales. It was bad enough that they kept building on additions to the Sun Devil Stadium for a college team.

But now they are going to build skyboxes high on top and then spend millions more to lower the playing field. There will be another million spent on clubhouses. Who knows, next it could be multi-story garages with decks on top for pre-game parties.

It will all end like J. Fife Symington's "world class" Esplanade, which will give us fancy Texas department stores but block out our view of the mountains.

When you and your gang are finished, the football stadium will be as crass as a Las Vegas casino and will totally obscure the role a large state university should play in modern society.

★   ★   ★

You were brought up with a silver spoon in your mouth. That is odd, because the family money came from second-rate racetracks like Sportsman's Park in Chicago, where the behavior of the horses was often questionable.

They sent you to Georgetown Prep, and you discovered the turn-of-the-century dress style that has become your trademark.

The *Chicago Tribune* ran you out of town by ignoring you because George Halas, owner of the Bears, was editor Don Maxwell's best friend.

In St. Louis you became an urban hermit who yearned for solitude in which to count your money. But the money never came through the doors in big enough bags to satisfy you.

So, you fell in with the troika of Burton Barr, Karl Eller, and Keith Turley, who lured you to Arizona with the promise you could break all the rules of decency in the pricing of tickets.

Barr, Eller, and Turley weren't consciously trying to mislead you. All three have become wealthy and powerful by overpricing their own services for years.

If you had brought the New York Giants to town, people would still be complaining about the ticket prices. But you brought a derelict joke of a team here with you.

In all the years of the NFL, who ever heard of a slow-footed place-kicker like Al Del Greco attempting to make it into the end zone on a fake place-kick? The Cardinals could have lined up against North High School and that particular play would not have scored.

There is a joke around town. The Cardinals now have one thing in common with the Pope of Rome. Both drew 70,000 people to Sun Devil Stadium and made them stand up and shout in full voice: "Jesus Christ!"

You have brought us a team that is like the Flying Dutchman of ancient myth:

It was a ship on which a horrible crime took place. Plague broke out among the crew. No port would allow the ship to enter.

The Flying Dutchman wandered about like a ghost, doomed to be eternally tossed by the sea, never more to enjoy rest.

You're Bill Bidwill, whose parsimony has created a floating garbage scow of a team that still has not found a permanent home.

On the Ropes

by Jerry Lodriguss of the Philadelphia Inquirer. Michael Spinks lies helpless against the ropes after being knocked down in the first round by Mike Tyson during a 1988 heavyweight title fight. Copyright © 1988, Philadelphia Inquirer.

Head Start

by Louis DeLuca of the Dallas Times Herald. Cleveland's Dennis Meapham goes to the air and heads the ball away from Dallas' Kevin Smith during action in a 1988 Major Indoor Soccer League game at Dallas. Copyright © 1988, Louis DeLuca, Dallas Times Herald.

Road Warrior

OFF-ROAD RACING

By _MALCOLM SMITH_ with _LEE GREEN_

From Playboy Magazine
Copyright © 1988, Playboy Magazine

JANUARY 4, 1988—HASSI-MESSAOUD, ALGERIA

Not for nothing has this Paris-to-Dakar rally acquired an unrivaled reputation as the most miserable piece of work an off-road racer will ever see. People die in this thing. And don't let anyone tell you the course is 8,000 miles. It may be 8,000 miles on the rally map or in the official route book, but when you're out here for real on this endless expanse of boulders and sand dunes and dry lakes, zigzagging through Algeria and Niger and Mali and Mauritania and Senegal, screaming helter-skelter through the Sahara Desert at 120 miles an hour, the mileage mounts with every wrong turn and miscalculation. And God knows, there are plenty of those. This is only day four of 22, but already I feel as though I've seen more of Africa's sand than Rommel did.

The media in Europe, and especially in France, where the Paris-Dakar rally is regarded with no less reverence and awe than the Super Bowl is in the U.S., think Americans are too soft for this sort of endeavor. Fortunately, Camel Racing Service and Range Rover's people don't feel that way, so they hired me to drive one of the four cars that make up the Camel Range Rover team. Still, the European pundits don't expect me to do well, even though I've had the good fortune to win more than my share of grueling desert races, including the Baja 1000, off-road racing's version of the Indy 500. In fact, I've managed to win the Baja 1000 six times—three times on a motorcycle, three in a car. I've won the Baja 500 four times, the Mint 400 twice, the Roof of Africa Rally twice, and just nine months ago, I captured the Rallye L'Atlas in Morocco. But as the lone American in the 1988 Paris-Dakar, I'm regarded as nothing more than a rookie with fancy credentials. I don't mind. I'd rather be underestimated than overrated. I just want to do well. A top-five finish would be nice.

Along with my navigator, Alain Fieuw of Belgium, I was sitting ninth among the race's 420 cars and trucks at this morning's start. As usual, the rally's motorcycle division, 183 strong this year, started ahead of us. The 155-mile racing section of today's stage traversed intricate sand-dune valleys and canyons. Lots of tight twists and turns, very technical stuff. Creep along in low gear at 10 miles per hour, hard turn, then 30 miles per hour, another hard turn—that sort of thing. Without having to work too hard, I managed to work my way past five cars and was running third when two motorcycles in front of me, vying for the same narrow passage between two dunes, bumped each other and went down in a heap. I swerved to avoid them and, for my trouble, ended up planted atop a dune, my rear wheels spinning in place and spewing geysers of sand, my front wheels cantilevered over the edge of the dune's sharp drop-off. Welcome to Paris-Dakar.

The motorcyclists got up right away. Since I'd spared them the indignity of riding out the race enmeshed in my front grille, I thought they might come over and give me a little shove to get me going again. No chance. They hopped onto their bikes and took off. Can't say I blame them. After all, they're in a race, too.

Alain and I weren't exactly happy about being stuck, but we were prepared for the eventuality, thanks to the mechanics at Halt'Up!, the French company that assembled and prepped Camel Range Rover's cars. A conventional jack is useless in much of the soft African sand, so Halt'Up! had given us a device I had never seen before, a large canvas air bladder that lifts the car as it inflates when you attach it to the exhaust pipe and rev the car's engine. Inasmuch as I have managed to race in the desert for more than 20 years without benefit of one of these heavy, cumbersome things, I was tempted to pitch it in Paris when I was packing our already-overloaded car. I'm glad I didn't.

Sprawled on either side of the Range Rover, Alain and I dug with treasure-seeking ferocity, while below us, competitors zoomed past, wondering, perhaps, why some idiot would attempt to drive *over* this dune when there was a perfectly good route around it. While the rear wheels were held aloft by the jack, we jammed six-foot-long fiberglass boards—common accessories in this race—under them for traction. My job was to rev the motor, pop the clutch and hope six feet was enough for take-off. As usual, Alain's responsibilities were more demanding and less glamorous. He was to gather everything up and chase the car until I found a hard spot in the sand or a downhill where I could stop without getting stuck.

Within 30 minutes, we were on our way. Within 20 miles, we were lost.

The route book indicated a right turn at a specified kilometer.

What we had failed to consider, distracted as we were by our earlier misfortune and all the ground we had lost, was that while stuck on the dune, we had spun our wheels enough to throw off our odometer reading. No longer in sync with the route book, we took a right turn at the wrong place and drove 16 miles out of our way, squandering 20 minutes.

Our mishaps notwithstanding, by day's end, we dropped only five places. Fourteenth overall, 42 minutes off the pace. It could have been worse: One hundred and thirty-nine drivers, more than a fifth of the field, had their rally hopes prematurely dashed today. Some made it to the finish too late and were disqualified; others had mechanical problems or got stuck in the sand or had accidents and were injured. Among the scratches was one of my Camel Range Rover teammates, Salvador Canellas of Spain, whose car had suddenly and inexplicably quit on him.

So we are three now. My other teammates, Frenchmen Patrick Zaniroli and Patrick Tambay, are running third and fourth, respectively. Tambay is a Formula I racing hero in France, so well known there that he can't walk down a street or sit in a restaurant without being gawked at and pestered. I suppose his good looks don't hurt in that regard. He's quite friendly, willing to share whatever he knows about this race with me, though this is only his second go at it.

Zaniroli, by contrast, is taciturn and unhelpful. Not unpleasant, just unhelpful. This is his ninth Paris-Dakar—he missed only the first one—so he knows more about this race than the rest of us put together, but what he knows, he keeps to himself. I thought perhaps he wasn't confiding in me because of the language barrier. I asked Tambay if Zaniroli shared his expertise with him. "No," he said, "he doesn't tell me anything."

I get the feeling that Zaniroli is as intent on beating us as he is on beating anyone else. He won this race in 1985 and he has finished second three times. I sure would love to know what he knows.

JANUARY 5—BORDJ OMAR DRISS, ALGERIA

It strikes me as the height of irony that in a race that regrettably has earned a reputation for death and injury, a race stage would be canceled due to unsafe conditions. Unsafe conditions? This entire race is an unsafe condition. Nevertheless, because of road-maintenance excavations on the dusty oil-pipeline route we were to have followed today to the village of Bordj Omar Driss, the stage was downgraded to what the French call a liaison, a nonracing transit to get the cars safely from one place to another, usually to avoid endangering bystanders in populated areas. The first three days of the rally were liaisons, taking us from Paris to the southern coast of France, across the Mediterranean to Africa by ferry and into the open desert.

But even the liaisons can be dangerous. Two nights ago, while sailing along at 90 miles per hour on an open highway on the approach to El Oued, I narrowly avoided plowing into a herd of camels crossing the road. The reporters would have had a ball with that one: "CAMEL CAR DEMOLISHED BY CAMELS." On today's liaison, Jacky Ickx of Belgium and Formula I racing fame took a sharp turn too fast and rolled his car. He complained tonight that the route book should have warned us about the turn, but I noticed nobody else had rolled there.

If liaisons are meant to be easy, the race segments are meant to be tough. Especially yesterday's. The organizers figure they may as well weed out the weak cars and the weak drivers before they get too far into the heart of darkness.

JANUARY 6—TAMANRASSET, ALGERIA

Another 114 drivers bowed out during today's cruel but incredibly beautiful 496-mile race, the sixth and longest stage of the rally. Alain and I placed a respectable 10th for the day, and we've moved up to eighth in accumulated time. But by the time we rolled into this desert oasis, I was ready to go home. And I probably would have if there had been a flight out of here.

The problem came near the end, after we'd spent nearly 14 hours winding through rocky passes in the Ahaggar Mountains and through spectacular sand dunes. We're talking 2,000-foot-high dunes, maybe higher, with descents of about a 40 percent grade. You could never ever think about going back up them. And if you were going fast and got cockeyed, you could easily roll over.

This was my kind of terrain. I felt confident, drove well and managed to pass everyone except former World Rally champion Ari Vatanen of Finland, the race leader and last year's winner. It probably didn't hurt that I got lost once and undoubtedly cut off a little part of the course, which is legal as long as you don't miss a check point. The race is rerouted somewhat every year—this year, it's about 85 percent new—but Alain has ridden a motorcycle in six Paris-Dakars and he knows this section. His French accent rose above the whine of the Range Rover's noisy transmission and reached me through my intercom headset. "I can't find the course right now," he said without apology, "but if you just head along the mountain range over there, we'll run into it." Bull's-eye. I wish it were always that easy.

Eventually, we found ourselves on a dry lake bed, flat as Formica and utterly featureless. We cruised at 120 miles per hour on the compass reading specified in the route book, but it soon became apparent that we were off course. The finish-line check point wasn't where it was supposed to be. "I don't know where it is!" Alain shouted after double-checking the route book. He seemed certain that he wasn't in error, but I wasn't so sure. He was insistent: "They show it as being here and it *should* be here! The book is wrong!"

By then it was dark and we were darting around the dry lake like aimless idiots, three kilometers this way, five that way. I was steamed. Here I had moved up to second place in the rough section, and we were blowing it on terrain that should have been a cakewalk. "This is a goddamn French Easter-egg hunt!" I wailed. "This is stupid! They call this a race, but all we do is wander around the desert looking for check points."

Out of desperation, we finally resumed the specified compass heading and hurtled through the Algerian night like fugitives. Twenty kilometers down course, we saw the blinking blue light. The organizers had moved the check point without bothering to change the route book, an oversight that didn't seem to faze some drivers but cost us a half hour. I was inconsolable.

"Well," Alain reasoned, "this is Paris-Dakar. These things happen. Later on, somebody else will have trouble, and you won't, and you'll make that back."

To make matters worse, our team lost one of its three support trucks today because it couldn't get through one of the narrow mountain passes. Support trucks hauling spare parts are utilized by all the big-money teams, but the rules require them to follow the race route. So it's a race for them, too: If they don't arrive at each night's camp early enough to supply their team mechanics with parts, they're not doing anybody any good.

Something like 30 percent of all the support trucks were knocked out today for the same reason ours was. We undoubtedly would have lost all three of ours if Zaniroli, who remembered the Ahaggar passes from a previous year, hadn't warned Pascal Vigneron, Halt'Up! owner and team manager. Vigneron rerouted two of the trucks; they missed a check point and were assessed a three-hour penalty, which means that tomorrow they'll have to start farther back in the field, behind slower trucks. But at least they are still in the hunt. Lose those trucks and our entire team may as well fold up its tents and go home.

To be sure, no one has it easy in this race, but the support-truck drivers probably have the worst grind of all. The mechanics are flown from camp to camp by the Halt'Up! team, but the support-truck drivers have to slog it out on the ground, well behind the race cars.

Here's how our team works it: When Zaniroli, Tambay and I arrive at each night's destination, we wake up our mechanics and they take the Range Rovers apart with tools we carry in our cars. Then we all have dinner and go to bed. Later in the night, the support trucks finally roll in and the team manager wakes up the mechanics again. They work on the cars through the night, while the truck drivers grab some sleep, and then we do it all again the next day. Since the truck drivers never stay anywhere long enough to get decent sleep, three drivers are assigned to each truck. While they're on the move, which is most of the time, they take turns sleeping. The idea is to make sure no one takes his turn sleeping while he's driving.

JANUARY 7—DJANET, ALGERIA

I was doing 70 in a dry wash when suddenly, I heard a blast from a horn right behind me. I couldn't see anything behind me, because the little aerodynamic side mirrors are worthless and the rear window is always covered with dust. The side windows are always covered with dust, too, so my field of vision is limited to the 90-degree view the front windshield affords. If I want to see behind me—to look for a navigational landmark we may have missed, for instance—I have to do 360s.

I assumed the horn behind me belonged to one of the Peugeots. Peugeot has reportedly invested $10,000,000 in this race, far more money than any other sponsor, and its cars are, without question, the best and fastest on the course. During the first racing stage, I passed every car ahead of me but one and thought I was going fairly fast. All of a sudden, Ari Vatanen's Peugeot 405 whooshed past me so fast, I felt as if I were driving a golf cart. Vatanen hit a dune and was airborne for a moment; as soon as I saw his car land smoothly and easily, I knew our cars weren't competitive with his.

Which is ironic, because these Range Rovers aren't exactly cardboard-and-glue jobs. The custom Kevlar/carbon-fiber bodies house a 300-horsepower, V8 engine that can take the car from 0 to 60 in less than five seconds or cruise her at 130. The navigational instrumentation includes digital-readout compasses and odometers that we calibrate with onboard microcomputers. Range Rover and Camel spent $250,000 on each vehicle.

I pulled over to let the Peugeot pass and was startled when I was passed instead by a huge DAF truck—a race entry, not a support truck—belching black smoke from its skyward exhaust pipes, all four tires spinning viciously and spitting gravel in every direction. This 10-ton monstrosity resembles a garbage truck; it must be 10 feet high and twice as long. Absolutely shocked that this thing had overtaken me, I decided to just hang back and watch a while. What a sight! It was straddling boulders I had to dodge. It was mowing down bushes and small trees. On straightaways, it pulled away from me, packing 1200 horsepower in twin engines.

In a sandy wash, after tailing the DAF truck for about 100 miles, I tried to pass it and hit a boulder obscured by the dust. Flat tire, broken shocks and springs. Alain and I hastily did some creative repairs and limped the rest of the way in. We were 23rd for the 328-mile stage but still managed to climb from eighth to seventh in the overall standings. Thirteen motorcycles, 19 cars and 10 trucks gave up the chase today.

To our team's profound disappointment and dismay, Zaniroli, who was running third overall, was among them. I encountered him near the end of today's race stranded atop a dune. Blown engine. It was a bizarre scene up there. Zaniroli was very upset, of course, but his navigator, Igo Fenouil, had stripped to his black bikini underwear and was merrily doing cartwheels in the sand. I don't know how those two ever got teamed. Zaniroli is so serious, Fenouil so wacky. I don't think they were hitting it off all that well, and they still had two weeks to go. No wonder Fenouil was doing cartwheels.

JANUARY 8—DJADO, NIGER

For some reason, the medical cars weren't in position today, so the organizers decided to change the 460-mile race to a liaison stage.

That was only slightly more surprising than the shock that awaited Alain when he woke up this morning. As usual, we slept on the ground in the compound where our cars were required to remain overnight. Our heads were adjacent to a chain-link fence, and our cars and mechanics were no more than 25 feet away. Yet Alain's duffel bag, which he had placed under his head for safekeeping, was nowhere to be found. In the middle of the night, someone had actually lifted his head, substituted the duffel with a jacket and set his head down.

Theft in our overnight camps is not unusual. A few nights ago, several motorcyle riders lost their helmets and boots. A lot of racers prudently threw their wallets to the bottom of their sleeping bags, only to lose them to thieves who boldly cut the bags at the foot and reached in.

It's amazing that anyone in our camps sleeps long enough or soundly enough to get ripped off. Mechanics are usually working through the night, so there's the constant clanging of parts and tools, the revving of engines, the incessant drone of generators. And there's no escaping the glare of floodlights. Even if things quiet down a bit, it's just a matter of time before another support truck rumbles into the compound.

JANUARY 9—ARLIT, NIGER

I have just survived a day in which I easily could have been killed. It left one racer dead and another paralyzed. Three or four motorcyclists broke their legs.

I've been out in the wilderness all over—snowmobiling in Colorado, biking, racing cars in Mexico—and I've never had the sort of eerie feeling I experienced today in Niger's Tenere Desert. I think it was the first time I'd ever been truly fearful. Oh, I've been scared for an instant before, but today's fear was constant. When I started racing motorcycles in the 60s, the thing that scared me the most was not the fear of injury but the fear of failure. I faced those same apprehensions going into this race, too, but at the age of 46, I sense my mortality more than I used to—I have more of a sense of my limitations. And I have a wife, and four kids to think about. So now I also fear injury. Not so much a broken leg or arm; those I could recover from. But a head or spinal injury really scares me. I stopped racing motor-cycles seriously years ago because of that. I'd seen too many people paralyzed or brain-damaged.

The problem today was depth perception. Or any other sort of perception, for that matter. I drove 370 miles before I saw anything. There were no people, no wells, no trees, no bushes, no roads, no sign-posts, no fences, no abandoned cars, no dilapidated shacks—nothing. There wasn't even a horizon. The Tenere is a surrealistic place where the eye can't distinguish between the white sand and the white sky. I couldn't tell if the terrain in front of me was uphill or downhill, smooth or rugged. It was like driving in a thick fog. I couldn't see the bumps; I'd just feel the car jump. At 120 miles an hour, that's a rath-er unsettling sensation. I slowed to 80. We shouldn't be doing this, I told myself. This is stupid. Yet I didn't sense that Alain was uncom-fortable in the least. He just kept one eye on the route book, the other on the digital compass and calmly called out his conclusions: a little more right, a little more left, still more left. We sailed across the dunes like a cloudship.

Suddenly, we were airborne. We probably flew for only two or three seconds, but it seemed like a month and a half to me, because I had no idea what sort of surface or gradient we were going to land on. Uphill? Downhill? A gaping hole? Anything too radical could eas-ily result in a flip or a roll, which, given our speed, could have had unspeakable consequences.

The answer came gently and was lifegiving: a smooth landing, the downhill glide of the car conforming nearly perfectly to the downslope of the dune that received us.

Enough. I cut our speed way down and made a 90-degree turn to the north, hoping to find someone else's tracks to follow. When it's all solid white out there and there are no tracks, the whiteout is intensi-fied. But as soon as there are tracks to concentrate on, you can kind of tell whether the terrain is going up or down or whatever's happen-ing with it.

Alain wasn't happy with my decision. "It's gonna cost us too much time," he said. It didn't seem to occur to him that a little too much recklessness in this dune field could cost a man *all* his time.

Presently, we came upon some fresh tracks. I altered our course to follow them.

Car tracks in sand tell me what's happening ahead. When the car ahead slows down or brakes suddenly, the tracks widen, because the vehicle is no longer planing on the surface.

The tracks guided me for about 60 miles and then suddenly wi-dened. I slammed on my brakes. The Range Rover's tires bit into the sand and we skidded to the brink of a plummet, a sharp dune drop-off of 30 or 40 feet. At the bottom lay a Mitsubishi—or what was left of one—that obviously had descended the grade in violent fashion. Fiberglass sections were strewn everywhere. In contrast to their car, the driver and his navigator appeared to be all right, so I kept moving to avoid getting stuck.

In Arlit tonight, we learned that one of those monster DAF trucks had flipped over and ejected the navigator through the windshield with his seat and seat belt still strapped to him. DAF management's response to its colleague's death was to pull its other entries from the race. Sudden, unexpected death always brings with it a flash of perspective. For now, spending all this money so we can tear across the sand dunes in these expensive cars seems absurd.

JANUARY 11—AGADEZ, NIGER

A layover day among the Taureg tribespeople in this distinctly African city, whose mostly dirt streets wind among mud-and-stone structures and whose black denizens are robed and ornamented in silver jewelry. Agadez embraces the rally with open arms. I'm told that half of the city's annual income is derived from the rally's brief stop, which makes me wonder what the place is like the 363 other days of the year.

We have gone nearly 4,000 miles—halfway—since New Year's Day, hence the scheduled day of much-needed rest. A swirl of press and TV crews has flown in from France. I'm running seventh overall. Most of the reporters tell me they are surprised to see that I'm still running at all.

JANUARY 12—NIAMEY, NIGER

Our team is staying in a hotel in this cosmopolitan city on the Niger River, and I've just enjoyed the pleasure of a hot shower, only my second during these 12 days of Mad Hatter scurrying. I continue to hold on to seventh place overall. My sole remaining teammate, Patrick Tambay, is sitting 12th, about two hours behind me in cumulative time. Inasmuch as I'm five hours and 48 minutes behind Vatanen, who is still wearing everyone out with his pace-setting Peugeot, my competitive gaze is quite naturally shifting to the factory-Mitsubishi team. The Peugeots are really out of our league, but the Mitsubishi team is quite comparable to ours, by any measure—drivers, cars, monetary investment, preparation. Vatanen's Peugeot teammate, Finnish countryman and World Rally champion Juha Kankkunen, is in second, an hour behind Vatanen, but the four other cars ahead of me are Mitsubishis. I don't have much of a chance of catching the Peugeots, unless they have serious mechanical or navigational problems, but at least two of the Mitsubishis are within my reach. Plus, I'd like to crack the top five.

JANUARY 14—TESSALIT, MALI

One of the difficulties of this race is the unusual character of the

Sahara sand. It's soft and fine-grained, almost like talcum powder in some places. You'll be driving along in fairly hard stuff, and suddenly, you'll hit a pocket of powder and the car will just stop and bury itself. You never want to stop intentionally, because you may not be able to get going again. At check points, instead of stopping, drivers gear down and just keep rolling. The navigator holds the daily time-card out for the check point official, who runs alongside and tries to stamp it. If he misses, you have to circle around and make another pass. A lot of times, there'll be three or four cars circling, and another two or three stuck.

Another of this race's formidable difficulties is finding your way. The organizers make it difficult on purpose, but I think they went a little bit overboard today. First, they had us searching for a nonexistent check point near the Algerian border. Then the route book advised us to take the second road to the right as we passed through a remote village, when, in fact, we should have taken the third road to the right. The guy who made the route book instructions either had a perverse sense of humor or spent hours lost in the Sahara and perhaps never made it to Dakar. He'd better not be in Dakar when this race ends, because I know a lot of navigators and drivers who would like to get their hands on him. Tambay, for one, who ended up in the wrong country today and eventually hired a camel herdsman to sit on his navigator's lap and guide him back to Mali.

Navigating in this race isn't easy. We're flying along, bumping and turning sharply, and poor Alain is trying to look at the route book, look at the odometer, look at the compass and communicate instructions to me. It's not an enviable job, tougher than the driving, I think, because the driving comes by instinct.

One of the Mitsubishis was lost for more than three hours today, so even though Alain and I were lost for more than an hour ourselves, we managed to move up to sixth place.

JANUARY 15—GARA JAKANIA, MALI

Earlier in the race, after hearing me grumble about lousy directions in the route book, Jacky Ickx, the Belgian driver, said to me in a very stern tone, "If everyone got lost, you could blame the route book. If only some of you got lost, it was your own fault." That makes sense. On the other hand, once a few front runners take the wrong line, it screws up the entire race, because everybody follows them. If the route book says to take the left fork but all the tracks seem to indicate that just about everyone ahead of you has opted for the right fork, it's damn hard to ignore the tracks. Especially when the route book has been such an unfaithful guide. All the Paris-Dakar veterans are saying that the route book is usually vastly superior to the one we've been saddled with this year.

That wasn't much consolation to Alain and me during today's 433-mile race, as we caromed around the futile end of a box canyon after arguing about which way to go at one of those forks. It *was* consoling, however, to note that virtually all of the other leaders except Tambay were bottled up in the same canyon, swarming around like angry honeybees. Vatanen and Kankkunen had topographic maps spread out on the hoods of their Peugeots and were hunched over them like confused vacationers, a summit meeting that quickly drew a crowd and sparked debates in three languages. The canyon seemed to offer no escape except via the route by which we had entered. Alain and I headed back toward the spot 20 miles distant where we had taken the wrong turn. We were not happy campers.

Managing to stay clear of the box-canyon debacle, Tambay beat the field by almost an hour and catapulted from 12th place to sixth, while I fell two places to eighth. Vatanen and Kankkunen are still one-two, even though they, like me, squandered two and a half hours today.

JANUARY 16—TIMBUKTU, MALI

The organizers arranged for locals from Timbuktu to truck gas up to us in the desolation of Gara Jakania last night. The organizers did not, however, arrange for the locals to charge us a reasonable price. The option was pay or stay. We paid $1,200 to fill our car, a modest $18 per gallon.

Here in Timbuktu, Alain introduced me to a Belgian friend of his who had raced Paris-Dakar two or three times on a motorcycle. A couple of years ago, his motorcycle broke down here. He met a black woman, fell in love, married and is now raising a family here.

JANUARY 17—BAMAKO, MALI

Tambay won the 234-mile race out of Timbuktu—he has now won two of the past three stages—and I was third, so it was a good day for Camel Range Rover. Andrew Cowan, who has probably won more long-distance off-road races than anyone else in the world and was fifth overall entering today's stage, blew the engine on his Mitsubishi. I've enjoyed the affable Scotsman's humor and hate to see him go, but at least there's now one less Mitsubishi Tambay and I have to contend with. We're sitting fourth and fifth, respectively, with only the Peugeots and one Mitsubishi ahead of us.

JANUARY 18—KAYES, MALI

Somebody strolled into the car compound just before dawn today and drove off in Vatanen's Peugeot 405. Somebody drives off in his Peugeot 405 every morning, but usually, it's Vatanen. This time, it was someone with a business proposition, conveyed by phone, for Peugeot team manager Jean Todt: If Todt wished to reclaim his front runner's car, he should start raising capital, because it would cost him 500,000 French francs—almost 100,000 U.S. dollars. Todt assumed he was the victim of a joke until he checked the compound and found daylight where Vatanen's car used to be. The Peugeot manager had prepared himself for a variety of problems in the Paris-Dakar, but this wasn't one.

As it happened, Todt's immediate problem was short-lived. It seems that the thief was ignorant in the ways of race cars and didn't know how to open the main fuel-tank feeds. The car was soon found not far from where it had been stolen.

Now the Peugeot team has another problem, and no small one at that. By the time the missing car was located and recovered, Vatanen had missed his start time for today's race to Kayes, 316 miles of narrow, winding roads, ruts, washouts, river fordings and dense jungle vegetation—a thoroughly delightful little motor tour of western Mali. The organizers allowed him to race the stage late and, for now, he is still the event leader, but apparently, the Peugeot driver may be disqualified. I, for one, would hate to see a participant who has held the overall lead in this rally the entire way—all 15 days since the opening racing section in Algeria—disqualified because someone stole his car. The word here is that the Paris-Dakar organizers want to let Vatanen continue, but, as the European press speculated, FISA (Federation Internationale du Sport Automobile) president Jean-Marie Balestre, still brooding over an old legal battle FISA lost to Peugeot, wants him out.

JANUARY 19—MOUDJERIA, MAURITANIA

Vatanen has officially been disqualified, but Peugeot has lodged a protest and asked that the Finn be allowed to continue until a final ruling has been made. The organizers have agreed to that.

There were no roads where we crossed the Mali-Mauritania border this morning, just washes, footpaths, horse and cattle trails—those sorts of things. It was a splendid place to get lost, and we did.

The rally is down to its last three days, and although we still have 827 miles to cover, only 371 of them are in race sections. The Camel Range Rover strategy at this juncture, as decreed by our team manager this evening, is to drive conservatively and make sure both of our cars get to Dakar. We're not going to catch the three cars in front of us, anyway, unless they have trouble, and going fast won't make them have trouble any sooner. With seven support trucks, an observation plane, 62 mechanics and enough spare parts to rebuild a car from scratch, how much trouble can Peugeot have?

JANUARY 21—RICHARD-TOLL, SENEGAL

Yesterday, the entire rally was swallowed up in a sandstorm. We were stuck in a bunch of dune canyons in the Mauritanian desert, everybody driving every which way, trying to find a way out. It's a wonder we didn't have some head-on collisions. Finally, the race stage was canceled and a local camel herder was helicoptered in to lead us out. However, we ran out of daylight and ended up on an impromptu bivouac, everyone sharing what water and food he had. We start out in a race and end up on a picnic.

The camel herder led us out this morning, but every few miles he became disoriented and it took more money to clear his mind.

Vatanen was part of our sandstorm folly, but he is no longer part of the race. His disqualification stands and he won't be allowed to make the final glorious run into Dakar tomorrow. I feel for the guy. He won this rally and everyone here knows it, including Kankkunen, who seems a little sheepish about accepting the victory.

JANUARY 22—DAKAR, SENEGAL

Dakar at last. This is a classy uptown coast resort, big city all the way, an apparition after all the mud huts I've seen in the past three weeks. This is a city a lot of Americans would like. Find a different way to get here, though. Maybe it's just me, but the route I took seemed indirect.

Of the 603 of us who took that route, only 151 made it all the way. For the leaders, today's race—50 miles along the beach—was pretty much just a formality, since no one could possibly make up enough time to move up a spot. With Vatanen's banishment, Tambay was third and I finished fourth, five hours and 52 minutes off of Kankkunen's winning pace. I figure that Alain and I were lost a total of six hours and drove at least 200 unnecessary miles, but what the heck. People do that in a single weekend in L.A.

For all the personal satisfaction I'm feeling and the carnival mood that embraces this city, like so many others associated with the Paris-Dakar, I can't help but be affected by the sorrows this race has wrought. Yesterday, a car being used by a film crew hit a mother and child and killed them both. Earlier, in a village in Mali, a 10-year-old girl who was watching the race was struck and killed. Other accidents killed three competitors and left two paralyzed. Fifty more were injured. In 10 years of Paris-Dakar, there have been 26 deaths. Obviously, the tragedy here is not that Ari Vatanen's victory was stolen.

It's going to be hard to go back to reality. The race is so long, it's like a war: You go out every day to do battle; you have a purpose, a direction, a specific goal that must be accomplished. That sort of focused effort can be intoxicating.

At the same time, there's no getting around the onslaught of discomforts and unpleasantries this race inflicts. You're hot, you're cold, you're thirsty, you're lost. You sleep on the ground nearly every night, surrounded by a mechanial cacophony. You're gritty and dirty with no shower in sight, and you're eating dinner out of a can. . . .

Would I do it again?

I can't wait.

The John Thompson Way

COLLEGE BASKETBALL

By *BRUCE LOWITT*

From the St. Petersburg Times
Copyright © 1988, the St. Petersburg Times

John Thompson was speaking about the youngster who was doing poorly in class, whose father could not read or write, whose mother was concerned about her son's potential. Eventually the youngster was kicked out of Catholic elementary school. The teachers told his mother he was retarded.

She brought him to a professional educator, a doctor who invited the youngster into his office and asked him to identify objects around the room.

"Radio," the boy said. "Telephone."

Then the boy, overly shy, froze and fell silent.

"You shouldn't be embarrassed," the educator told the woman, "because it's not your fault. But this boy isn't educable."

The boy earned his bachelor's degree in economics and his master's degree in guidance and counseling.

"This little boy," John Thompson said, "is talking to you."

★ ★ ★

He is far more than the coach of the Georgetown basketball team playing in the Holiday Invitational Wednesday and Thursday at the Sun Dome in Tampa. He is a complex man, an amalgam of emotions, a man who elicits a full range of emotions from those whose lives he touches.

He is driven to win, but even more to excel. He will needle, threaten or bench his star players if they fail to produce grades in excess of minimum standards—the National Collegiate Athletic Association's, Georgetown's and his own.

Some critics say he is more than driven. They say he is an ogre.

He shelters his players as much as he drives them. He protects them in abbreviated locker room interviews—sometimes timed to the second by a stopwatch—and often houses them in relative isolation on the road.

Some critics say he is more than sheltering. They say he is paranoid.

He coached the United States basketball team at the Summer Olympic Games in Seoul—the bronze medalists, the first American team to *conclusively* lose the gold (as opposed to the 1972 team that wound up with silver in a controversial game against the Soviets).

Some critics say he ignored offers of assistance and assembled a flawed team. He has denied it and has said he would do it all again.

John Thompson, 47, is black, with an exclusively black team at a predominantly white school. Over the years, he has seen and heard both subtle references to his color and the most blatantly racist slurs. If it hurts, he doesn't show it.

★   ★   ★

"To be nobody but myself—in a world which is doing its best, night and day, to make you everybody else—means to fight the hardest battle which any human being can fight, and never stop fighting."

That passage from e.e. cummings, says George Raveling, basketball coach at the University of Southern California, is one of Thompson's favorite quotes.

Raveling also was one of Thompson's assistants at the Summer Olympic Games at Seoul. "I've heard John say, and I think it's true, how amazed he is that in America, supposedly founded on individual freedoms, people want to deny him the right to be who he is. He dares to be different in a world of sameness. That, more than anything, is why I respect this man."

Two rhymes, say those who have known John Thompson well and long, reflect what drives him.

One was sung to him in childhood by his mother:

You can do anything you think you can.
It's all in the way you view it.
It's all in the start you get, young man.
You must feel you are going to do it.

The other is a verse from *The Ladder of St. Augustine* by Henry Wadsworth Longfellow:

The heights by great men reached and kept,
Were not attained by sudden flight.
But they, while their companions slept,
Were toiling upward in the night.

★   ★   ★

Thompson has seen professional educators overlook potential in others—in himself—and he is a professional educator.

From Charles Smith to Alonzo Mourning and everyone in between, his players aren't attending Georgetown for the sole purpose of winning basketball games.

The Rev. Edward Glynn, now president of St. Peter's College in Jersey City, N.J., was Georgetown's faculty representative to the NCAA early in Thompson's tenure. "From Day One," Glynn recalls now, "he was dedicated to making sure his players would leave school with more than the ability to shoot a basketball."

"He'd tell them there are too many people hanging around street corners with nothing but their newspaper clippings, heroes in high school or college and nothing after that."

Raveling and Thompson have known each other since 1957, when Raveling was a student at Villanova. "What you find in John Thompson," says Raveling, "is a person who doesn't see his responsibility to his players confined to the basketball court. What I mean is that while most people might look at it as a basketball court, he sees it as a classroom, a place where he can teach them lessons more valid, more important, than blocking shots and making the outlet pass. So many people criticize him, but we really have to ask ourselves, isn't this what we want for our own children? Wouldn't we want someone like him to teach our children?

"A lot of the way he is is that he is at peace with himself. He has been able to answer two most relevant questions: 'Who am I and what am I capable of being?' He knows who he is and he understands what he is capable of being. . . . John sets his own standards. Be they right or wrong, they're his," Raveling says, "and he should be respected, not ridiculed, for establishing them."

★   ★   ★

For a few of his players—Patrick Ewing, Reggie Williams, Sleepy Floyd, Michael Graham and others—life after Georgetown meant professional basketball. For Ewing in particular, it meant millions of dollars and guaranteed stardom in the National Basketball Association.

It could have meant the same for Graham. He, too, had that gossamer quality of potential. But Thompson said Graham was wasting his time at Georgetown.

As a freshman in 1983-84, Graham was a major factor in the Hoyas' national championship season. Nevertheless, Thompson dropped him from the team the following season. Graham wasn't measuring up to Thompson's academic standards, the coach said, even though Graham had met Georgetown's and the NCAA's. In the long run, Thompson said, he would have been hurting Graham by permitting him to continue playing.

Graham left Georgetown, transferring to the University of the District of Columbia, sat out the obligatory season, then left without playing a game there, without earning a degree. He was drafted by the NBA's Seattle SuperSonics and never signed a contract or played for them or anyone else in the NBA. Today he is earning less than $10,000 playing for the Rochester (Minn.) Flyers, his fourth team in three seasons in the Continental Basketball Association.

Graham will not talk publicly about Georgetown or Thompson.

Glynn remembers an evening midway through the 1974-75 season, Thompson's third as Georgetown's coach.

"He'd lost a game up in Fairfield (Conn.)," Glynn said. "He hadn't brought along one of his star players because of academics and wasn't starting another one because he'd skipped some classes. John told me, 'I may not be able to keep my values and be a successful coach, but if I have to make a choice, I'm going to keep my values.'"

★   ★   ★

Hoya Paranoia is a headline writer's dream, and it has it's genesis in fact—Thompson's zealous protectiveness of his players and his program.

His team practices are closed to everyone. On the road, the team often stays in out-of-the-way lodgings, sometimes outside the city in which they are playing.

At the annual Big East media day at the Grand Hyatt Hotel in New York, the schedule calls for two one-hour sessions. The coaches meet with the print media, the players with the electronic media. Then they switch for the second hour.

Eight of the teams adhere to that schedule. Georgetown does not. Georgetown's players stay with Thompson, grouped around him at his table. If people want to talk to Charles Smith, they must do it with Thompson at his side.

After each game, the Hoyas media guide points out, "the Georgetown locker room will be open for 15 minutes to the press. Precisely at the end of the 15-minute period, the locker room will be closed and no more interviews will take place." Thompson's post-game news conferences last 10 minutes, concurrent with the players' interviews, "and after that period the coach will not be available to the press. There will be no exceptions to this procedure."

★   ★   ★

Thompson was on the Archbishop Carroll (Washington, D.C.) High School team. He would spend hour upon hour in neighborhood pickup games practicing his 15-foot jump shot, refusing to pass to the other kids on the team, ignoring them, working on the shot until the rest of them quit and went home.

After his two seasons as backup center to Bill Russell on a pair of Boston Celtics championship teams, he was left unprotected in the 1966 NBA expansion draft. He was claimed by the Chicago Bulls and wooed by the New Orleans Buccaneers of the new rival American Basketball Association. He knew he wouldn't have been in control of his destiny, he said, so he turned them both down and came home.

In his first coaching job, at St. Anthony's (now All Saints) High School in Washington, D.C., his teams played highly physical, full-court-defense games from start to finish. More than 20 years later, Georgetown plays the same in-your-face game.

Red Auerbach was Thompson's coach with the Celtics. Thompson, Auerbach said recently, "is the way he is because he doesn't want people to get too close to him. He picked that up from me and Russell—take control, stay in control, put everyone else on the defensive."

He is, by his mere existence, a black role model. But while others —from Martin Luther King to Jesse Jackson—have preached change through social programs and legislation, Thompson's message is that the elimination of racism can best be achieved by eliminating poverty.

"I think more change has come about because of economics," he told the *Washington Post* last August, "because people totally disregard color barriers if you have economic value. . . . Put yourself in a position of power where you create a need for yourself that has an economic effect on somebody. The world is not black or white as much as it is green."

That he is black and the team is black spawns criticism that race is a determining factor in Thompson's recruitment process. He rejects the idea out of hand. "I don't know of any white player who qualified to play on my teams that I've turned down," he says, and his supporters say Thompson does recruit white players and doesn't discriminate against them.

"I'm not going to . . . demean myself by trying to explain myself and justify myself," Thompson says. "I'm not going to do that because some ignorant person said I'm prejudiced. I'm not interested in apologizing for being a black man. I'm as proud as I can be of that."

His critics also point to Thompson's unwillingness to schedule games against other area schools—George Washington, American, UDC, Howard—which might benefit financially with a game against Georgetown.

When the Rev. Timothy Healy, president of Georgetown, once suggested a game against George Washington, a crosstown rival, Thompson rejected the idea, saying GW's fans had shouted racist remarks at Ewing. Healy didn't push the matter.

But others accept Thompson's public explanation.

"He plays enough tough games in the Big East and one or two intersectional games with schools like LSU and Texas-El Paso," said Coach Ed Tapscott of American, which was dropped from the Georgetown schedule two years ago. "A local game would be just another tough, emotional game and he doesn't need another game like that. . . . If he beats American or George Washington or Howard, so what? He's supposed to. But if he loses, all of a sudden it's , 'What happened?'

"He's not discriminating," Tapscott said. "Effective scheduling is a part of coaching. When one has the advantage, one must press it. John does it. . . . Every coach does what's best for his school, for his team. He's just a bigger target than everyone else—literally as well as figuratively."

★   ★   ★

Under Thompson, Georgetown's image has become one of a street-wise, street-tough team. In the motion picture *Colors*, one of the gang members wears a Georgetown jacket. The Hoyas have engaged in their share of on-court fights.

During a nationally televised game last season, a melee broke out between Georgetown and Pittsburgh players. Former Seton Hall Coach Bill Raftery, broadcasting the game on CBS, said over the air during the brawl: "John Thompson has to control his team. There are too many incidents over the years."

Thompson says he opposes fighting but points out that Georgetown plays an "aggressive" game. "We cover the full court for 40 minutes and that brings about and creates frustrations in ourselves and in other people at times."

Healy acknowledges the team's negative image and Thompson's adversarial relationship with the media, but explained in the *Washington Post* interview: "He runs a large program. He's got guys doing things very well. The things he doesn't do well strike me as so much less important than the things he does well. I'm going to leave him alone."

Thompson runs one of the most successful basketball programs in the nation. Because of it, he earns perhaps half-a-million dollars a year. He is a coach, he runs a summer basketball camp, he endorses Nike athletic products, he has his own local television program, he is a highly sought-after and highly paid speaker (ProServ, the sports marketing group that represents him, says Thompson does about a half-dozen such appearances a year at about $15,000 apiece) and he lives in a house given to him by Georgetown alumni.

★   ★   ★

It was early in the 1974-75 season, Thompson's third as head coach of the Hoyas, one which would culminate in Georgetown's first trip to the NCAA Tournament since 1943.

He had inherited a team which, the year before he arrived, had won three of 26 games. This season, it had won seven of its first nine. But Thompson was not happy.

His players were required to sign a book verifying they had attended all their classes. His top scorer, Jonathan Smith, had signed—but he had cut some classes. When Thompson found out, he benched his star player without explanation.

Georgetown lost six consecutive games. The predominantly white student body was in an uproar. During one game, a bedsheet was unfurled. It read: "Thompson The N----- Flop Must Go."

The next day, The Rev. Robert J. Henle, then the president of Georgetown, called a news conference and apologized to Thompson. Then Smith revealed at the news conference why he had been pulled from the starting lineup. He supported his coach.

Felix Yeomans, then the youngest player on the team, followed Smith to the microphone and listed what Thompson had done for

him and for each of his teammates. "If this is what it is to be a n-----
flop," Yeomans concluded, "this is what we want to be."

Georgetown won 11 of its next 12 games, including the championship of the East Coast Athletic Conference (forerunner of the
Big East Conference), and was invited to its first NCAA tournament
in 32 years.

★   ★   ★

Bill Stein is the athletic director at St. Peter's College in Jersey
City, N.J. He was one of Thompson's assistants at Georgetown during 1972-82. They also were teammates and roommates on the road
at Providence College.

"John recruits only certain types of people," Stein says. "I know
he has refused to go after players who wound up as All-Americans.
Whether someone is white or black has nothing to do with it. Whether a person can fit into his program, into the kind of style he wants to
play, that's what matters.

"People can make a big deal about how he's a black coach with
an all-black team. A white coach with an all-white team, that's ac-
ceptable. Nobody thinks much about it. A white coach with a black
team, they'd say, 'What a great guy!' "

Thompson knew, even before Georgetown won the NCAA title in
1984, that one question would inevitably rise—how he felt about
being the first black coach to win a national championship. His answer was cool, reasoned, but not without a tinge of bitterness.

"When you think about it," he said, "the question is insulting.
What is implied by the question is a great big blank before the first
one came along. And that's a lie. Plenty of other black coaches could
have won an NCAA national championship if they had ever had the
opportunity. It's not the brains and talent that were missing until I
came along. Those have always been there."

★   ★   ★

When he recruited Ewing, Thompson knew Patrick's mother
was interested in academics first. They spent the better part of an
hour in the Ewing household discussing the subject.

Then Patrick spoke up. He asked about the social life in Washington, D.C.

"With your schoolwork and the athletics," Thompson replied,
"you won't have much time for a social life."

Patrick's mother made up her mind. Her son would attend
Georgetown.

★   ★   ★

It happened in the early 1980s, as Georgetown was emerging as a
national power. The season and the tournament were over. The team
was returning home.

In the rear of the bus, several players were carousing. From the
darkness, one voice floated toward the front: "I guess this means we
don't have to see you tomorrow, Miss Fenlon."

Mary Fenlon, seated beside Thompson, turned and replied: "The
basketball season is over, but you're still freshmen. If you want to be

sophomores, you'll be there tomorrow."

The bus fell silent for the rest of the ride.

When Thompson took over at Georgetown, three assistant coaching positions were open. He filled two of them with assistants to work on basketball. But the first person he hired was Mary Fenlon, academic coordinator. She had taught English and Latin at St. Anthony's when he coached there.

"She was a teacher, not a temporary mother or guardian," Thompson said in the Georgetown media guide, "and she got the students to do what they were supposed to do in school without the pretense of being overly affectionate with them."

At Georgetown, she is the players' tutor, their confidant. They trust her implicitly. She declines all interviews, saying politely that they "would impair my relationship with the students."

She doesn't call them players.

She also rides herd on Thompson. "If I start to interfere with the players' studies," he says, "she will let me know."

She has as much say as Thompson about who goes on road trips and who stays home to improve grades. Thompson says she also is his alter ego, his conscience. At all games, home and away, she sits on the end of the bench. She was there, too, in Seoul, at the Summer Olympic Games.

Under NCAA rules, a coach is permitted to take only full-time assistants on recruiting trips to screen and assess prospects.

John Thompson takes Mary Fenlon.

★   ★   ★

Since Thompson took over as head coach, 53 of 55 basketball players who have played four years at Georgetown—96 percent— have graduated. In all, 67 students have played basketball at Georgetown in the Thompson era. Ten transferred to other schools and two dropped out. That reduces the graduation rate of the school's basketball players under Thompson to 79 percent.

Overall, about 70 percent of each year's entire entering freshman class graduate from Georgetown within four years, and about 80 percent eventually receive a Georgetown degree.

The NCAA said that in a recent survey of all Division I-A private schools (those major institutions such as Georgetown without Division I football programs), the graduation rate of all entering basketball players was 60 percent, the graduation rate of non-athletes 56.7 percent.

The numbers—even the discussion of them—annoy Thompson. Athletes, he says, should not be looked upon as somehow different.

"We have an educational problem in this country," he once said when the subject of basketball players' grades arose, "and I'm sick and tired of people focusing in on athletes as if that's the only place there's a problem. Athletics just reflect a small part of our society.

"The kids that we have that are participating in athletics come out of society as a whole. . . . I'm sick about all this bull about athletics being looked at educationally. That's a bunch of hypocrisy. It's easy for people to discuss athletics."

Thompson recalled a television program he had seen in which educators were discussing whether a student with a 2.0 grade-point average in his school should be allowed to play basketball. "Big debate!" Thompson snorted. "All these people from academic circles. I said to myself, 'Maybe I'm wrong, but I think there are other kids in educational systems who are having problems.'

"Personally, I think the athlete is fortunate. People focus in on him because of the public interest in him. Some little kid who doesn't play anything and doesn't have a 2.0, nobody gives a damn whether he has one."

★   ★   ★

When Thompson arrived at Georgetown in 1972, there wasn't much interest in the basketball team. The Hoyas had had only one winning season in the past five. More to the point, Maryland had a virtual lock on the Washington, D.C., media.

At the time, Thompson was Georgetown's best resource—a local star high school player, a member of two Boston Celtics championship teams and a coach at St. Anthony's.

He personally sold the Georgetown basketball program. He told Bill Carpenter, then the general manager at local television station WTTG, "Come with us now, because we'll be good some day and we won't forget where we started."

WTTG began televising the Hoyas' games. There was little viewer or sponsor support. Some station executives considered dumping Georgetown. Carpenter stayed with it. Georgetown has since turned aside more lucrative offers and has stayed with WTTG.

"Loyalty," says Betty Endicott, WTTG's current general manager, "is one of John Thompson's strong suits."

Dennis Donaldson, an assistant basketball coach at the University of South Florida, saw Thompson's sense of loyalty in action as an assistant during the selection process for the U.S. Olympic basketball team.

"John was kind of hurt that a few players he would have liked to try out for the team stayed away because they thought it might hurt their pro careers, how their stock might go down (in contract talks because of poor performances), that they might get hurt or something. Like Derrick Chievous (from Missouri, now with the NBA's Houston Rockets) and Gary Grant (from Michigan, now with the Los Angeles Clippers)," Donaldson said.

"There were seniors there who weren't going to make the team, who everyone *knew* weren't going to make the team, but John wanted them around just to help their pro careers. There were guys who pretty much knew they didn't have a chance (to be selected to the Olympic team) but John was so honored that they had been willing to come to the Trials that he gave them an extra shot at making it. He kept them past the first cut.

"I think what he was doing was looking to make them look better in everyone else's eyes, maybe to look better to their agents, to the media. John was trying to help them along in life. Fennis Dembo (out of Wyoming, now with the Detroit Pistons) was one for sure," Donaldson said. "He had a lot of hype coming out and was disappointing in the Trials. John told me, 'I'm not going to cut him early. I'm keeping him around. He thought enough to come here, to put the pro stuff aside, I'll help him out.'

"John's got some very interesting thought processes. They run a lot deeper than most people's."

Dwayne Schintzius likewise saw a softer side of Thompson. When the 7-foot-2 University of Florida center first showed up at the Trials, he was out of shape, overweight.

"A lot of coaches might have just gotten rid of me at the first cut. But he sat me down, told me I had potential, told me he liked me and that I should go home, work on my game, lose a few pounds and come back."

He did, dropping about 20 pounds. Thompson then worked with Schintzius, on his game and on his attitude, and put the former Brandon High School star on the U.S. Select team that made a six-game tour of Europe in June. Schintzius survived to the final series of cuts. "I can't believe how much I learned from him," Schintzius said. "I knew I wasn't going to make the team, but he was very fair, gave me a very fair shot."

★   ★   ★

After the United States lost 82-76 to the Soviet Union in the Olympic semifinals, Thompson bore the brunt of the criticism because he had selected a feisty, defense-oriented team similar to those he assembled at Georgetown. He should have selected more outside shooters, the critics complained.

The only pure shooting guard, Hersey Hawkins, was injured and missed the Soviet game. And Danny Manning, one of the U.S. team's acknowledged stars, spent most of the game on the bench in foul trouble. He didn't score a point.

"The things that were done were things that we thought were in the best interest of what we were trying to accomplish," Thompson said the day after the game. "I think if I had to do it over again, every player I selected I would select again, every staff member, everything that we decided to do. You make decisions, and then you have to go with those decisions."

Stein, an assistant coach (along with Raveling) at the Olympics, said the Americans "played as well as they could have. We just had a bad game. The guys were a little tight. Our boys had played 16 games together. The Russians played something like 120. They'd been together six years with one change in personnel."

"If we played those guys 10 times, we'd beat them seven or eight (times)," Stein said. "Too much was made of one game."

Raveling said: "I think there were a lot of personal prejudices—

as opposed to racial prejudices—exhibited before, during and after the Olympics. One writer told me not long after that there were some writers rooting against the U.S. team because Thompson was the coach. There's a sickness in that, that someone could actually root against his own country because of the composition of a coaching staff. No one should dislike anyone that much."

★   ★   ★

John Thompson is a 6-foot-10, 300-pound bear of a man, his countenance generally more contemplative than menacing. But perhaps because of the way he covets his private life, his insular program, and because of his size and blackness, he is sometimes characterized as a villain.

"People are just jealous of him," Auerbach, president of the Celtics and long a friend of the Georgetown coach, said earlier this month. "I don't care what anybody says, John Thompson is a dedicated guy who really cares about people, about the players who play basketball for him. Whether they become pros or not, they've got the basics to be successful in life."

"I'm not going to win many popularity contests," John Thompson once said. "I don't have to explain myself. I don't do things for other people. The people who know me know the way I am.

"I think sometimes my friends feel they have to explain or apologize for me. That's unfortunate. I don't see the need for that, but I feel affectionate toward them for doing it."

Strange Wins U.S. Open

GOLF

By *THOMAS BOSWELL*

From the Washington Post
Copyright © 1988, the Washington Post

Everyone in golf who knows Curtis Strange knew where his thoughts would turn as he walked up the 18th hole of The Country Club with the U.S. Open championship safely in his hands today.

He would think of his father Tom and their years together in his boyhood when golf was their bond and passion and almost a blood vow between them. He would think of the man who died when he was 14, nearly 20 years ago, leaving a paternal memory of superhuman size and demands, deep-carved demands, that would drive and lash Strange all his life.

Everybody knew, almost to the word, what Strange would say as soon as he had finished the work of beating British Open champion Nick Faldo, 71-75, in this 18th-hole playoff. Strange would not talk yet about putts and sand shots, about "sheer guts," about how he ignored 10 visits to the rough and five trips into sand traps. He would not talk about how he kicked the ball all over wind-whipped eastern Massachusetts, but willed his way to a dozen one-putt greens.

"I think you wait for a moment like this in your life to thank the people who've given you the advice, enthusiasm and knowledge to continue on," said Strange, picking every word, pausing as much as 10 seconds between phrases as he cried quietly. "I have to thank my dad. This is for my dad." Then he waited.

"And that's all I can say. I've been waitin' to say that a long time," said Strange. "I just wish he could have been here. . . . I screwed up the '85 Masters. But let's not be bringing that up. Let's be havin' fun. . . . This is the greatest thing I have ever done . . . the greatest feeling I have ever had. My two kids don't even know (yet) what the hell this means to me."

This U.S. Open meant everything to Curtis Strange. More, perhaps, than it ought to mean to anybody. Even he has admitted that countless times, talked about the coiled spring of ambition inside him that drives and torments him, even as it pushed him to Arnold Palmer scholarships at Wake Forest and seasons as the No. 1 moneywinner on the PGA Tour. "I'm too hard on myself," he says. Yet this week, he has barely slept. His eyes are bloodshot. And, Sunday night, after coming so close to throwing away this Open, he couldn't even eat. For nearly 24 hours, he was a taut bow, "Waiting to go." Waiting to atone.

Faldo should have finished Strange when he had the chance, when he had all those cozy birdie putts on the back nine Sunday. He shouldn't have waited until this nasty, windy afternoon when both he and Strange would, inevitably, be blown off the short grass into the high heather and have a war of hearts, not swings. Eleven times Faldo missed the green and six times he ended up with bogey—five times in the last six holes as the long battle just wore him out.

Strange, the grinder's grinder, the bad boy with a bit of a sneer, just kept holing those heartbreakers. Three feet, six feet. Sorry, Nick. No lip-outs today. Strange only hit seven greens all afternoon, but three times he set the huge crowds roaring with birdie putts of 10, 22 and, finally, 29 feet at the fifth, seventh and 13th holes.

Strange never trailed, not for a second. When he birdied the 13th, it was the day's kill shot. Faldo three-putted for bogey a moment later to put Strange ahead by three shots. "The turning point," said Strange, who never led by less than two shots thereafter.

The door only opened once after that, for a second at the 15th hole, when Strange was trapped and had to bogey. But Faldo slapped that door on his own foot. He fragged an easy chip shot all the way across the green into the fringe and bogeyed himself.

"I don't know what happened on that one," Faldo said.

Now Strange could come home on cruise control. When Faldo, gambling for birdie, bogeyed the 17th, Strange thought, "It's over."

More than a golf tournament was over for the 33-year-old who has won $3.6 million but, until today, never a major championship. Always money. Never glory. Never what his father, the romantic, valued most—stature in the game.

"We all have our egos and we want to be respected, not just as a person, but as a golfer," said Strange. "This (Open) means Curtis Strange might be looked at a little differently. . . . It means I got to that next level, damn it."

The earnings at the next level aren't bad, either. Strange pocketed $180,000 for the victory; as runner-up, Faldo received $90,000.

Strange is the player that fellow pros on the tour always have worried about. Tears and fury ran just beneath his skin. His mask always was full of cracks, the rage or hunger waiting to erupt. Friends worried when he got publicly scalded by Palmer for bad temper at the Bay Hill Classic a few years ago. They worried when he blew that Masters after being four up on the back nine. Think what that would do to any player. Imagine what it does to Strange.

The final round of the U.S. Open always falls on Father's Day—another bad break for Strange, who tries too hard, berates himself too much, on the best of days. Once, on an Open Sunday, a fan approached Strange between nines and said, "Win it for your dad."

"That did it," recalled Strange. "I was in tears on the 10th tee."

Now, the friends of Curtis Strange—a group that has grown enormously in the last three years after he met the indignities of Rae's Creek with fresh dignity of his own—don't have to worry anymore. He's come into the clearing.

Because he faced the worst when he lost the Masters, because he discovered that people forgave him, empathized with him and even liked him in failure, Strange was able to cope with his near collapse here on Sunday. But it was far from easy. A night to regroup helped.

"After my (three-putt) mistake at the 17th on Sunday, I didn't want to lose today. . . . I just didn't want to face you guys if I lost. I hate to admit that, but it's true," said Strange at the postmatch news conference. "(A loss) would have been something I would have had to get over. But it would have been tough. Those things affect us."

Faldo seemed unfazed by his defeat. In fact, he seemed so proud that his nerve had held on his long shots—"I had it going in the right direction all day"—that his ineffectual putting hardly seemed to enter his mind.

"I just never put enough pressure on Curtis. . . . It felt like a helluva long day," he said, after roasting in the mid-90s heat. "(And) I think my five spectators did a helluva job."

For Strange, the path to this Open title has been a long one. Along the way, he learned—although he'll be the first to concede not completely—how to relax, how to enjoy others, how to forgive himself, how to fail and how to carry himself like a champion of the game. "That Masters wasn't going to intimidate me or ruin my career," said Strange. "It even motivated me, to a point. What I've done since says, 'This was not going to devastate Curtis Strange.' "

As he came down the 18th fairway this hot, breezy evening, the throngs straining against the ropes to praise him, Strange raised both hands above his pepper-gray head in salute. In the gallery, his twin brother Alan, almost a golf pro, hugged Curtis' wife Sarah. Then, after the final putt, after he had joined Francis Ouimet and Julius Boros as Open playoff winners at The Country Club, it was Curtis' turn to hold his wife, tight and saying nothing for a long time. Finally, Strange's lips moved. He seemed to whisper, "I made it."

And if he didn't, he might as well have.

Run, Lindsay, Run

COLLEGE FOOTBALL

By *TOM JUNOD*

From Atlanta Magazine
Copyright © 1988, Atlanta Magazine, Inc.

The people in this state love football, and if you play for the University of Georgia, you'll never be forgotten, whether you make it in the pros or not.
— A Georgia coach to a prized recruit

There are no second acts in American lives.
— F. Scott Fitzgerald

He sat on the step and waited for the end of the rain. All summer, the sun had squeezed Statesboro dry, and now for three days straight, a deluge had come sweeping over the town's blistered lawns and blighted fields every time he donned his shorts and sneakers and set out to run. Once, he had been a football star and could count on the lightning in his legs. Now the lightning sprang from the clouds and spat thunder, and Lindsay Scott was earthbound amid a clot of men trying to stay out of the rain.

The men were not athletes. They were doctors, lawyers, railroad workers. They sported bellies and beards and smoked enough to spread a carpet of cigarette butts from the step to the parking lot. They did not like to sweat, and while a few of them had tried running with Lindsay, not one had stayed with the routine very long. In general, they preferred to sit and smoke under the overhang, to drink Cokes and coffee, to swap jokes and stories about their lives as alcoholics and drug addicts.

"This is a crazy place, man," Lindsay said, shaking his head. "Animal House." He lounged against a wrought-iron trellis and stretched his legs and laughed along with the other men. Finally the clouds untangled, and sunlight blew across the train tracks and overgrown lots and lit up the peeling green paint and crooked shutters of the halfway house. A car swung into the parking lot, squishing cigarette butts under its tires, and a visitor emerged in sneakers and shorts. "You ready?" he asked Lindsay.

One of Lindsay's compatriots rose from the step, a tall, freckled black man who, as a cocaine addict, had been known as the Taster. "You gonna run with Lindsay Scott?" he asked the visitor. "You can't run with Lindsay Scott. He gonna bust your heart. Lindsay Scott been running all his life. You try running with him, he bust your heart!"

The Taster laughed and watched Lindsay stand and stretch. So did the others. Although he was 20 pounds overweight, and worked now not to recapture his speed but merely to sweat, the former Georgia Bulldog still had the thick legs of a sprinter, the tiptoe, prancing walk, the showy grace, the glow. Oh, Lindsay Scott could run, all right. As a boy, he ran roughshod through the south Georgia sandlots, and as a high school hero he ran for touchdowns by the dozen. As a Bulldog, he ran far enough to become the greatest receiver in Georgia history and fast enough to snare a million-dollar contract with the New Orleans Saints. As a pro, he ran through cars, a condo and cocaine, and in a few years, when cocaine was all he had left, he ran to a hospital in Statesboro. Now he lived in the halfway house, and when he turned to trot down the rain-soaked street with his visitor, the Taster and the stubble-jawed men under the overhang cried, "Bust his heart, Lindsay, bust his heart!"

But Lindsay Scott did not spring loose, did not bust anyone's heart. He jogged down a side street, his short, childish steps turning into a slow canter, and talked about his addiction and newfound sobriety. He carried his hands high, drew breath through a wide-open mouth and let the sweat slick his face and stain his Atlanta Hawks T-shirt. He said, "I don't know what's next for Lindsay Scott. I just know one thing. If I was doing that shit, I wouldn't be doing this. I wouldn't be running. I'd be locked in some room in Atlanta looking crazy." The putrid tang of some far-off paper mill blossomed in the sun, and rainbows slid down the oily streets. "I just want to do God's will," Lindsay said. "I don't know what God's will is going to be. I just know what it's not. It's not doing that cocaine."

He kept running, an easy two-mile jaunt, and as the sun gleamed off his face, people began to look at him. To notice. A child stumbled toward him, and Lindsay patted his head. A man waved from a driveway, and Lindsay waved back. A foxy woman in a Mustang checked him out from head to toe, and when Lindsay said, "Yo! Slow down!" she hit her brakes. No, they didn't know who he was. They just knew he was *someone.* Eight years earlier, against the University of Florida, he had pulled lightning from the sky and scored the touchdown that secured destiny's hold on a team headed for the national championship; once a man does something like that, he acquires a *look* that only the blind can miss.

Buck Belue back . . . third down on the 8 . . . in trouble . . . got a block behind him . . . gonna throw on the run . . . complete to the 25 . . . to the 30 . . . Lindsay Scott . . . 35, 40 . . . Lindsay Scott . . . 45, 50 . . . 45, 40 . . . RUN, LINDSAY . . . 25, 20 . . . 15, 10, 5 . . . LINDSAY SCOTT! LINDSAY SCOTT! LINDSAY SCOTT!

No, once a man gets a taste of magic, it's hard for him to give it up, no matter how far he runs or where he tries to hide.

★   ★   ★

This is a Bulldog story. It is the story of a man, a team and a moment. It is a story about fate and magic and the gifts the gods choose to bestow or withhold. It is about the thunderclaps that control the course of events in football games, and the slow, brooding clouds that rule the arena of real life. It is about our heroes and the burden of our expectations. Finally, it is a story about Lindsay Scott and Buck Belue and the most famous play in Georgia history—the 93-yard touchdown that beat Florida in 1980 and led a young man to believe, if only for a while, that he was blessed and had access to miracles.

On November 8, 1980, when the University of Georgia played the University of Florida in Jacksonville's Gator Bowl, the Bulldogs were ranked second in the nation. They had a freshman back named Herschel Walker, a banshee defense and a love affair with Dame Fortune. In the first game of the season, they nursed a one-point lead against Tennessee, watched the Volunteers march to their 5-yard line in the final minutes of play and salvaged a victory by recovering a fumble just shy of the goal line. In a 20-16 triumph over Clemson, they intercepted a pass in the end zone as the clock wound down, and in a 13-10 win over South Carolina, they jimmied the ball from Heisman Trophy winner George Rogers in the shadow of the goalpost. Undefeated over eight games, the Bulldogs had but two major obstacles standing between them and a No. 1 ranking—top-ranked Notre Dame and the Gators of Florida.

Two minutes into the Florida game, Herschel Walker did what he had been doing all season long and put Georgia ahead with a 72-yard sprint. In the second quarter, quarterback Buck Belue hit a skimpy fullback named Ronnie Stewart with a touchdown pass, and the Dogs went into halftime with a 14-10 edge. In the fourth quarter, however, Georgia stalled, and Florida took a 21-20 lead. The gods had begun conspiring. With less than two minutes left in the game, Florida's punter chipped the ball to the Georgia 8, and the Bulldogs faced the challenge of traveling 92 yards in an offense designed around Coach Vince Dooley's preference for gaining ground in four-yard increments. On the sideline, Lindsay Scott spoke to Buck Belue in words fusing the imperatives of plea and command: "Just get me the ball."

The two players were not strangers. Indeed, from the moment they had begun playing football, they had been locked in destiny's embrace. Buck Belue, the quarterback of south Georgia juggernaut Valdosta High, and Lindsay Scott, the wide receiver for rival Wayne County. Buck Belue, the curly-haired charmer groomed for leadership from a young age, and Lindsay Scott, the high-stepping scoring machine. Once they completed their high school careers, college coaches recruited them in tandem, and the boys often called each other to compare notes. The most coveted athletes in the state, they were the touchdown twins, similar in height and build and even in appearance: both of them with broad, handsome faces, thickly muscled jaws, expansive cheeks, strong chins, pug noses, and small eyes set deep under dark brows. Although one was white and the other black, they might have been carved from the same genetic code.

Eventually, they decided to attend the University of Georgia, lured by tradition and the promise of forging a passing combination —Belue to Scott!—that would liberate the stodgy Bulldog offense. It never happened. Over the years, Buck Belue would forsake the habits of his freewheeling Valdosta days and become the prototypical Georgia quarterback—an image of competence and modest talent, a master of execution rather than innovation. In 1980 Herschel Walker arrived in Athens as the most heralded athlete in the state's history, and Buck learned the bittersweet joy of winning ball games in which he threw seven passes and completed two—in which he stayed out of the way and let the Big Dawg eat.

On the road, Buck and Lindsay roomed together and talked about their dreams of sudden strikes and big numbers, wondering what had happened to the touchdown twins. If Buck the gambler had learned to minimize mistakes and hand off to Herschel, then Lindsay the gazelle had learned to block and keep his mouth shut, and turned his talent to turmoil. In his freshman season, he caught 36 passes—a Bulldog record for first-year players—and returned an LSU kickoff 99 yards in a play still featured in highlight films. In his sophomore year, he caught 34 balls in a mediocre 6-5 season. Then, in the spring of 1980, when the Dogs had begun to prepare for the fall campaign, Lindsay's life unraveled. On a Thursday night during the week of final exams, he argued with his girlfriend in his dorm room, and when an academic advisor tried to intercede, Lindsay shoved him to the bed. The following Monday, he met with Vince Dooley and returned to the dormitory to watch *The Young and the Restless* in the TV lounge. His teammate Ronnie Stewart was waiting.

"What happened? What did he say?"

Lindsay shook his head, as if dazed. "He said he had to get my attention."

"Well, what did he do?"

Lindsay slumped in his chair. "He took my scholarship, man," Lindsay said. "He took my scholarship."

It was only the beginning. That summer, he fell asleep in his Datsun 200 SX on a road between Soperton and his hometown of Jesup, and woke up three days later with a severe concussion and a managled foot. Although one doctor said Lindsay would never play football again, he recovered in time for fall, outfitted with a special helmet. In the first two games of the season, he caught a total of three passes. Then, against Clemson, he came up empty, and after the game a reporter corralled Lindsay and split end Amp Arnold and asked them if they were unhappy with Dooley's conservatism. Yes, the two receivers said, they were. The story ran in the newspapers the next day, and once again Dooley called Lindsay into his office. "If you don't like what we're doing here," he told his flanker, "then there's the damned door." Two weeks later, Lindsay showed up late for a team meeting, was demoted to the second team and became a seemingly permanent fixture in "Dooley's Doghouse."

On the eve of the Florida game, he reflected on a season that had produced just 11 catches and no touchdowns, and in the dark of his hotel room he spoke to his roommate out of the frustration of failed promise. "Wouldn't it be great," Lindsay Scott said to Buck Belue, "if we could break our drought against Florida? If we could do all the things we'd been recruited to do?"

With one minute and 35 seconds left to play and the ball buried on the 8-yard line, they finally got their chance. On first down, Buck Belue lost a yard scrambling, and on a second down, he threw incomplete down the sideline. Georgia was dead, and Florida's defensive backs danced the funky chicken to shame the corpse. Mrs. Belue left her seat and headed to the locker room to console her son. Loran Smith, the Bulldog Club director who had signed a contract two days earlier to produce a book about this championship season, cursed himself for his hubris, and Larry Munson, the radio announcer, gravely intoned in the Gator Bowl's rickety pressbox: *It'll take a miracle now. . . . Do the Dogs have it?*

Third and 93. One minute, 20 seconds to go. From his perch atop the stadium, offensive coordinator George Haffner radioed a play to the sideline, and an assistant coach used hand signals to relay the play to Buck Belue—left 76, a short-yardage, high-percentage pass. *Florida in a stand-up five. . . . They may or may not blitz. . . . They won't. . . .* Belue took the snap, rolled to his left and saw the play collapse, his line engulfed in a wave of Gator orange. *Buck back . . . in trouble. . . .* He reversed field, sprinted right, picked up a block and dodged a Florida ambush and then spotted Lindsay Scott, No. 24, tucked behind a linebacker 15 yards downfield. *Gonna throw on the run. . . .* The quarterback pointed a finger to the left, then twisted his hips and shot a lumpy spiral high into the gap. At the 25, Lindsay obeyed Belue's command, slid to the seam, jumped straight up in the air and cradled the ball in his belly, his knees as high as his hips, his feet pressed together, his heels tucked under his butt, his eyes already looking for an avenue of escape. *Complete to the 25 . . . to the 30. . . .* He was a shadow now, a man floating through the air in a gesture at once skittish and protective, and when he touched ground again he became a ghost, watching enemies fall at his feet.

Lindsay Scott ... 35 ... 40. ... Some have said that he stumbled. He did not. He spun around and leaned so far forward that his free hand brushed the turf, and his shoulders almost touched ground. While all those around him were standing straight up, Lindsay Scott cut upfield in a cougar's crouch, his body bent in an angle that defied physics, and when he reached the sideline he began his kick. *Lindsay Scott ... 45, 50 ... 45, 40 ... RUN, LINDSAY! ...* He didn't see Vince Dooley knock Loran Smith to his knees and race 40 yards along the sideline, didn't know that Buck Belue had followed him downfield, couldn't imagine that Larry Munson broke his chair, or that George Haffner fell down and lost his headphones, or that about a half dozen Florida players drew a bead on him and somehow missed their target. He simply began to *run*, just as he had all his life, his arms swinging high, his cleats scraping his seat, his shoulders propelling him forward. *25, 20 ... 15, 10, 5 ... LINDSAY SCOTT!* He took one sidelong glance at his pursuers and pranced over the goal line, reversing the angle of his torso, allowing his shoulders to lag far behind his white shoes, his body bent like a stick in the wind. *LINDSAY SCOTT!* He raised the ball over his head and fell under the weight of his teammates and the explosion of sound that burst from the crowd like a storm and seemed to rip the stadium in two. *LINDSAY SCOTT!* The touchdown twins could hardly stand. On the 50, Buck Belue collapsed to the field and "felt the ground shake," and in the end zone two teammates draped Lindsay's arms around their shoulders and dragged him back to the bench, his toes bouncing off the turf.

A half hour later, Vince Dooley stood before his team in the locker room and announced that Lindsay Scott had his scholarship back.

★ ★ ★

At the end of the 1980 football season, when the University of Georgia conquered once-beaten and once-tied Notre Dame for the national championship, ABC Sports judged Lindsay Scott's scoring sprint the play of the year, and a few years later, a fan poll voted it the greatest play in Bulldog history. How could it be otherwise? Yes, there had been a legacy of plays almost as unlikely, almost as sudden and spectacular. Yes, there had been Fran Tarkenton's across-the-field toss against Auburn in 1959, there had been flea flickers and Hail Marys, and there had been the play that immortalized a fullback named Theron Sapp as "the man who broke the drought"—a one-yard touchdown that in 1957 snapped Georgia's string of eight losses to Georgia Tech. No other single play, however, had established a Georgia team as a friend of fortune, had pushed the Bulldogs to the pinnacle of college sport, had stretched so far into the folds of football history. No other play had been so damned *beautiful* or had demonstrated so conclusively the power of speed and grace. And no other play entered so deeply into the lives of its principals or rendered so indistinguishable the extremes of promise and perdition.

Indeed, The Play—it deserves capital letters—changed everything for Lindsay Scott. On Nov. 7, 1980, he stood merely as an exemplar of unfulfilled potential. On Nov. 8, he emerged as a star and came away from Jacksonville convinced of his personal magic, his ability to summon divine intercession. "It was the timing of that play that made it special," he says. "I was down and out in a lot of ways. I was having a lot of turmoil, I was off scholarship, the ball wasn't coming my way. But I plugged and plugged, and the release came when Lindsay needed it. It shot me over the hump. . . . Things have always happened for me when they needed to happen, you know. I needed something big to happen that day, and it happened. That's why I'm optimistic now. I just have to make something happen. . . ."

People started calling him. Since Lindsay had first joined the Bulldogs, professional scouts had acknowledged his gifts and projected him as a relatively early selection in the NFL's annual draft of college seniors. Against Florida, however, he established himself as a game breaker and a potential big-money man, and the agents began circling. After his junior year, he met a Los Angeles attorney and sports agent named Mike Trope, who, Lindsay says, flew him out to the coast. "Here I am, this boy from south Georgia, and he's showing me Sunset Boulevard and Jacuzzis. It blew my mind." After his junior year, Lindsay says, he kept an off-campus apartment and drove a nice car and "wanted for nothing."

For the first time in Lindsay's Georgia career, "everything fell into place," and that summer he stayed in Athens to work with Buck Belue and prepare his assault on the record books. The quarterback and the wide receiver had finally "come together" on the field against Florida, had finally "realized what we had been talking about when we used to call each other in high school," had finally established a chemistry. All summer long, Buck pitched and Lindsay caught, and by the time the 1981 season began, the touchdown twins could anticipate each other's movements as if by telepathy. The effort paid off in the fall. On a team still built around Herschel Walker, Buck Belue passed for 1,603 yards and Lindsay Scott caught 42 passes to become, in the words of Vince Dooley, "the best receiver we've ever had," the man with the most catches, touchdown receptions and receiving yardage in Georgia history. Four months after Lindsay's last game as a Bulldog, the New Orleans Saints selected him as the 13th player in the NFL draft, and Lindsay Scott, who by now had stopped attending classes, became a millionaire.

Pocketing a $350,000 signing bonus, he moved to New Orleans in 1982. Like most boys, he had dreamed of this opportunity; now, unlike most boys and even most of his teammates, he could realistically contemplate a *career* in football, as "the kind of receiver who catches 70 or 80 balls a year," as an All-Pro, a superstar, a possible Hall of Famer. In his moment of triumph, he didn't know, couldn't possibly have imagined, that fate had frowned on him. He couldn't foresee that his quarterbacks would be either washed up or burnt out, that his coach would be the resolutely unimaginative Bum Phillips, that tailback George Rogers would dominate the Saints as completely as Herschel Walker had dominated the Bulldogs, that New Orleans would pass the ball about as often as Georgia. He didn't realize that the NFL would go on strike his rookie season, that the Saints would founder and that a cabal of players would salve the humiliation of losing with good times and cocaine. He didn't suspect that he would become one of them, or that in the friendly river town of New Orleans he would be so far from home.

★   ★   ★

As Lindsay Scott crossed Florida's goal line in 1980 and the entire Gator Bowl shook and spasmed, it is safe to say that only two men in the stadium voiced little surprise. The first was John Donaldson, who as Lindsay's high school coach had seen the same kind of legerdemain countless times and who surveyed Florida's secondary at the instant of the catch and said, "They'll never catch him." The second was Raymond Scott, Lindsay's father. "Not to be bragging," says Mr. Scott, "but I knew my son. He always believes he can, whether he can or can't, and it always seemed he could do the impossible."

Indeed, from an early age, Lindsay Scott could easily achieve what other boys couldn't, and even as a working-class black kid from the wrong side of the tracks, he was pampered and indulged by the townspeople of Jesup, Ga. As a Little League baseball player, he had toured the state with a traveling all-star team; as a basketball player, he had scooped up a shelf of trophies; and as a football player, he was, in the words of John Donaldson, "the *prettiest* receiver I've ever seen. A racehorse. Quick hands, and that spring in his legs. He'd catch the ball, tuck it in and—*bam!*—he'd be gone. There was nobody like him."

In his junior year in high school, Lindsay scored an astounding 26 touchdowns for the Wayne County Yellowjackets, and although saddled with rag-armed quarterbacks, Donaldson kept finding ways to feed him the ball. "I would tell my quarterback, 'Throw the ball down the field as far as you can, Lindsay will get it. Throw it inside, throw it outside, he'll get it.' When we played Savannah's Benedictine Academy, we were behind with a minute and a half to go. Their entire secondary hung back, waiting for the long one, but Lindsay caught a short pass and sprinted 62 yards down Benedictine's sideline for the winning score. People got so frustrated they threw things at him."

On May 5, 1982, Jesup declared "Lindsay Scott Day" with a parade down the town's main drag. Lindsay and Vince Dooley sat in the backseat of a convertible, waving to the crowds, and people remarked that never before had Jesup honored a black man in such a grand manner. At the time, Lindsay had just been drafted by New Orleans, and the town's 12,000 citizens wanted to salute the hometown hero as he embarked upon his journey to stardom. These days, Lindsay lives an hour away, in a Statesboro halfway house, and some of those same townspeople express shock, sadness and even anger over what has befallen their champion. There is John Donaldson, tanned and lined and retired now, wincing and clenching his fist every time he mentions Lindsay's addiction: "The boy's in the pits now. He has to fight his way out. Damn! I don't even like to think about it. It's distasteful. I thought I had done a better job with Lindsay." There is Jimmy Sullivan, a white-haired Bulldog booster who owns Jesup's finest clothing store and has acted as Lindsay's adviser and patron: "It's hard to believe that this has happened to his family. He comes from a good family. His father is a good man and his mother is a fine woman. . . . It wasn't like they were out running around." There is Len Hauss, who was a center for the Washington Redskins for 14 years and now is a loan officer in the downtown bank: "I don't think athletes deserve special privileges. So Lindsay Scott didn't make it in pro football. Whose fault is that? Society's? Bullshit." And, finally, there is Lindsay's father.

In the 1940s, when Wayne County still maintained segregated schools, Raymond Scott was a compact speedster and a star running back for all-black Wayne County Training School. Although he went to work rather than to college, he always believed he possessed the ability to make his mark as a ball player and passed both his talent and his ambition to his sons. Today he works in the paper mill on the banks of the tea-colored river outside town and lives with his wife, Johnnie Mae, in an immaculately kept brick house in a neighborhood of unpaved roads and spilled trash cans. At night, he works the midnight shift, and during the day, he will sometimes pad about his house in pajamas and mocassins. Mr. Scott is a thick, squat man with graying hair and a mustache and a deep croak of a voice, and when visitors come inquiring about Lindsay, he is gracious and wary, often apologizing for his slow, deliberate manner of speaking.

For Mr. Scott, Lindsay's touchdown in the Gator Bowl was "a dream, the happiest day of my life," and for months afterward, he says, his co-workers revered him as the father of the miracle man. Sitting on a couch in his neatly paneled family room, he folds his hands between his legs and gazes at an astonishing array of athletic memorabilia generated by Lindsay and his other sons. There are three shelves of trophies, and plaques cover the walls. There is a portrait of Lindsay on black velvet, a pencil drawing of Lindsay in high school, an assortment of photographs, a plaque certifying Lindsay's run as the play of the year, and another recognizing Lindsay as the Bulldogs' "best-conditioned freshman athlete." When talk turns to Lindsay's tenure in New Orleans and subsequent addiction, Mr. Scott does not change his tone; reflective, resigned and hopeful, he says he does not care if Lindsay ever catches another football if only his son can "be himself again, and achieve something in his life." He gestures around the room. "We love sports," he says, "and we love all this, but we love Lindsay first."

Still, sometimes he cannot help but shake his head, for he had always tried to warn his son of the perils of promise. "We thought he could handle it," he says, speaking of Lindsay's move to New Orleans, "but it was too big a step. Not everybody can handle that kind of success. I'd always told Lindsay, 'You can't take nothing for granted, son; you got to get out there and fight for it every single day.'" He shrugs. "Maybe he had to find that out for himself."

★   ★   ★

In the first game of his rookie year with New Orleans, Lindsay Scott caught six passes for 103 yards and one touchdown. It was his best day as a Saint and the last touchdown he would score as a professional. Over the next four years, he would play less and less, and watch other, hungrier receivers pass him by. The most stylish receiver ever to come out of the state of Georgia became just another player, and the writers covering the Saints mocked him as "Mr. Touchdown" and later, simply as "Mr. T." As suddenly as it had come to him, the magic was gone.

There have been abundant explanations for his failure. He wasn't fast enough, some say. As a product of the University of Georgia, he wasn't skilled enough for the complexities of the pro passing game. He was high-strung and put too much pressure on himself. He got off on the wrong foot, and just never regained his step. He was a small-town boy lost in the New Orleans fast lane. He was frustrated by Bum Phillips' decision to develop a power game and to use his receivers as blockers and decoys. He was just a poor draft choice, a player whose stock had been drastically overvalued by a fluke touchdown against Florida.

Although Lindsay Scott recognizes the merit of all those theories save the first and the last, his own is simpler and more encompassing: He lost his edge, the ability to sacrifice. At the University of Georgia, he had grown accustomed to discipline and supervision; in New Orleans, he was left to his own devices and could not find it within himself to work. "Bum Phillips was a laid-back coach," Lindsay says. "He gave you a lot of rope, and he allowed you to hang yourself. In the pros, nobody will pamper you. You're a man, and you've got a job, and if you can't do it, they're going to find someone who will. They're paying you, and you're not doing them any favors. It's like, 'Can you play for the Man? If you can't, the Man's gotta do what he's gotta do.'"

In high school and college, Lindsay relied on his speed and simply ran past defenders. In the pros, *everybody* could run, even the linemen, and he had to add another dimension to his game. He could not, and to this day he speaks admiringly of those who could. "I saw guys who got better because they *worked*. But I had the money, I had the cars and the home. I took for granted that I had the ability and that I would stay at that level because I had always been at that level. The NFL is the real world, man, and I wasn't ready for the real world. I felt that God was smiling on me, and it was just a blessing to be able to do the things I could do."

As Lindsay felt himself slipping into oblivion, he grew desperate, and during conferences with Coach Phillips tears came to his eyes. What could he do to turn things around? He groped for magic and couldn't find it; dreamed of stopping his slide with a big play, and couldn't manage one. Eventually, he turned to chemical lightning, and became in his words, "a snorting man." In his freshman year at Georgia, he went to a package store with a carload of teammates, and they laughed when they caught the kid from Jesup dribbling his beer out the window. Now, in New Orleans, a city where convenience stores sell bottles of liquor along with diapers and dog food, Lindsay partied in earnest and found in the rush of cocaine and alcohol that old feeling of immensity and grace. For as long as he could afford the view, Lindsay Scott was once again on top of the world.

While he claims not to have used cocaine during the season, he acknowledges that as his drug use increased, his attitude, physical prowess and reputation inevitably declined. Finally, during a game broadcast on national TV, Lindsay stood on the sidelines watching his team "do the same stupid stuff" in a loss to the Minnesota Vikings, and about 20 seconds before the final gun, he jogged off the field alone and headed for the locker room. The cameras zoomed in, and the newspapers interpreted his premature departure as a gesture of disgust and surrender. A few days later, the Saints released him. Six games short of completing four seasons in the NFL, he had caught a total of 69 passes for 864 yards and one touchdown. He would never catch another, and the worst was yet to come.

Over the next two years, Lindsay would drift between his old haunts and havens—Atlanta, Athens, Jesup—and watch his life splinter into shards of rumor and deception. He would become a borrower and a deadbeat; "he was always a charmer," says Vince Dooley, "to the extent that people would go out of their way to cash his checks." (Lindsay himself prefers not to discuss the details of his financial misadventures.) He would try out for the Falcons and, physically and mentally unprepared to play, would be released before the opening of training camp; he would try his hand at sales and would become that saddest of figures, the ex-athlete who deems himself above the world of work; he would spend a good deal of his money and split with his wife, a former Georgia cheerleader who is now a schoolteacher in Athens. Worst of all, he would admit to no one that he was in trouble and tried to use cocaine to preserve his ebullience and maintain appearances.

"In my wildest dreams, I never would perceive cocaine use getting to the point where I was out of control," says Lindsay. "But cocaine—that shit *calls* you, man. It's good to you for so long, and then that shit turns into the devil—it says, 'I *got* you now,' and you cross the line where it's killing you and you can't stop it.

"It took me all those years to build what I had and took three years of cocaine to destroy it all."

He freebased. He tried crack. And when he finally cried out for help, he did not seek Vince Dooley or Herschel Walker or Buck Belue, who since college had bounced around from minor league baseball to USFL football to a broadcast booth in Jacksonville to a coaching stint in Valdosta and was presently working to get a college degree before his 10-year high school reunion. He did not seek any of the stars. Instead, Lindsay sought out the man he calls "the little fullback," Ronnie Stewart.

★   ★   ★

As a Georgia Bulldog, Ronnie Stewart, more than most of his teammates, seemed to have a line on what "the real world" was all about, and Lindsay Scott had always looked up to him. Once, when Lindsay heard him make a simple observation on the ways of this world, he asked, "Man, how do you know all those things?" Ronnie Stewart responded, "Because I take life just a little slower than you do, Lindsay."

Stewart learned about the real world early, as a boy growing up poor in Tampa, and later as a Georgia Bulldog. Although he had arrived in Athens with the standard dreams—"I said, 'Yep, I'll play awhile for Georgia, and then I'm going to play me some pro ball' "— he was a player whose desire outstripped his talent, and with the emergence of Herschel Walker, he became a 205-pound blocking back, bloodying himself to clear tacklers from the superstar's path. Undrafted by any NFL team, he tried out with the Saints as a free agent, wrecked an ankle, tried out again with Tampa's USFL franchise, lasted two weeks ("long enough for coffee and doughnuts"), signed with Jacksonville, and this time lasted only long enough for coffee. He got the message. "I finally got my butt back into school," he says. "I wanted to be remembered as a name on a degree, not as a number on a jersey." Eventually, he became the 15th black male athlete to get a degree from the University of Georgia, bought the southwest Atlanta franchise of a company called ServPro—a firm specializing in flood and fire cleanups—and is now one of the most prosperous members of the 1980 championship team.

He is not surprised that Lindsay Scott and Buck Belue have had difficulty adjusting to life after Georgia. He remembers the touchdown twins strutting into the Bulldog dining hall, checking out the menu and saying, "Shit, hamburger patties? Let's go eat at Cleve's (an Athens restaurant)." Says Stewart: "I always knew that when it came time to roll up the shirtsleeves, those guys were in trouble. With Lindsay, everything had to be *fast*. If the train he's on is running good, he's going to stay on. If it breaks down, he's going to get on that other fast train, without looking where it's going. In high school, he was the big fish in the little pond. At Georgia, he was one of three big fish—along with Herschel and Buck—and I was a minnow. Then he goes to New Orleans, and he's a minnow, so what's he gonna do?"

One night, while watching the Saints on Monday Night Football, Stewart listened to an announcer talk about Lindsay's tendency to run erratic patterns and drop easy passes. "A light went on in my head," he says. "Something didn't add up. I turned to my wife and said, 'Lindsay's doing something he has no business doing.'" Stewart was right, of course, and in time he had to fend off Lindsay's attempts to borrow money, barring his friend from his home. Finally, when Lindsay had touched bottom, Stewart heard from Matt Simon, a Bulldog understudy who had roomed with Lindsay in Athens. "He's mentioned your name, Ronnie," Simon said. "I think he wants to see you."

Stewart drove to Simon's apartment and met Lindsay at 8:30 in the morning. The three men went out to breakfast, and Stewart had to pay the bill for a man who had made a million dollars. "It brought tears to my eyes," he remembers. "I told him, 'Lindsay, you are headed for one of two places. You're either going to jail, or you're going into the ground. There's no middle of the road for you anymore.'" That day, Stewart telephoned Vince Dooley, some former teammates and some Georgia alumni for financial support; that night, he boarded the private plane of Willingway Hospital at Peachtree-DeKalb Airport and flew with Lindsay to Statesboro. On the way, Lindsay Scott said to Ronnie Stewart, "You know what I was going to do today, Ronnie? I told some guy I'd meet him at 4 o'clock. We were going to hit that horse." Heroin, that is—the horse that runs forever.

★   ★   ★

On Jan. 15, 1988, Lindsay Scott checked into Willingway Hospital and remained in the inpatient unit for six weeks. Although at first he cut the figure of the depressed and embittered ex-athlete, he applied himself to the 12-step program prescribed by Alcoholics Anonymous and earned the right to live in "the men's lodge," or halfway house. By August he was the lodge's assistant manager and lived like a chastened bachelor in a small apartment full of scarred furniture and AA literature. He ran errands for his cronies, bought the groceries and vacuumed the shag carpet. He watched sports on TV and rooted for players who had also been in rehabilitation; he ran in the morning and smoked cigarettes in the afternoon. In short, he had become a civilian.

A few months earlier, he had traveled to Tampa for a tryout with the Buccaneers—a tryout arranged through Vince Dooley's intercession—and had faced, in the heartless precision of the stopwatch, hard evidence of physical decline. Fifteen pounds heavier than his best playing weight, he had run the slowest 40-yard dashes of his adult life and had returned to Statesboro without a contract. Now he sat in front of his TV, cigarette dangling ludicrously from his long fingers, and acknowledged that "my playing days might be over," speaking cheerfully of his aspirations beyond the game of football. "I still have some big-ass dreams," he said. "That's what keeps me motivated."

For all he has been through, Lindsay Scott does not inspire pity. He has had to hurt to grow, he often says, and swears that his trials have made him "a better person." For his entire life, he had managed to hide behind his stardom and, in his words, "was never forced to deal on a bare-bones level with Lindsay. Money, cars, beautiful wife . . . you have all these things and you're supposed to be happy. So I would try to project this image that I was so fine, and meanwhile something's tearing me up inside. There's a void there, and I tried to fill it with cocaine. But that void's so deep, you ain't never going to fill it. My addiction stripped me of everything and forced me to come face-to-face with Lindsay Scott. Not Lindsay Scott, Bulldog, or Lindsay Scott, Saint—just Lindsay Scott."

That night, he went to an AA meeting in Statesboro and drove afterward to the Shoney's on the main drag for soup and salad. He wore a long-sleeved pink oxford-cloth shirt, a pair of dressy gray shorts with pink pinstripes, and tasseled black loafers with no socks. Once again, when he walked back and forth from the salad bar in that funny prancing posture, he turned heads. But he didn't notice. He sat in a booth, ate his clam chowder and talked about his sobriety ("the most important thing in my life"), his intention to write a book about his experience ("won't mean a damn thing if I don't stay sober"), his anti-drug speech to Erk Russell's Georgia Southern football team, and the possibilities of a career in counseling. He talked about NFL wide receivers, Tony Casillas, Buck Belue and Ronnie Stewart. Then he looked up. A little man in a plain shirt was standing over him.

"Were you talking about Ronnie Stewart?" the man asked.

"Yes," Lindsay said.

"Are you related?"

"No, Ronnie's a friend," Lindsay said. "I played football with him at Georgia."

The man didn't pause a second. "I own the ServPro franchise in Statesboro, and Ronnie's a ServPro man in Atlanta. He's a fine fella."

As the man left, Lindsay shrugged, and the conversation turned back to football and his friends at Georgia. "I went to school with some crazy guys," he said. "It was a once-in-a-lifetime opportunity, and we had some good times." He smiled dreamily and started talking about the morning after the Florida game and his miracle touchdown, when he and his buddies went to the Waffle House in Athens after partying all night long, ordered as much food as they could and then didn't eat a bit—they just sat there, watching eggs and pancakes pile up on their table, and laughed so hard they could barely raise their forks.

He looked away, shaking his head slowly. "Wild times," he said. Then again: "wild times." Again: "wild times." Finally, his companion interrupted the reverie: "Lindsay . . ."

He looked up, smiled sheepishly, and shook his head briskly, like a man trying to snap out of a spell. Then he smiled again, this time broadly and confidently, because what the hell, the times *were* wild, and there is nothing anybody can say or do to make Lindsay Scott forget them.

Too Many 10s in Gym

GYMNASTICS

By *LARRY ELDRIDGE*

From the Christian Science Monitor
Copyright © 1988, The Christian Science Publishing Co.

This year marked the third consecutive Olympics in which a teen-age female gymnast captivated a worldwide audience and won the most gold medals, only to see a rival walk away with the all-around championship. The latest victim was Daniela Silivas, who lost to Yelena Shushunova of the Soviet Union via the closest vote in the history of the event.

As is frequently the case in this sport, the result in Seoul was tinged with some questionable judging. And for the Romanians, it must have seemed like one too many cases of *deja vu*—marking the third straight Olympics in which their star missed out by the tiniest of margins.

In 1980 it was Nadia Comaneci, only 18 and still in peak form four years after her triumph in Montreal, performing so magnificently that even the partisan Moscow crowd seemed ready to concede the gold medal. But in complicated and controversial voting that threw her coach, Bela Karolyi, into a histrionic frenzy, she was edged by the host country's Yelena Davydova. Nadia did win two apparatus finals to emerge as the only double gold medal winner, but that hardly made up for the inequities of the all-around.

Four years later in Los Angeles it was a 17-year-old sprite named Ecaterina Szabo who lost a razor-thin decision to home favorite Mary Lou Retton. Szabo, like Nadia, came back to stake her own claim to top honors, winning three of the four individual apparatus events.

Now this year, incredibly, another Romanian won the most medals (5) and the most gold medals (3)—but not the big one. Silivas, an elfin, 18-year-old crowd-pleaser, appeared to match Shushunova in technical proficiency while outshining her in terms of dynamic performance. So why didn't she get the gold?

Where partisan crowds were factors in Moscow and Los Angeles, the culprit in Seoul was the modern penchant for giving out "perfect" 10s at the drop of a hat.

It was in Montreal, for Nadia, that Olympic judges first broke the unwritten rule against awarding such scores. The crowds loved it, and perhaps in itself the change was all right. Maybe the time for an occasional 10 had come. But since then, they have become far too common in both men's and women's events. This year's judges, for example, awarded an incredible 41 "perfect" scores, including some for obviously flawed routines.

In the uneven bars, East Germany's Dagmar Kirsten ended an otherwise fine routine with a little jump on her landing. The gymnast herself appeared downcast, and reacted with disbelief when her score was posted—looking as though even she didn't really want such an "imperfect 10," as one commentator described it.

Shushunova, in the same event, threw her arms forward to avoid a fall—prompting a TV announcer to joke that she looked like somebody deciding at the last minute not to dive into the water—but she got a 10, too.

These two judging generosities took place in the apparatus finals, and didn't affect the all-around outcome, but there were problems in the latter, too.

The big mistake here came in the floor exercise—and again was related to the proliferation of perfect scores. Shushunova, who preceded Silivas, did well and deserved good marks. But when she got a 10, it left no margin if her rival should follow with an even better routine—which is exactly what happened.

The Romanian brought the crowd to its feet with a spectacular performance, but all the judges could do was give her the same score. Thus the two gymnasts came out equal—and it didn't matter that one was "more equal" than the other.

Unfortunately for Silivas, the same situation didn't prevail in the final event, the vault. Shushunova did better and got a higher score, which gave her the gold.

Clearly it is time for changes in the way gymnasts are scored. Politics and hometown bias may always be with us, but the system itself shouldn't impose additional inequities. The solution is to go back to the idea that you don't give out 10s except in the rarest cases —thus keeping the door open to mark the best gymnast highest in any particular event.

Beyond 'Bull Durham'

BASEBALL

By *MIKE D'ORSO*

From the Virginian-Pilot and Ledger-Star
Copyright © 1988, the Virginian-Pilot and Ledger-Star

The owner is a politician, a three-time city councilman and one-time candidate for state senate who is partial to white cowboy hats.

The general manager can't tell left field from right, but she *has* learned to read a scoreboard. She, too, wears a cowboy hat, a black one.

The operations manager wears flip-flops and shorts. When he's not mowing the ball field, he's dreaming up promotional schemes, most of which have not worked. For example, the team got a good deal on its TV ads—unfortunately, they run at 2 in the morning.

The director of program sales rides a scooter to work—a push scooter. She wears barrettes and, during meetings, does headstands on the conference room couch. She's 9.

The director of beer sales is a 340-pound recovering alcoholic who goes by the name of Tiny. He has an assistant who works here because she has to—it was either this or go to jail for stealing a fire hydrant.

The grounds crew is one man, the ticket taker's son. He is the fourth grounds crew the team has had this season. The first—the general manager's ex-husband—was fired two days before the home opener.

The director of communications travels with the team, broadcasting games on a radio station whose frequency shrinks to near nothing at dusk. The first three innings or so come through loud and clear, he says. After that, you can either drive toward the station or read about the rest of the game in the morning paper.

The team's trainer has had a tough time. The home run leader is out with a separated shoulder. The best hitter has torn ligaments in his right hand. But worst of all, the clubhouse manager quit two weeks ago, so now the trainer has to do the laundry.

The players are kind of confused. They're not happy having to count coat hangers the way the general manager wants. And they don't think they should have to give her their wornout caps so she can sell them as souvenirs. They were embarrassed the night a game began and someone noticed home plate had been put in backward. But worse than all that is the pitching staff, which, unlike the rest of the ballclub, has no contracts with a major league team. The pitchers are free agents, signed and paid by the front office here. The horrendous pitching, say the players, is the reason the club won only 18 of its first 70 games, dropping 15 straight during one nightmarish stretch.

The manager has his own problems, what with the pitching situation and the injuries. And he doesn't have much experience of his own to draw on, seeing as how this is the first professional ballclub he's ever managed. He doesn't want to get into a war of words with the general manager, but they've had their battles over everything from the hats to when the players get paid. Their relationship wasn't helped when the general manager fired the third grounds crew—that was the manager's brother.

The fans don't know what to make of it all. Some have been coming out to this ballpark since it was built in 1948. They've seen winners and losers, but they've never seen anything like this. One night this season, a total of 25 people were in the stands at game time. As a tribute to their loyalty, the management introduced each one over the P.A. system, which, that night, was working.

This is the world of the Virginia Generals, arguably the worst, possibly the most woeful, and certainly one of the wackiest organizations in professional baseball.

★　　★　　★

It is early Monday afternoon. The Generals are due back from a road trip the next day, when they will open a home stand against the Salem Buccaneers. Today, the owner himself is visiting the front office.

The front office, like the wall that surrounds this stadium, is made of cinder blocks painted in Generals shades of white, blue and gold. The paint is new, but it cannot hide the fact that War Memorial Stadium, perched on a weedy lot at the industrial end of Hampton's Pembroke Avenue, is just plain old.

The war this stadium remembers is WWII. The Dodgers who first put a farm team here were in Brooklyn. Gil Hodges and Duke Snider roamed this grass. Satchel Paige once stood on that mound. Johnny Bench and Lou Piniella played here. So did Gary Carter. Over the past 40 years, with parent clubs ranging from the Dodgers to the Phillies to the Expos to the White Sox, this creaky structure has been home to one of the older and prouder minor league traditions in the nation.

But lately that pride has taken a beating. In 1983, an average of only 541 of War Memorial Stadium's 4,330 seats were filled for each home game played by the Peninsula Pilots, forerunners of the Generals. In 1984, all of 28 season tickets were sold. There was talk of the team leaving for good.

That talk caught Gil Granger's ear.

People in Williamsburg know Gil Granger. He's not quite home-grown, but he's been a local ever since he graduated from William and Mary in 1957. He raised three kids, built a nice little accounting business, bought property around town and got elected to the City Council three times. He's a Kiwanis kind of guy, described by friends as "affable, outgoing, eager to please."

But Gil Granger is not the type of guy you'd guess would be the savior of pro ball on the Peninsula. As of the end of the 1984 season, he'd never been to a game. So it seemed sort of strange when he appeared virtually out of nowhere that winter and, for $160,000, bought himself a baseball team.

It's odd to watch Granger walk around his ballpark. He swears he has no intention of giving up his team, but as he surveys the stadium, you'd swear he's ready to rid himself of the whole mess. "It's . . . adequate," he says, gazing up at the weathered edifice. "We've put a lot of money into this place, but there are still some things that are the pits."

For instance, he says, the parking lot has room for only 700 cars. "When we have a crowd of 3,000," says Granger, "we're in trouble."

Fortunately—or unfortunately—that is a problem the team rarely faces. Home crowds this year have averaged a paltry 678. The real-life Durham Bulls, one of the Generals' rivals in the Carolina League, are averaging 3,800, thanks in large part to the success of the current film "Bull Durham."

Someone tells Granger the scoreboard, mounted above the center field fence, looks pretty good with its new coat of paint and Generals logo.

"Oh, it *looks* great," says Granger. "But it doesn't work."

Eric Rosenfeld, the flip-flopped operations manager, corrects him.

"*Parts* of it work," says Rosenfeld. "Balls and strikes work, but the outs don't. The innings will light up, but there's no telling what numbers will appear."

Granger turns toward the grandstands, where old seasoned bleacher boards are shored up here and there. "We didn't have to replace all of them," says Granger of the planks. "Just the ones people were falling through."

Finally, he eyeballs the pigeon droppings splashed on seats throughout the stadium.

"Eric," he says, nodding toward the mess, "we've got some *work* to do before tomorrow."

★   ★   ★

In most places around the nation, bush-league baseball is booming.

Twenty million people attended minor league games last season, up 25 percent from 1981. Owners like Miles Woolf, who bought the Durham operation in 1979 for $2,500, are grinning as their clubs' values multiply—the Bulls are worth more than $1 million today. An estimated three-fourths of North America's 166 minor league clubs operate in the black.

Gil Granger, however, has seen nothing but red.

While major league teams typically ante up for minor league players', coaches' and managers' salaries, expenses, uniforms and equipment, it is up to the host lower-league organization to provide the stadium, as well as transportation, lodging and part of the meal costs on the road.

With that standard setup, Granger's operation lost $25,000 its first season. The next, it lost $15,000. Last year it lost $45,000. This year, with the added costs of the free agents he pays for as part of a co-op arrangement with the Kansas City Royals, Granger figures to lose $100,000. Entering this season, he already had sunk almost $350,000 into his investment. Last year a group from Raleigh offered to buy the team for $500,000. Granger refused, prompting some to question his sanity.

But he seems to enjoy the confusion. When asked why he got into this business and why he refuses to get out, he sits back in a closet-sized conference room, sips a soft drink and drifts through a variety of answers, ranging from glib to seemingly sincere.

"Stupidity," he says at first, when asked what moved him to buy this baseball team. "Sheer stupidity."

Then he gets serious, citing regional loyalty: "If we ever lose baseball on the Peninsula," he says, "we'll probably never get it back."

Granger says he has plans in hand for a new stadium, perhaps near Newport News' Patrick Henry Airport. His dream ballpark would seat 8,000, he says, "with the ability to push 12." The cost, he says, would be "not an astronomical amount—basically $1.2 million."

Granger apparently has plenty of money. He pooh-poohs the price it took to buy this ballclub, saying, "I'd paid more money than that for filling stations."

He then reels off a tale about growing up in Philadelphia, watching the old A's and Phillies play and telling his wife back before they were married that he would someday own a baseball team. But he had virtually no contact with baseball between then and the day he decided to buy the Peninsula team.

Income taxes, indicates Granger in an offhand way, are perhaps one reason he won't let go: "If I sell for $500,000, that's $150,000 I've gotta pay taxes on. Why give the government that money? What will they do with it, send it to Iran?"

But the most telling of Granger's reasons is his children. As he talks about them, it begins to sound as if this team might ultimately amount to little more than a legacy for his kids.

"None of my children will ever be a CPA," says Granger. "That's not in their nature. But I think the baseball business is a nice business, an interesting one to get them involved in."

And that may have been what prompted this announcement last winter:

The new front office manager of the new 1988 Virginia Generals would be Gil Granger's 29-year-old daughter, Gilinda.

★　　★　　★

Gilinda Granger is the first to admit her background is not exactly that of a budding baseball executive.

"Last year I learned to read a scoreboard," she says. "This year I learned how to read stats. And I know the names of the positions now, although I'm still not sure about right or left field. Is that facing the outfield or looking in?"

Granger's office is cluttered with boxes of used balls and old baseball hats—all of which she plans to recycle. Many of the baseballs are ones she retrieved from kids who gather outside the stadium at game time to catch fouls.

"Those kids aren't there for sentimental reasons, they're out there for money," she says, describing the kids selling stray balls back to her employees for 50 cents apiece.

"Those balls cost me $5.25 each," she says. "It costs me between $12,000 and $18,000 a season just for baseballs. That's the price of a *car.* So every time one of those kids takes a ball, he's basically taking a taillight off my car.

"People think I'm being crude about this," she says, tipping back the brim of her black hat, "but that's the stand I'm taking. And I *have* saved $8,000 in balls this year.

"I may not know baseball," she says, "but I know business."

Actually Granger's business background is somewhat sketchy. After graduating from high school and attending college awhile, she came back to Williamsburg, ran a hot dog shop, bought a camera store, met and married a Navy man in Norfolk named Roger Phillipe, sold the camera store and moved to a farm on the Eastern Shore, then moved to Virginia Beach where she worked as a live-in nanny. Somewhere in there, she also got into another line of work—selling synthetic drugs.

"At one point I decided I was going to make money on my own and do whatever I could to make it," she explains. "I wanted to be somebody besides Gil Granger's daughter. In Williamsburg I was always Gil Granger's daughter."

When she and Phillipe were charged in 1982 with distribution of marijuana, Phillipe pleaded guilty. She did not. The two were married that spring, and two days after their wedding, Phillipe was sentenced to nine days in jail. Granger got 30, which she spent writing wedding thank-yous. Now, she has a framed certificate signed in February by Gov. Gerald Baliles, removing "political disabilities" resulting from her conviction. Granger says she's proud of the pardon and sorry for her past.

"I was not selling illegal drugs," she says, "but I was walking a very thin line. I was found guilty of crossing over that line. I was stupid, and I've never come near that line again."

Neither, she says, will anyone in her organization. This year, says Granger, the Virginia Generals are the only team she knows of in the Carolina League that has a policy of drug testing.

Granger is ready to hang the governor's pardon right alongside her autographed photo of Cincinnati Reds owner Marge Schott. Schott, a controversial figure herself, is one of only three women executives in major league baseball. Granger is one of only five in the minors. It seemed natural that the two should meet, which they did, says Granger, in Dallas last winter. And when things got rough early this season, Granger flew to Cincinnati to meet with her mentor again.

"I needed some motivation," she says. "Kansas City was not pleased with what they were hearing about me. And I was catching a lot of flak around here."

Only someone like Schott, says Granger, could understand her problems: "There's a lot of things we both have in common—feeling left out by the old boys network."

The moment Granger says she remembers best from that visit was sitting with Schott at a Reds game and watching her fine outfielder Eric Davis $50 for tossing a baseball to fans.

"That made me feel so good," says Granger, eyeing her boxes of balls. "I can't *tell* you how good I felt."

★   ★   ★

It is Tuesday afternoon, and the Virginia Generals are trickling onto the field. Some pitchers are jogging out in right field. A couple of infielders are playing pepper by the dugout. Manager Joe Breeden is out by the mound chatting with an instructional coach from Kansas City. Things look tidy, sharp, organized . . . *professional.*

"Yeah, that's the way it's supposed to be," says trainer Jim Stricek, sitting in the stands, where a crew of kids wearing Virginia Generals T-shirts are scrubbing pigeon droppings off the bleachers.

"To people who are around this game," says Stricek, "baseball is a religion. The field is a cathedral. The clubhouse is a confessional."

Then he pauses and glances in the direction of Gilinda Granger's office.

"And *her*?" he says. "She should be persecuted for blasphemy.

"She knows nothing about this game," continues Stricek, who at 31 is looking to a career in the big leagues. "The things she's tried to do are a mockery. To be honest with you, we're the laughingstock of the Carolina League. This team plays better and is more comfortable on the road, where there are less distractions. Everywhere we go, people want to hear the latest Gilinda story."

Infielder Deric Ladnier, who leads the team in home runs despite being sidelined with a separated shoulder, has plenty of Gilinda stories. The blond 23-year-old fully expects to be among the 10 to 20 percent of bush-league players who make it to the bigs. He was signed three years ago out of the University of Mississippi, where he played against the likes of Bo Jackson and Will Clark. In his Florida high school days, Ladnier was in a top-flight league that featured a pitcher named Dwight Gooden. Ladnier has come a long way from high school—but he didn't expect it to be a long way *down.*

"Odd?" he says of the Generals' organization. "This is about as odd as it gets."

Vacant bleachers. A field that was hardly in better shape than the gravel parking lot when the season began. And a general manager who, rather than concede a rainout, has leaped on the field during a thunderstorm and joined the 10-year-old kids struggling with the tarp. These things—along with the foul ball-chasing and the bat-collecting and the hanger-counting—says Ladnier, are "embarrassing" for the players.

"It's gone from 'Well, let's give her a chance,' " he says of Granger, "to 'There's no way.' "

Outfielder Pete Alborano, the only Virginia General selected to this year's Carolina League all-star team, says he can't believe what he's seen this season. He spent last summer at Eugene, Ore., in the Northwest League, where 2,000 fans would show up for batting practice and 6,000 would watch the games. Alborano says he was "scared" when he saw the setup here.

"It wasn't what I expected," says the 22-year-old Brooklyn native. "People just seem like they fly in and out of here. From the field crews to the pitchers, everything's so confusing. . . .

"When I was at the all-star game, I got the feeling everyone looks at us as a Mickey Mouse operation."

One person who sees it that way is Dave Rosenfield, general manager of Norfolk's AAA Tidewater Tides—one step away from the major league Mets. Rosenfield has had his eye on the Peninsula operation for years, fronting a group of investors interested in buying the Class A club across the water.

"With the proper operation," says Rosenfield, "the Peninsula could support a Class A club very well. I'm certainly willing to put my name and other people's money where my mouth is."

But, says Rosenfield, he hesitates to call the current Peninsula baseball organization professional.

"It's an *abortion,*" says Rosenfield. "As long as Gil Granger lets his daughter run that operation, it will never succeed."

★   ★   ★

At game time Tuesday night, 455 bodies are in the bleachers. Grandstand tickets for Virginia Generals games are $4—50 cents higher than Tides tickets and $1 more than it costs to see the major league Royals. But few fans on the Peninsula actually pay full freight—there are plenty of discounts, family packages and promotional gimmicks that slice the price.

"*Anybody* can get in for $1.50," says Gilinda Granger, noting the discount price for showing up an hour early. "All they have to do is watch batting practice."

Nobody showed for batting practice, but by game time, Elton Futrell and Leroy Quick are settled into their seats, two of the few actual fans among this year's 922 season ticket holders—most season tickets are bought by local businesses and few of those seats are actually filled with bodies. Both Futrell and Quick, retired from Newport News Shipbuilding, have been coming to this ballpark for 40 years. Both have their names painted on their seats. But as he watches Salem score three runs in the top of the first inning, Quick looks like he's about ready to take his name off that chair.

"I don't know what the holdback on them is," he says, watching a catcher's errant throw sail into center field. "But I just haven't seen the ball being played like it should. Last night they won two games up in Prince William. And now look at them."

Futrell is a bit more forgiving.

"I've seen 'em all," he says, fingering the cowbell he's been ringing the past 40 years, "and this is the poorest club I've ever seen here. There's some that says it's the management, but I don't know about that. Me, I'm just a fan of baseball. I come out, win or lose. I don't care about anything else but the game on the field."

The game on the field does not go well this night. The Generals commit four errors, adding to their league-leading total. The final score is 6-1, Salem. The players trudge back to the clubhouse. Gilinda Granger is in the front office, counting receipts. And Herbert "Tiny" Woolston is in his beer room, drawing drafts for the last of the evening's customers.

"The people that come in here do think this is a really different year," says the former Army sergeant and Air Force mechanic who was a fan here for 20 years before Gilinda Granger asked him if he'd like to tend bar this summer.

"They talk about the management not knowing what they're doing," he says. But Tiny is not ready to pass judgment on the woman who gave him his job.

"People always look for a place to put the blame," he says, pulling the tips out of his jar, "when things are going bad."

But somehow, down here in Tiny's Place, underneath these old right field stands, with the green ballfield glowing out there under those white lights, with a cool drink in hand and the sound of crickets drifting in from the darkness beyond, all the problems disappear and the timeless magic of an empty minor league stadium on a summer night takes over.

Somehow, for the moment, things don't seem that bad at all.

Kimball Faces Silent Protest

DIVING

By MIKE DOWNEY

From the Los Angeles Times
Copyright © 1988, the Los Angeles Times

Cherie Beck wrote this letter herself. She intends to send a copy to anyone of influence, Ronald Reagan included. She and her daughter and her daughter's friends called an impromptu news conference here Thursday at their hotel, after traveling 1,000 miles together in two cars to protest Kimball's decision to compete.

His participation, their letter insists, is "outrageous and insulting to the families and friends involved in this tragedy, and it is equally abhorring (sic) that you would consider presenting Bruce Kimball to the United States and the world as the best America can offer."

They are here and they are mad and sad. They have the support of Mothers Against Drunk Drivers (MADD). They have support from Students Against Drunk Drivers (SADD). For the time being, at least, their alliance is more specific. For the time being, they represent mothers and students against Kimball's participation at the trials.

"Maybe we'll let Bruce Kimball know that you can't just run away to follow your dreams," Chuparkoff said, "without the broken dreams of the people you've hurt following *you.*"

★　　★　　★

They say his son killed two people. They say he seriously hurt six more, including the teen-aged girl whose lacerated body already has undergone six operations, and the boy whose leg was transported separately from the scene of the accident by police helicopter. They say his son ran them down with a car, hurtling 70 to 90 m.p.h. down a dead-end street. They say his son has little right to be walking the street, much less representing his country in the Olympic Games.

"People are ready to crucify him," Dick Kimball said.

Father and coach to Bruce Kimball, he watched from the sidelines Thursday as his expressionless 25-year-old son did all of his 11 qualifying dives without incident. Springboard is not Bruce Kimball's specialty; platform, which begins Saturday, is.

It is unlikely Kimball will qualify for the Olympics in both events, but all of his first-round springboard dives were efficient, and by day's end he stood sixth among a field of 12.

"He did very, very well," Dick Kimball said. "A lot better than he did four years ago at the trials.

"It's been very difficult. It hasn't been easy for him. I think he's really been trying hard to concentrate. I think it was real important to get that first dive in, and once he got that in and saw that there wasn't any (visible or audible protest), he knew everything was going to be all right."

Bruce's teammates have been supportive, his father said. None of them has said anything negative, to him or about him. Not so, though, the MADD woman who shouted "Go home, Bruce!" at his son's news conference Tuesday, or the journalists who, Dick Kimball claims, continue to ignore the darkly lighted, overpopulated scene of the accident, exaggerate the traveling speed of Bruce's auto, refuse to research all the facts.

These facts all will surface at Kimball's arraignment in Florida on Aug. 29, where he is expected to plead not guilty to the charges. Two weeks later, if he is free and entitled to do so, Bruce Kimball would leave for South Korea and the Games if he finishes among the top two at the trials.

For the moment he is free on $10,000 bond, a complete surprise to Bill James, state attorney from Hillsborough County, Fla., and, by sheer happenstance, former equestrian from the 1952 Olympics. James never expected Kimball to keep competing after the tragedy. "I thought he'd announce he was pulling out because of more pressing problems," James said. "It shows he has ice water in his veins."

Or something. Kimball endured after a 1981 accident in his hometown of Ann Arbor, Mich., in which a drunk driver swerved her van directly into his path, smashed into his car and left him with a face that had to be rebuilt from scratch.

A year later, he returned to the same pool at Indiana University for the National Sports Festival, wearing a T-shirt that read "The Comeback Kid." Kimball placed second to Greg Louganis, who pulled him up to the top pedestal of the victory stand to share the moment of triumph.

Such is what Kimball was referring to Tuesday when he said, with cracking voice and trembling hands: "I've dealt with adversity in my life. I've dedicated 21 years of my life to the sport of diving. I've made incredible sacrifices. I won't give up and I don't give up. I can't live with myself if I do."

They sit there in the stands, staring. The man on the springboard bounds up and down. Their eyes never leave him. Kathy Chuparkoff,

17, rubs 20-year-old Dawn Berrios' shoulders, comforting her, because she knows that Dawn knows that the man on the springboard is the man who faces charges for driving under the influence in an accident that killed the boy Dawn was going to marry.

Jennifer Beck, 17, also cannot remove her eyes from him. He is the man who gives her bad dreams, the man who scares her awake, shaking, in her bed at night, because she keeps hearing his voice saying that he cannot give up, that he has to carry on with what he does, even though some of Jennifer's closest friends no longer can carry on with what they do, because they are hurt or dead, because of the accident.

Cherie Beck, Jennifer's mother, studies the man on the springboard. Up and down he goes. Up and down. All she can think of is R.J. Kerker. Poor, suffering 16-year-old Raymond (R.J.) Kerker, confined to a Florida hospital bed since the first day of August, a hospital where doctors have attempted to re-attach R.J.'s severed leg. Cherie Beck can think of nothing else except that R.J. Kerker cannot do what the man on the springboard can—jump up and down.

They sit there and stare. They fixate on him, soundlessly. There is a voice 10 rows above them, the voice of a female diver, Kelly McCormick, yelling encouragingly, "Come on, Bruce!" and momentarily Jennifer Beck swivels her head for a look. Then she turns back and stares at the man on the springboard.

Bruce Kimball dives. A forward somersault, into a pike. The water ripples as he breaks its surface. It is his first dive of the day, first dive of the men's U.S. Olympic springboard trials, first dive since the 1984 Olympic platform silver medalist announced Tuesday that he would not withdraw from the competition, in spite of the fact that he is charged with five felony counts for driving under the influence in Florida, for which he faces a maximum sentence of 45 years in prison.

Kimball has come to dive, so dive he does. He, too, says not a word, to anybody. He will not discuss his situation beyond what he said in Tuesday's news conference. He climbs up, splashes down, resurfaces, climbs out, then ducks into quiet seclusion until his next turn.

The judges post his first marks of the day: 8.0, 7.5, 7.5, 7.5, 8.0, 8.0, 8.0.

On a 10-scale, not bad, not bad at all. Bruce Kimball calms down. The natatorium at Indiana University is quiet, except for the whir of an occasional camera and the polite applause of no more than 300 spectators when the dive has been completed. If there is protest to his presence, it is a silent one. He can handle this. It is not as bad as it might have been.

What he does not know is that the Becks and Dawn Berrios and Kathy Chuparkoff, Shari Wilson, Craig Diemer and Blake Bishop, the tight-knit, tight-lipped friends focused upon him from the stands, have driven all night from Brandon, Fla., just to make it clear that

Bruce Kimball's presence here does not go unchallenged.

He does not yet know that they have organized a petition that already, they say, has more than 5,000 names on it, and that they have written to Olympic swimming and diving officials, asking that Bruce Kimball not be permitted to represent America in the Olympics, should he qualify to do so here at the trials.

Colleagues understood. Wendy Williams, a top U.S. diver, for one, said: "I wish it (the accident) never happened, but we can't let it distract us. He's here, and he isn't letting it distract him." Indeed, practically every diver present, including Louganis, emphasized that they were so focused on their own efforts that they could not take time to be distracted by Kimball's.

Kathryn Owen, on the other hand, was outraged. A MADD member from Hamilton County, Ind., whose daughter Teri, 18, was killed coming home from a high school football game by a drunk driver who got off with a one-year work-release program sentence, Owen is the one who hollered "Go home!" to Kimball at his news conference, and she was still on the premises Thursday to side with the protesters from Florida.

"Nobody knows how it feels until you go see a zippered plastic bag and have identified the broken body of your beautiful child," Owen said. "What he (Kimball) did wasn't an accident. It was a crime. It's arrogant, pompous and self-centered of him to compete. *I work hard, I won't give up.* Hey, he made two people give up permanently. They don't have any choices anymore. They're gone. He took their choices away."

★   ★   ★

On the night of Aug. 1, on an isolated stretch of highway called Culbreath Road that young people from Brandon use as a hangout and refer to as "The Spot," police say Bruce Kimball's sports car came zooming down the dead-end road. How fast is in question, but he almost certainly was in excess of the posted 25 m.p.h. speed limit. How drunk he was also remains in question, but empty beer cans were found in the car.

Kimball's car at first careened off parked autos, then started hitting bodies. Ken Gossic, 16, was killed. So was Robbie Bedell, 19. While surveying the wreckage afterward, a sheriff's department deputy of 19 years said, "The last time I saw anything like this was in Vietnam."

Kimball was found, virtually uninjured, pounding the ground and screaming: "Why me? Why me?"

Robert Bedell, the dead boy's father, came forward later to mock the fact that even then, Kimball seemed concerned mostly about himself, and to say he had no idea how the young man could proceed with his Olympic plans as if nothing had happened.

Dawn Berrios, Robbie's girlfriend for 4½ years, wrote a statement in longhand Thursday and read it, nervously.

"Robbie was the essence of my life, and we have to rectify this injustice," she said. "His love will live forever in my heart. My life is re-directed now, because it has to be. But I'm here for you, Robbie. At least when I go back home, I can say that I did something about your death, that I tried. That's why I'm here today. This one's for you, Rob."

Cherie Beck read her letter, "The aspirations and dreams of the youth of America ride on the shoulders of each Olympic participant," it began. "The special talents, the high moral character and the 'role model' image truly are worthy guidelines for our youth.

"Bruce Kimball does not meet these requirements! He may possess the talent; however, based on his pattern of life, he does not possess the quality and requirements of an Olympian.

"He has a horrible record of flagrantly violating the traffic laws in Michigan. His disregard for traffic laws and his driving habits have been similar in Florida. While in training for the Olympics, he has admitted to drinking in local bars. His reckless, careless and thoughtless actions on the night of Aug. 1, 1988, have resulted in the death of two teen-agers and injuries to six others. His actions have devastated hundreds of lives. . . .

"The youth of America will hopefully see through the shallow meaningless image that you are about to present to them. We sincerely hope that the American people's image of an Olympian is not tainted by Bruce Kimball."

Jennifer Beck plans to go to law school at the University of Florida. She does not mean to present herself as judge and jury to Bruce Kimball; he deserves a fair trial. What he does not deserve, she believes, is to attend the Olympic trials, at least without opposition.

"We won't heckle him. We won't say a word when he's up there on that board," she said. "I'm not going to say, 'I hope you fall off the edge of the diving board,' even if that's what I'm thinking inside. We're not here to harass him. We're just expressing our opinion of him."

Shari Wilson nodded, standing next to her friend. "He's supposed to be so emotionally ill over what happened," she said. "If he felt that bad, he wouldn't be out there. Diving takes a lot of training and thought. You saw him today. Did he look like somebody who had anything else on his mind? Well? Did he?"

Down But Not Out

by Jeff Guenther of The Chattanooga Times. The referees probably did not think much of this routine, but this unidentified coach, letting the officials know exactly what he thought of their work, had at least two of his players in stitches. Copyright © 1988, Jeff Guenther.

Heavy Hitters

by Brian Peterson of the Minneapolis Star Tribune. Minnesota's Al Tuer (left) and Chicago's Dave Mackey take time away from their hockey pursuits to engage in a different kind of competition during a 1988 National Hockey League game in Minneapolis. Copyright © 1988, the Star Tribune.

No Majority Rule

PRO BASKETBALL

By *FILIP BONDY*

From the New York Daily News
Copyright © 1988, New York News, Inc.

An Unequal Partnership
(First of three parts)

The National Basketball Association does not have a single black owner. Unlike the other major sports leagues in America, it had a very good opportunity to get one last spring.

Wilt Chamberlain, who earned his formidable reputation and fortune in the NBA, organized a syndicate to bring an expansion team to Toronto. His bid was legitimate, even generous, in the $20-$25 million range. Toronto was a proven sports city, one that would provide a stable home for a franchise.

But demand was high; higher than supply and high enough to mean windfall profits for the established owners. League commissioner David Stern hiked the expansion price tag from $25 million to $32.5 million. Chamberlain dropped out, and the NBA lost its shot at the first black club president in the history of major professional sports. Instead, Charlotte, Minnesota, Orlando, and a shaky Miami group were awarded franchises.

"The owners got greedy," said Chamberlain. "They were asking for numbers I couldn't believe. We had the best city, we had the fans, and we had the facilities. I don't think the league gave us the consideration it should have. I don't know if that was because a black was involved, but I didn't come out of that experience with too many positives."

Despite its image as a racial groundbreaker among professional sports, the NBA is not leaving its black players, executives, or fans with too many positives. Their perception—and it is backed by nearly every statistic available—is that this sport comprised of 72.1% black players (as of March 28) is being marketed by, and for, whites. Whether this is an economic, or philosophical, apartheid is open to debate. The numbers are not.

The league's portfolio suggests anything but an equal partnership among the races:

• White ownership of every franchise, in a league that earned $250 million in revenues last season and is expanding within two years to 27 teams.

• Only four high-ranking black executives on the existing 23 teams.

• Four whites in the four most powerful league office positions.

• Reverse tokenism at the end of the bench, where the lowest-scoring player on 15 of the 23 teams is white.

• Fewer black players on teams based in cities with small black populations than in those with high black populations.

• A large majority of white local broadcasters, many of them employees of the clubs. At the network level (CBS), two all-white broadcast teams.

• The nurturing and disproportionate national exposure of the Boston Celtics, a team built around Larry Bird and top-heavy with white players.

The NBA's exclusive policies begin at the top, with ownership, where executives, coaches, and players are hired, fired, and bartered. Despite entrepreneurial interest by such former greats as Julius Erving and Oscar Robertson, Chamberlain doesn't think a black will ever own an NBA team under the present system.

"There are too many whites who get a vicarious thrill from being in control of players, who are willing to pay too much money for a team in order to say, 'Michael Jordan plays for me,' " Chamberlain said. "If a black guy wants to rub shoulders with Jordan, he just goes to the disco. The white guy buys him."

Once he's plunked down his millions, the white owner has not yielded power to minorities. This season, there were only four black executives with notable power: Wayne Embry in Cleveland, Elgin Baylor with the Clippers, Bill Russell in Sacramento and Al Attles in Golden State. Attles' clout was significantly softened last summer when owner Jim Fitzgerald imported a close personal friend, Don Nelson, as executive vice president and as a 10% minority owner. Despite Nelson's reputation as a franchise molder, the Warriors collapsed upon his arrival.

"If a black executive is in the right place, he may move up within his organization," said Attles, demoted from general manager to de facto superscout. "But there is virtually no movement between teams, not like there is with whites."

There were six black head coaches this season: Russell, who was kicked upstairs after an aborted four-month trial; Bernie Bickerstaff in Seattle; Lenny Wilkens in Cleveland; K.C. Jones in Boston, and midseason replacements Wes Unseld in Washington, and Willis Reed with the Nets. The NBA receives great credit for this statistic, because football and baseball have no head coaches or managers. But with the exception of Bickerstaff, who is arguably the best and most qualified of the black coaches, these men were offered jobs only after Hall of Fame careers.

"If you're black, you need a couple of championship rings before you get an offer to coach or be an executive," said Mike Glenn, the former Knick and Hawk who received no offers after his retirement from the game two years ago. "That's just the way it is."

The six black coaches this year had a total of 22 NBA titles and 57 seasons of experience as players. Three of them got their first shot at head coaching in the city where they starred. A fourth, Jones, is coaching now in Boston, where he played for nine seasons.

By contrast, 12 of the 22 white head coaches this season (original and interim) never played pro ball. Only Doug Collins in Chicago, Gene Shue of the Clippers and former Bullets coach Kevin Loughery had particularly distinguished playing careers.

Since few pro coaches lately have been plucked directly from the pool of collegiate talent, the NBA can't use the universities' poor racial hiring record as an excuse for its own. Potentially strong black coaching candidates with mediocre NBA playing careers are being ignored, even when it comes to assistants' posts.

White coaches are pre-schooled in coaching. Blacks are not. This unequal selection process leads to another stereotype: Black coaches are unprepared and unqualified celebrities. Blacks can't win, because the sport won't let them.

Russell, perhaps the greatest player in NBA history, personifies this Catch 22. He landed coaching jobs at Boston, Seattle, and Sacramento without knowing how to diagram a play. He was the object of great media scorn, mocked for his substitution patterns and his work habits.

Russell, once outspoken enough to brand Boston "the most bigoted city in America," is suspicious of a white reporter probing black issues. Commissioner Stern isn't comfortable with the issue for a different reason.

"We don't want to get in a situation where every hire is examined and re-examined, where people wonder whether a particular person was hired just because he is black," Stern said.

"We've had progress, and it wouldn't have come without input and considerable pressure from the league," Stern said. "We've been forwarding resumes, working behind the scenes. NBA hiring has far exceeded baseball and football."

It has, sort of. In the NBA office itself, there is a black director of community programs, a black director of security, a black attorney, and, most recently, Julius Erving, the league's overseas marketing director. But the four chief policy makers—commissioner Stern, executive vice president Russell Granik, general counsel Gary Bettman, and vice president of operations Rod Thorn—are white.

This may explain, in part, why the NBA agreed to sell a $50-million package of games to Turner Broadcasting in November while that cable network was in the midst of a war with the NAACP over hiring policies. In any case, the league-wide rate of minority hiring, for prestige jobs, is not high enough. Few black players have a realistic shot at making a career of it in the NBA, of rising above the status of assistant or director of community relations.

"The positions they create are easily dismantled—like community relations director (Nate Thurmond in Golden State and Billy Knight in Indiana)," said Glenn.

"Black players will kid a white player, 'When you make coach, make me an assistant.' "

Players Association executive vice president Charles Grantham, who is black, thinks disenfranchised blacks are paying now for sins of omission.

"Twenty years ago, the pressure groups didn't pressure sports into minority hiring. They just pressured corporations," Grantham said. "The NBA was more like a Ma and Pa business. The league would say 'Hey, we have 70 percent black players. We gave at the office.' That was supposed to be enough."

"Remember," Grantham said. "You have 23 different franchises responding to their own market, like a Wendy's or a McDonald's. It's difficult to get a hold on them."

And even more difficult to instigate change.

Reverse Tokenism on Bench
(Second of three parts)

Pro basketball is a game dominated by black players, everywhere but at the end of the bench.

Twenty-one of the 23 NBA teams are led in scoring by a black player. Seventeen of the top 20 scorers in the league are black. Eight of the top 10 rebounders are black. Nine of the 10 leaders in steals, assists and blocks are black. Twenty-one of the 24 All-Stars in Chicago—all but three Celtics—were black.

"Speaking as one of the blacks," kidded Boston's Kevin McHale, in Chicago, "I don't feel self-conscious at all."

Experts and non-experts alike argue about the physiological, cultural and motivational reasons for this dominance. They might never find the correct rationale. But team owners, general managers and coaches have come up with the perfect solution to what they perceive as a dire marketing problem. It is called "reverse tokenism" by some; among black players, it is called "stealing."

"The general consensus is that the white player is going to get the nod for a marginal position unless the black player is a lot better," said Mike Glenn, who retired two years ago from Atlanta. "They are stealing roster spots."

"Stealing" is evident everywhere. On 15 of the 23 teams, a white player has the lowest scoring average. The six players receiving the most minutes on the Mavericks are black. The six players receiving the least minutes are white.

Of 297 players in the league on March 28, 214 were black, 83 white—a breakdown of 72.1%-27.9%. Yet among those three players on each team receiving the least minutes per game, the ratio was significantly smaller—38 were black, 31 were white (55.1%-44.9%). In other words, 37.3% of all the white players in the league, 31 of 83, could be considered "token whites," players who are around more to cheerlead than to hit the jumper.

The trend is toward more tokenism, not less. Five seasons ago, a racial analysis reveals, 73.2% of NBA players were black. For the final three spots on each team, 62.3% were black. Twenty-six of the 74 white players in the league (35.1%) were among the last three players on their teams.

These numbers are no coincidence. Ted Stepien, the outspoken former owner of the Cavaliers, once was upfront about the matter.

"This is not to sound prejudiced," he said, back in 1979. "But half the squad should be white. I think people are afraid to speak out on that subject. White people have to have white heroes. I respect them (blacks), but I need white people. It's in me."

Four years after Stepien's flight from ownership, NBA franchises playing in the three cities with the smallest black populations —Salt Lake City, Phoenix and San Antonio—have more than twice as many total white players (16-7) on their rosters than those from the three cities with the highest black populations—Washington, Atlanta and Detroit.

"I tell my black players they have to be a little bit better than the white guys in order to make the pros," said Larry Brown, who won the NCAA championship this month. "They're better off knowing it ahead of time. That way, they're motivated to work harder."

In theory, white players not only make season tickets more palatable for corporations, they make white coaches more comfortable. They provide company at home and on the road. In return, the fringe performer receives job security or at least a job.

Rick Pitino said Billy Donovan was "like a son to me." John MacLeod, now coach of the Mavericks, was known to socialize with his players on the Phoenix Suns. The white players. Truck Robinson, a black power forward, complained that MacLeod asked Paul Westphal to his house for dinner.

"I wouldn't have known where his house was if I drove right past it," Robinson said.

Marginal white players seem to hang on for an extra season: Rick Carlisle, John Stroeder, Marc Iavaroni, Jeff Lamp, Chris Engler. Chuck Nevitt has become a 7-foot-5 mascot for the Pistons.

Utah coach Frank Layden has seven white players on his roster.

One of those players is Kelly Tripucka, acquired from Detroit for star Adrian Dantley in a 1986 deal that infuriated the tiny black population of Salt Lake City.

"Trading AD was a slap in the face to the black community," said Lenoris Bush, a member of the NAACP for Ogden and Salt Lake City. "He was respected. He talked back to Layden. He took himself out of games."

"His problems here harked back to the master-slave relationship," said Bush. "When the Jazz marketing people would go out to the community businesses, they would hear people say, 'We don't want to watch any million-dollar nigger.' "

Dantley himself isn't quite so sure about that.

"I was treated well by almost everyone in Salt Lake City," he said. "I think it was just a personal thing between me and Layden."

Bernard King, a black player who faced assault charges while in Utah, also wouldn't confirm racial problems there.

"If any black player feels he's a victim of prejudice, my advice to him is, 'Make the jump shot,' " said King. "If he does that, they can't keep him off the team."

White executives can, however, pay the black player less and cause him more headaches.

"The Celtics tried for three years to give Danny Ainge my spot when he came into the league, but he couldn't earn it," said Gerald Henderson, the former Celtic and now a guard for the 76ers. "They gave him $500,000 a year when he got there. They never brought me up to that level, and when they traded me, Red Auerbach talked about his salary, my salary, and said he didn't want an unhappy player on his team."

★   ★   ★

Black or white, the pay is still outrageously good. The NBA players share in 53% of all revenues. The average salary is more than $500,000, and the mean salary is about $300,000. Blacks are paid as well as whites, overall, perhaps because they are generally the better players. There are even some commercial endorsements.

But the extra dollars don't help the black player get through the next bus ride or the next hotel stay. The isolation is real, eight months a year. Management and coaches are mostly white. The trainers and the public relations directors are all white. Forty-six of the 55 newspaper writers who cover the NBA teams for major newspapers are white. The players endure stares at the airports, stray racial comments and affronts from mascots like the Phoenix Gorilla and the San Diego Chicken—an "expert" at mimicking the soulful strut of black players.

Socially speaking, there is little mixing of the races on teams. Families of black players are often not invited to parties thrown by families of white players. On the road, black players eat breakfast with black players; white players with white players. Finger-pointing is often cross-racial. When Boston went into a mild slump this season, several white players complained privately that Darren Daye wasn't executing the plays. Daye was soon dumped.

Instead of socialization, there is suspicion and misunderstanding. Some black players are viewed as inscrutable or worse. There are crazy rumors. Two GMs asked agent Bill Pollak whether one of his black clients were a transvestite. Blacks feel singled out by the predominately white media on the drug issue. When Micheal Ray Richardson learned that Chris Mullin had entered an alcohol, not a drug, rehab program, he said, "There's no way they'd let me get away with that."

★   ★   ★

Among the other complaints from black players interviewed this season, given with the assurance sources would not be identified:

"When a black player sits out because of an injury, he's supposed to be dogging it. When a white player sits out, it's OK."

"Even after Isiah Thomas (discussed the issue), the broadcasters are still calling black players 'athletes' and still saying white players are the smart ones."

"Black players can't speak out. They get traded if they do."

Those are some of the perceptions. They ought to count for something.

The Celtics Story
(Third of three parts)

In the minds of many black basketball players, racial injustice is headquartered at rickety Boston Garden on Causeway Street.

Here, the sweet odor of stale beer, spilled and re-spilled on every wooden seat in the house, mixes with the sour taste of prejudice. Drunk white fans, a few dressed as leprechauns, hover near the visitors' bench. After games, they heckle near the locker room. Too close for comfort. Where are the black fans?

"Not many blacks come to games in Boston," said Gerald Henderson, a starting guard with the Celtics until he was traded four years ago in a cold, but shrewd, move by Red Auerbach. "Tickets are sold out for years, so it's who you know and who you are to get in. When blacks do get in, they get hassled."

When the Celtics were losing, in the late '70s, they happened to have a majority of black players. "The city turned on its own team, on guys like Billy Knight," said Len Elmore, the former Knick and Net forward. "Fans would walk past the bench and say, 'Cowens, Havlicek, you're great. The rest of you guys ain't worth a damn.' "

This season, the Celtics have been winning with between seven and 10 whites on their roster. That number includes the only three white All-Stars in the NBA—Larry Bird, Kevin McHale and Danny Ainge—plus former All-Stars Jim Paxson and Bill Walton.

Boston games are broadcast by an all-white radio team of Glenn

Ordway and Johnny Most. On local television, on Channel 56, the white team of Gil Santos and Bob Cousy calls the shots. On cable, the white team of Mike Gorman and Tom Heinsohn does the job.

In the stands, in the high-priced seats, sit the power brokers. Alan Cohen, vice chairman of the Celtics. Jan Volk, general manager. And yes, Auerbach, president. All white. All imperious, dynastic.

"The Celtics recruit the best white guys who play the game," Henderson said. "They're catering to the paying fans. It's a format that's worked for them for years. Why go against it, if it's accepted by surrounding society?"

It is accepted, arguably ensured, by the NBA—which installed a salary cap on team payrolls that virtually froze player movement since 1984 and facilitated the Celtics' stability and dominance. League officials insisted the cap would promote parity. In fact, NBA teams are moving up or down an average of just one place per season in the standings, far less than in baseball or football. Boston has won eight division titles in the last nine years.

★   ★   ★

The Celtics have been a windfall for the entire 23-member league. They mean sellout crowds. The last two finals, both involving Boston, have brought record Nielsen ratings to CBS. That means bigger network and cable contracts. The Celtics, representing only the 10th largest market in America, have been on 10 of the 50 regular-season cable games shown this season by Turner Broadcasting— a number equaled only by Ted Turner's own Atlanta Hawks.

"The Celtics are popular because of the winning and tradition," said one CBS official. "And being white doesn't hurt."

Can the successful Celtics be held responsible for what others wish to see in them? Do they pander to the racist element? Auerbach, stogie in pocket and on a recent pre-game walking tour of Madison Square Garden with Volk, did not want to debate the issue. "You've got the wrong guy," he said, brushing off a questioner without missing a step. "I don't want to discuss it."

Because he was a coach and then general manager for a team considered a pioneer in integration during the '50s and '60s, Auerbach often is granted immunity from criticism for the Celtics' questionable racial record in recent years. Wilt Chamberlain, an old rival, says such special consideration is undeserved.

"I don't like Auerbach," Chamberlain said. "He coached five blacks, and he had insights about playing them. But he didn't have anything to do with getting them. Never did. That was done by the old owner, Walter Brown. Brown was the guy who said it was OK to have five blacks on a team in Boston."

Auerbach gave black power forward Cedric Maxwell a five-year, $3.5 million contract for the team-oriented skills that helped win two titles in the early '80s. But after undergoing arthroscopic surgery on his left knee in 1985, Maxwell found out the Celtics didn't have much patience for black players in physical rehab. He was traded to the pathetic Clippers.

"The guys who left Boston on negative terms were all black—Don Chaney, JoJo White, Paul Silas, myself," said Maxwell during a game this season at the Meadowlands. "We were always traded in a negative atmosphere. It was always more positive when they traded Paul Westphal, Dave Cowens, guys like that. That can't just be coincidence.

"By the time I left, I was tired of being there and the people were tired of me being there," Maxwell said. "The sendoff wasn't exactly on the Queen Mary with flowers. In my case, management kept saying, 'Oh, he got hurt in the first year of a five-year contract. He didn't work hard in rehab.' They just feel the fans are looking for a role model, a Kevin McHale driving a Bronco truck, for the middle-class fans. I don't know if that's racist, it's more economics."

Auerbach has a black coach, K.C. Jones. That hasn't been enough to alter the image. "Whether or not they're a white team, that perception is there," said Al Attles, the Warriors' vice president. "The perception is what matters."

Last season, in the playoffs, the Celtics' thin white bench might have cost them the title. No reserve averaged more than five points per game. Auerbach tried in the offseason to sign Bernard King and Antoine Carr, two blacks with real impact. He eventually signed Dirk Minniefield and Artis Gilmore, two blacks he needed. When the resin dust cleared at the end of the bench, however, the pale faces of Fred Roberts, Brad Lohaus and Mark Acres were still most visible.

"Why do they have whites at the end of the bench? I don't know," said Mike Glenn. "It's different if they had to have them. But they have all the other guys already; the good whites who can flat-out play."

The Boston brass has its economic incentives. Despite eight straight titles in the '50s and '60s, the club built around Bill Russell did not draw well. The Celtics averaged under 8,000 fans per game during five of those seasons, and played second fiddle to the Bruins until the day Bird arrived on the scene in 1979. They have sold out the arena ever since. Cable TV money poured in, as the Celts took advantage of their new popularity throughout predominantly white New England.

★   ★   ★

In December of 1986, Cohen and Celtics' chairman Don Gaston unveiled the ultimate money-making scheme. They put up for sale on the New York Exchange a 40% limited partnership in the club, representing $48.1 million in stock purchases. The team's broad appeal, and the color of its public face, was more critical than ever. As the sale approached, the Celtics went from five whites in 1984, to six in 1985, to eight in 1986. All the shares were purchased within days, underwritten by Smith Barney. White America had taken the bait.

Despite such marginal acquisitions over recent years as Roberts, Conner Henry and Greg Kite (Kite was drafted ahead of solid big man Mark West and future All-Star Doc Rivers in 1983), Jones says the Celtics don't stockpile white players.

"The Celtics are not more marketable because we have some white players," said Jones, who says he approved of the decision to dump Sam Vincent and retain Jerry Sichting, "the better player," before the season. "You can't market a white team, in Phoenix, Dallas, or in Boston, unless you win ballgames. Winning titles makes you marketable."

Most, the beery-voiced radio man sees nothing wrong with the team makeup.

"To say the Celtics are prejudicial, that's totally erroneous," Most said. "It's a lefthanded way of thinking. We (Most is a Celtic employee) happen to have been in a position to get some great white players. Then, we happened to be drafting down low in a position to get some more."

Cousy, too, insists that, "Arnold (Auerbach) just sees names, he sees numbers on a 1-to-10 scale when he judges talent, not skin color.

"When you're drafting low, though, then that (race) might become a slight factor if everything else is equal," Cousy said.

If everything else were equal in Boston, the race issue wouldn't haunt the Celtics, as it continues to haunt the NBA and all of professional sports.

A Season of Futility

HOCKEY

By *KEN MURRAY*

From the Baltimore Evening Sun
Copyright © 1988, the Baltimore Evening Sun

Doug Shedden is among the last of the Skipjacks to emerge from the shower room, where he has tried to wash the residue of another dismal defeat from his mind. If it takes him longer than most, there is good reason. He has played in every Skipjack game this season, a cruel and unusual punishment.

"It's demoralizing," Shedden says, fingering a faded blue towel. "It's demoralizing to go into some rinks knowing you have no hope in hell (of winning). A lot of times we went in and had no chance. You know you're going to lose. The only question is by how many goals. You don't want to be embarrassed, but sometimes you are.

"You hang your head, and get out of there as fast as you can."

★ ★ ★

Murray Bannerman juggles an ice pack on his upper right thigh, fidgeting in the seat that his coach, Gene Ubriaco, normally occupies. The Skipjack goalie is trying to coax the soreness from a groin injury, and to revive an NHL career that slipped into a coma this year. He may not have enough time to do either.

"This is the first time I've ever played on a team that didn't make the playoffs," he says in a monotone voice that hides his pain. "If it's my last year, it's not a high note to go out on. (But) it makes you a better person. It humbles you. It gives you a different perspective on things. I met some good people here. . . . It hasn't been a total loss."

★ ★ ★

Keith Miller sits on a table in the corridor outside the Skipjack locker room and looks down at his swollen left ankle. Surgical scars run up and down either side. He broke it Nov. 10. Ten days later, pins were inserted. Three months later, he was back on the ice. Miller, an enthusiastic 21-year-old rookie, tries to explain why he rushed back to the Skipjacks.

"I wanted to play," he says. "I wanted to show them I'm not a quitter. I wanted to show them I could play in the American Hockey League."

★   ★   ★

These are your Baltimore Skipjacks, fans. Beaten, battered, bloodied, but somehow still on their feet. They have torched records for futility in the AHL this season, left a trail of incredulity in their wake. *Can they really be that bad?* But, if nothing else, they beat the odds.

The bright spot in a 12-56-9 season, coach?

"That we made it," Ubriaco said this week.

Their season of torment will come to an end in Glens Falls, N.Y., on Easter Sunday, appropriately enough. With three games to play, counting tonight's Fan Appreciation affair at the Arena, they are three losses away from becoming the AHL's all-time losingest team. The end will not come a minute too soon for Ubriaco.

"I'll be honest," he said. "It's been like wearing a mask all year. I'm tired of it. We've got the office staff, the players; I've got to stay positive. I can take the mask off Sunday."

It took Tom Ebright, the team's new majority owner, to keep pro hockey alive in Baltimore this season. Then it took a Dec. 1 appeal to the AHL to get players on loan to keep this season from becoming a financial bloodbath. As it is, Ebright stands to lose $250,000—"before taxes"—for his noble effort.

Along the way, the Skipjacks employed a revolving door. There were 53 players from 10 different NHL teams who graced their roster. But when the Pittsburgh Penguins pulled out their farm team in June, and then reneged on an agreement to supply the Jacks with competitive players in October, their lot was cast. They were destined to be losers.

"I didn't know what I was into until I got here the day before the season," said Shedden, a winger and veteran of 392 NHL games with Pittsburgh, Detroit and Quebec. "When I saw the talent, I knew it was bad. I told the fans not to expect much. We were getting everybody's second cuts."

Shedden, the team captain, scored the first goal in the first game against Hershey. "It's been all downhill since then," he said. "The toughest part was early in the year. Eighteen games (the Jacks' season-opening losing streak) put us out of the playoffs right there. You're looking at the first of November and you're out of the playoffs. That's a long year."

Bannerman arrived in November, exiled by the Chicago Blackhawks, for whom he had played 289 games over seven seasons. It was instant culture shock.

"Everybody here, nobody else wanted them," he said. "Myself

included. Being put in a situation like that, it's tough to have confidence to go out and play well. When I first got here, we'd go into the third period in a close game, tied or ahead, and there wasn't the confidence to go get another goal and win. My second game here, we had a one-goal lead and it was like, 'Hey, let's not screw this up.' "

Almost universally, the Skipjacks point to two January trades that undermined a chance they had of getting back to respectability this season. They were the trades that Montreal made to move Alfie Turcotte and Scott Harlow to other organizations.

When Turcotte was traded to Winnipeg Jan. 8, the Skipjacks had won four of their last five games. He had 19 points in his last seven games, 30 in his last 13, and was the league's second-leading scorer. No sooner had Harlow replaced Turcotte as the league's second-leading scorer than he, too, was traded. Harlow had 39 points in his last 18 games. The line of Turcotte, Harlow and Shedden averaged better than two goals a game when it was broken up.

"That was the low point for me," Ubriaco said. "It took a lot out of me. Spunk. It hurt the team. We had built something from nothing. Montreal helped us (by supplying decent players), but when they had the opportunity, they used us, too."

Quebec was the most generous with loan players, giving the Skipjacks 11 in all. Miller was one of them. But he broke his ankle in his fourth game before 40 relatives in Newmarket. It was his introduction to life in hockey's fast lane. For what it's worth, he says he has enjoyed it.

"I've learned nothing comes easy," said Miller, a hulking 6-foot-2 winger. "You've got to work for what you get. And nothing comes easy for the Skipjacks. Everyone wants to stick it to us. People make songs about us. But our fans have stuck behind us. The team has 12 wins and we're averaging over 2,500 fans. First-place Fredericton isn't over 2,500. This is a nice city and I've made some nice friends."

Miller is one of the few Skipjacks with a future. By Shedden's estimation, there are "five or six" players who won't be back in hockey next season. That fact, coupled with the endless losses, has tended to give the Jacks a "loose" atmosphere, Shedden said.

"The theme of the team is like that in the movie, 'Slapshot,' " he said.

"Slapshot," starring Paul Newman, was about a struggling minor league franchise that gained notoriety for its "Goon" antics. The Jacks aren't goons, but they do have Steve Carlson, the assistant coach who played the part of Steve Hansen in the movie. In perhaps his most memorable scene, Hansen beat up on a Coca-Cola machine.

"We were idiots in the movie, but these guys are hockey players," Carlson said. "I guess we're in the same boat, though, because in the movie we didn't know where we'd be next year. And a lot of these guys don't know if they'll be offered a contract for next year."

Bannerman and Shedden loom as most likely to get an NHL call. Having played out the option year of his Chicago contract, Bannerman will be a free agent June 1. He hopes for a "fair chance" to make it back to the NHL, but doubts he would settle for another stint in the minors.

Can he still play in the NHL?

"I think so," he said. "But I have to be realistic. I'd be deluding myself if I said I thought somebody definitely would sign me. The realistic view is it might not happen."

Nearly all the Jacks face an uncertain future after Sunday. For some, like Bannerman, it will be a bittersweet finish.

"I know it might be the last pro hockey I play," he said in that monotone voice. "That wouldn't be a happy situation. But I've been away from the family since I got here, and when it's over, I'll get to go back home (to Chicago)."

Shedden felt similar pangs of remorse and relief at the prospect of the season finale.

"I'm disappointed because there will be no playoffs," he said. "I feel relief, too. At the end of every year, you wonder where it went."

Dan Jansen's Sorrow

SPEED SKATING

By *HUBERT MIZELL*

From the St. Petersburg Times
Copyright © 1988, Times Publishing Co.

Lest we forget, life does transcend sport. Hours before his Olympic race, a moment Dan Jansen had worked a lifetime for, the American speedskater learned that his sister died Sunday of leukemia.

"I want," Jansen told a U.S. teammate, "to go out and win the gold medal for her." In a Wisconsin family of 11, Dan and sister Jane were especially close.

He's 22. She was 27.

At Calgary twilight, Jansen adjusted the hood on his sleek red-and-aqua racing suit and sucked in the millionth deep breath of a traumatic Sunday.

He tapped skates on the angel-white ice of the Olympic Oval, and lined up beside Japanese skater Yasushi Kuroiwa for their 500-meter race for glory.

The gun went off.

But, instantly, the two skaters were recalled. There'd been a false start. A minute later, the two athletes again sped away, and a standing-room-only crowd of 5,000 roared. Almost none of them knew of the death of Jane Jansen Beres.

Then, the unthinkable. . . .

For Danny Jansen, it was to be a Sunday with no departure from sorrow. On the first turn, his left skate slipped and the young man from greater Milwaukee fell hard, skidding into the padded outer wall and taking Kuroiwa down with him.

Jansen got up, not physically injured. He skated away slowly, face buried in hands. Alone with his thoughts and his multiplying distress. For a long, long time, Danny snailed his way about the 400-

meter track that had taken him down.

He paused for a second to shout encouragement as American teammate Nick Thometz sprinted by in the next heat. That didn't work out, either. Thometz skated poorly, and his medal dream also disintegrated.

Mike Crowe, the U.S. Olympic speed skating coach, came onto the ice and put a consoling arm around Jansen's waist.

Dan nodded, and skated on.

"I think he was trying, under the circumstances, to skate the hardest he could," said Thometz, who wound up in eighth place. "I think that may be part of the reason Dan went down."

Two weeks ago, the World Championships were held in Jansen's hometown. His West Allis neighbors chanted "Dan! Dan! Dan!" as Dan skated to three gold medals, the first American male to pull such a triple since Olympic hero Eric Heiden in 1981.

"I'm dedicating the season to Jane," Jansen said that night, his eyes glazing with tears. "She's fighting so hard, and I love her so. Jane is never out of my mind."

Jane Beres, a former speed skater, smiled at hearing of Danny's three wins. She was two miles from the rink in West Allis, at home with her husband, Robert, a Milwaukee firefighter, and their three daughters.

Jane's hair was gone, due to chemotherapy. But the crusty, competitive Jansen spirit had not eroded. "I'll be pulling for my brother to do it one more time, at the Olympics," she said.

That night, Dan visited.

There were 11 Jansens in all, including five daughters and four sons. Every one of them a speed skater. For mom and dad, keeping up with rink schedules was a two station-wagon job.

Jane's leukemia was detected in January 1987. Immediately, she needed a bone marrow transplant. Dan was eager, but doctors refused. He was recovering from mononucleosis.

"My sister, Joanne, gave Jane the marrow," the brother said in the athletic afterglow of the World Championships. "But now it's my turn. If Jane needs me, I'll be there, no matter what.

"If the call comes as I'm warming up for an Olympic race, I will be dressed in 10 minutes and heading for the airport. Compared to *her* needs, the Olympics mean nothing."

Then, six days ago, Jansen was in Calgary, practicing his techniques on Olympic ice. He stopped for a moment to talk with reporters about his medal chances . . . and about his sister.

"It's not looking any better for Jane," he said, gnawing at the lower lip. "She's just gone back into the hospital, for more chemotherapy. Her liver is now the biggest concern."

Saturday night, a dreaded call came from West Allis. Jane's condition was worse. Harry Jansen, a retired policeman, and his wife, Geraldine, had just gotten to Calgary to see their son skate. They never unpacked. They returned to their daughter's bedside.

Sunday morning at 6, just before Canadian dawn, Dan was called to an Olympic Village phone. He hadn't slept much. His mind was drenched with thoughts other than of the 500-meter finals, which by then were 11 hours away.

Jansen's brother, Mike, said the end was near for Jane. Dan spoke to his sister, but she was too weak to reply. "I know she understood me," Jansen said. "The reason I stayed to race was that I was sure it was what Jane would've wanted." Before the Sunday morning phone call ended, Mike Jansen gave Jane a kiss, and said it was from her brother at the Olympics.

Four hours later, she died.

It was 9:55, seven hours from Dan's race. Jansen's family asked him not to withdraw. He said he would remain in Calgary until Thursday, to skate the 1,000-meters.

The family was gathering back in West Allis, to grieve a daughter . . . and, late Sunday, to turn on the TV for a moment, to cheer a son. Their emotions, already complex, would see no relief.

Tyrant on Field, Populist in Classroom

HIGH SCHOOL FOOTBALL

By *PAUL RUBIN*

From New Times
Copyright © 1988, New Times, Inc.

His eyes slits, red cap pulled down hard on his forehead, the football coach at Mesa's Mountain View High hovers over his team in the losers' locker room.

He doesn't say anything for a terrifying minute. There is no escaping him. There never is.

"Do any of you really know how bad it hurts to lose a game?" Jesse Parker finally growls in his nasal Oklahoma twang.

"How bad it hurts? You know, we might have to play them again this year."

"We'll kick their ass," a player blurts from the group huddled below Parker.

"Oh, no, no, no, no, no," the coach counters, sounding like John Belushi. "I'd rather get some sort of petition to get them off our schedule because they're just too tough for us. What did I tell them before the season? That this was the most aggressive team we'd fielded at Mountain View? Why'd I tell people that?"

"You had faith," a player moans. Hallelujah. Parker runs with it. He says: "And you're eager to destroy that faith. I made a bad mistake, didn't I?"

He tells them what he did once after one of his teams was tied by a "half-assed" opponent: "We had a better game right afterward when we went out and scrimmaged. I would do that with you, but I don't think you're tough enough. The best thing to do is to get the season over, isn't it?"

Parker whirls and smashes a blackboard with an open palm. Boom. He smacks it again. Several boys are sobbing. A few feet away, a Parker maxim is taped to a wall. "Defeat is worse than death," it says, "because you have to live with defeat."

He glares at his team for another full minute, then continues:

"It's just a game, isn't it? It doesn't mean anything. You have to put your heart and soul into it. If you don't, it just becomes a game. We didn't, so it doesn't hurt very much. I've seen teams hurt, believe me.

"They came here and kicked our ass. This is the fourth time in the history of this school someone has scored more than 30 against us. We can get up off the mat or stay down like a bunch of cowards. It would be a lot easier to quit."

A player speaks up. "But you'd have to live with yourself."

Parker nods slightly. "So how many of you are willing to make a bigger commitment than you have so far? You'd better think twice. You better not lie to me—you'd *better* not do that. Tomorrow's going to be a bitch. Somebody's going to quit, I promise you. You're going to have to hate losing so bad that you just won't lose. I know it's hard in this society, where everything is just a game. How many of you don't want to pay the price tomorrow?"

Parker leans on the battered blackboard and whispers, "Eight o'clock. Full pads."

★   ★   ★

The teacher returns test papers one by one to his U.S. history class. Teacher and students banter easily as he strolls through the classroom in this clean-cut, suburban high school.

"That was an interesting effort, Dave," the teacher says.

"If it was so interesting, Mr. Parker, why didn't I get an A?" Dave asks, as everyone laughs. Jesse Parker can be forceful as a teacher. And his students say he's demanding. But he rarely raises his voice and the classroom is a friendly place.

In the classroom, the tyrannical coach becomes the intellectual. And a liberal—but not a squishy one.

"They are so conservative, so right-wing out here," Parker says, "and my goal is to try to make my students think. I don't mind what they think about, as long as they think. When we talk about Vietnam, I tell them it was a rich man's war fought by poor people. They call me a raving liberal.

"They'll say, 'The poor are jerks because they don't have any money.' I tell them I sympathize with poor people. It's not doing without a VCR or a big car. It's an attitude. It's 'I'm poor.' Our most serious problem is this unequal distribution of wealth. We're getting our asses kicked economically by the Japanese, not by Russia. The Russians can't even make a paper clip."

Parker complains about flaccid Mesa. "I don't want to come down too hard on this community, but it's yuppie," he says, making "yuppie" sound like a disease.

"Parents are getting softer and softer. What I try my best to do is to get the kids to believe beyond what they already believe they can do. I want them to say they've learned something—and not just to tackle. Most people have negative perceptions of themselves. The only way to change those perceptions is through achievement. Achievement does not come easily."

Parker not only hates sissies on the football field. He also hates them in his classroom. "I want you to be questioning about things," Parker tells his students. "Question. Question. Question. Question what I say, and question the way historians have written about our history."

But few question him in the classroom and fewer still on the football field. "If a player asks me why we're doing something, which they rarely do," Parker says, "I say that it's designed to make him tougher, a winner. Take it or leave it. That's football. In class, if they challenge one of my views and make a point, they gain new stature in my eyes."

Parker heads the social studies department at Mountain View and teaches two advanced-placement classes in history and an economics course. (Parker makes about $42,000 a year for teaching and $2,400 a year for coaching.)

"He's almost impossible to get an A from," says senior student Robert Brown, a would-be optometrist who doesn't play football. "He says, 'You aren't perfect. Why should I give you a perfect grade?' He describes himself as one of the four liberals in the entire city of Mesa, and some of his political views make people gasp. He makes us think."

And his students don't forget him after they graduate. A few years ago, for example, incoming Brigham Young University freshmen from his school voted Parker as their most influential high school teacher.

"He's very impressive, very intellectual, very analytical, and yet he's this legendary football coach," says senior Michelle Roseburrough, an aspiring political scientist and not a sports fan. "At first, everybody was in such awe of him. I didn't know what to call him—coach, sir, who knows. He's so imposing, he scares you to death. Then you find out that he's kind of a softy. He's a memorable type of teacher."

On this day, he is lecturing about how the idea of racial superiority seeped into American history books at the turn of this century:

"It was the 'white man's burden,' the whites had this 'duty' to take care of the rest of the world. If you think all of that is gone, listen to some of us today. 'We know what government is best for Nicaragua,' they say. 'Democracy is bound to be better. Wait till they get democracy.' "

That leads to a discussion of early 20th-century historians who wrote that economic conditions are what force societies to change. "You don't get much Progressive writing in your textbooks," Parker tells the class, "because that might shake up your parents.

"Progressives write that when Patrick Henry said, 'Give me liberty or give me death,' he meant, 'I want more money for myself and my class, the upper class.' You don't think that if you wave a few bucks at somebody, they won't change their ideals?''

★   ★   ★

High school football coaches and fans around the Valley probably rejoiced last month after Mountain View got thumped 31-7 by Westwood High. It wasn't so much that the top-ranked team in the state had been knocked off its pedestal. It was that *Jesse Parker* had been gored—at least that night.

He is the only head football coach Mountain View has ever had, and he has built a powerhouse. The Toros have won three state titles and more than 80 percent of their games since the school opened in 1976. After last week's victory over Tempe McClintock, Mountain View's record is 123-25-1. This season, the Toros are 9-1 going into the state playoffs, which begin this Friday.

Opposing coaches, however, have berated him. Tucson Amphitheater head football coach Vern Friedli says: "High school football is a game, but with Jesse Parker, it's not. It should be a learning experience. With Jesse Parker, it's not. Period."

(Parker says of Friedli: "We kick their butts again and again. He's a poor loser. When we get whipped, I say we got whipped. It's totally an ego problem.")

Some, like Friedli, see the 48-year-old Parker as a bullheaded jerk. They say Parker savors running up the score on opponents. They ridicule his explosive sideline antics, which they say intimidate referees and even other coaches.

At a 1983 meeting of Arizona football coaches, so one story goes, someone asked, "Why do people continue to idolize a coach who is a complete asshole?" The other coaches agreed with applause.

Parker will do anything to win, his enemies say, emphasizing the word "anything." They point to Mountain View's ban from the 1981 state playoffs for breaking the rules by using tackling dummies out of season. And they note that Parker was reprimanded by Mesa school officials this summer after someone complained about the savage drills he uses to punish wayward players.

Parker is sometimes maniacal during games, upbraiding his players or pulling them toward him by their face masks or jerseys. He frequently roams well beyond the designated coaching area and sometimes even strides onto the field until assistants pull him back.

"I grab face masks, I shove kids, I say things that probably aren't in anyone's best interests," he says. "I'm not concerned with my image on the sideline. The game is my sole focus. They say, 'He's crazy, he's this, he's that.' After we beat them, kill them, it's 'He cheats.' There are people who come Friday nights just to watch me. They say, 'How can you take a game so serious? A billion Chinese don't know about it. What's the big deal?' If this isn't serious, what is serious? I don't give a goddamn what people think. The only ones who matter over the long haul are your own players."

Gilbert High School athletic director Joe Pico, a former Parker assistant, sees it like this: "People love to say things about him—he's the bad boy, he's a madman. What he really is is an Oklahoma farm boy who was a poor kid coming up through life, and he somewhat resents kids having everything given to them."

Toro football teams are like their coach—dogged and serious. Parker is not interested in building character through defeat. "The world is not interested in the storms you've encountered," he tells his players, quoting from a poem, "but did you bring in the ship?"

The only "ship" for Parker is the state championship.

"I tell them," he says, "that the fun of it is in the success that we have, that there's nothing more glorious than to win the state championship. How you perform under pressure tells a person a lot about himself. Where else does a 17-year-old have to contend with such pressure except on the football field?"

★   ★   ★

It is Saturday morning, 10 hours after the Westwood game has ended, and the Toros are running wind sprints up and down their football field. They run in full uniform through debris left behind after last night's fiasco. Parker stands grimly at midfield, whistle in mouth.

It had been a miserable night. He got home after midnight, ate a pizza with his wife, Latsy, and fell asleep around two. He awoke about four and drove to a health spa for a 90-minute workout. Then he went to his coach's office to think things over.

"I thought about where I have failed this group of kids," he tells a visitor. "The 48th kid on the team, the kid who never gets to play, used to feel it the same as the guys on the field. During that Westwood game, some kids on the bench secretly said to themselves, 'I don't want to be part of this.'

"I've gone soft on these kids. Maybe it's because of all the criticism I've received. Maybe it's because I wanted to do things without being so tough, so hardnosed, whatever you want to call it. Some call it brutal. I decided to tell them, 'You're going to get your butt kicked.' I'm going back to the way I've always done it."

By 9 a.m., it's 90 degrees, and the players are suffering. One yells, "No pain, no gain" at a heavyset teammate who can barely move. The big guy curses. A player tries to throw up. Another falls dizzily to his knees. He tries to lift himself, but collapses. The school's trainer rushes over and hoses him down. He's done for the day.

After more than a half-hour of sprinting, the players get a water break. Then it's all-out hitting for another half-hour or so, offense versus defense in a scrimmage as intense as last night's game.

Former Toro Paul Kasprzyk, now a senior football player at the University of Arizona, remembers days like this: "We had what we called 'perfect plays': starting from the huddle, the snap, executing the play, running it just right. The coaches would say thumbs up or somebody goofed or didn't run hard enough. My senior year, we went 14-0, and we always attributed it to our 'perfect plays.' " Arizona's player of the year in 1983, Kasprzyk also recalls the rough stuff. "When you screwed up, you knew you were going to pay for it," he says. "My pain tolerance went way up."

Today, three players are ordered through the Gauntlet. It's brutally simple: One player squares off against two teammates. When Parker blows his whistle, the punished player barrels straight into his teammates from a three-point stance. Then he goes against two fresh teammates, getting mashed again and again, until Parker decides enough is enough.

Until this season, Parker also used something called the Circle Drill. Players who cut class, skipped practice or otherwise upset the coaches were punished by having to wrestle one after another inside a circle of hooting teammates. Those disciplined often wound up bruised, battered and bloodied. School officials this summer made Parker halt the Circle Drill, after someone complained anonymously to a Mesa weekly paper.

Bob Davis, now a junior defensive star at BYU, remembers those punitive drills—fondly. "I loved those days of banging bodies, banging heads," he says. "The Circle Drill was just another tough drill. Up at BYU, I get very intense for games. At Mountain View, I used to get just as intense for practices. Practices here are cake compared to high school. Every time you saw Coach, you'd start feeling intense. He just brings it out of you. I wouldn't want to get into a scrape with him."

Parker himself is unrepentant. "I told my kids that this school is turning sissy," he says. "The Circle Drill wasn't an issue until some anonymous crybaby wrote in. Then, it was 'Parker Abuses Kids.' The drill isn't designed to inflict pain for pain's sake. It makes a point about commitment to a team and to yourself."

Parker knows about pain. When he was a college player, knee and shoulder injuries plagued him. "I discovered something about myself," he says. "I was like most people: When I got hurt, I was kind of willing to stand on the sidelines. Then the coach asked me if I was going to play or what. I played. Nowadays, I'll never play a kid who even tells me he thinks he's hurt, but I discovered that we can overrate how much pain we have."

The Saturday-morning practice ends at 10, and the team staggers into the locker room. Parker tells his players before they leave that one of them will apologize to the student body Monday morning for the big loss.

★   ★   ★

Monday at nine, Brent Blakeman apologizes over Mountain View's public-address system. He tells the 2,500 students how embarrassed he and the other players are about the Westwood game and how it won't happen again.

As Blakeman, a three-year starter and straight-A student, speaks, Parker fiddles with papers in his classroom, not looking up to see how his class is reacting. Blakeman's confession mercifully lasts only about 30 seconds.

Some, like Parker's history student Michelle Roseburrough, hardly believe what they've heard. "It's like it was a national catastrophe and we're all supposed to be in mourning," she says. "It sounded like he was crying, so that got to some kids in class. I thought it was ludicrous."

Parker chuckles—a bit menacingly—when told of that. "I know some people think we go too far," he says.

Says Blakeman, "Coach Parker doesn't accept anything but winning. I didn't mind saying we're sorry."

★　★　★

Football is a seven-day-a-week job during the season for Parker. On Sundays, when he's watching game films, Latsy, his wife of 26 years, attends a Baptist church. Even there, she says, it's impossible to escape Mountain View football, especially after a loss. "All these wonderful people who love me and who I love very much caringly say, 'What happened? What did Jesse say?' And I don't even want to see people, because I don't want to answer the question."

Jesse and Latsy Parker's lives have long been wrapped around football—while they've raised three children: Kathy is a 25-year-old school teacher, and Robert, 24, is a radio announcer and a senior at Northern Arizona University. Jonathan, 11, is a ball boy at Mountain View's home football games.

When Latsy went to the hospital to give birth to Robert, Dad had a game to coach. He didn't get to the hospital until after Robert was born.

"I was brought up with football all around me," says Robert. "When I think back about it, Dad never told me, 'You're going to play football.' I played because I wanted to play more than anything. I wanted to be the best."

But Robert was no star. "I realized at some point that I was mediocre, though I wanted badly to shine for my dad," he says. "He never got on me except when I didn't try my best, same as anyone else. He wanted me to do more than I believed I could do. He wins because he gets that across and because he knows the game. I was a very emotional player, and I became obsessed with winning. When I moved up to Flagstaff, I brought that 'winning is the only thing' attitude with me. It took me a while to realize there is life after high school football."

Robert Parker says his dad never has spoken much about himself. "I'm just starting to get the details and they're really something," Robert says. "I can see more where he's coming from, both as a father and as a coach."

Latsy Parker adds: "You have to understand Jesse's upbringing before you can understand what's going on with him. Jesse loves to challenge people. He knows all about challenges.

★　★　★

Part of Jesse Parker still is in Idabel, a town of about 6,000 in southeastern Oklahoma. His past as a poor person is always in the back of his mind.

"Republicans are the worst thing that's ever happened to this country," he says. "I can't stand these Republicans who support big business. I don't emphasize my roots, but to me, being a Republican would be a denial of those roots. In a sense, it would be denying a lot of what I believe."

The Parkers were like many others in rural Idabel, scratching by in a poverty-ridden area known as Little Dixie. When Jesse, the oldest of six boys, was growing up, the family moved to a house in town. His sharecropper dad got a job at a gas station, but the clan was so poor the house didn't have running water. However, Parker's mother, Bert, saw a way out for her boys.

"She was determined we were going to a 'town school,' not a one-room schoolhouse," Parker recalls. "That's why we moved to Idabel. She feared we were going to drop out like everyone else in the family. She has a sense of loyalty, of toughness, and a quiet determination, and she just wouldn't let that happen."

So Parker became a student. "I read and read when I was a kid, though I often tried to hide that fact," he says. "I remember reading Nevins' biography of Rockefeller when I was in junior high, just to read it. I did not want to be known as a bookworm, so I'd slip around and read those books."

He tried to keep up that charade until he graduated.

"My mother wanted me to do well in school, so I tried really hard," he recalls. "But I didn't want anybody to know that I tried hard. I would never carry a schoolbook home, so I'd have to squeeze everything I had into the class and whatever time I could find. I gave off that air that I didn't care, and then they'd think I was so smart because I did not take books home. I was the epitome of insecurity."

The first person on either side of his family to finish high school, Parker won a football scholarship to little East Central Oklahoma State in Ada and went off to college in 1958. At East Central, Parker worked as a drive-in movie projectionist and delivered the Ada newspaper. He also met Latsy Ann Gooch, a cheerleader and the daughter of a pool-hall operator.

Parker graduated in 1963 with honors in history. Married to Latsy and with a baby to support, he took a teaching job in Amarillo, Texas. He also coached a seventh-grade football team. It won most of its games. During his four years in Texas, Parker spent summers trying to sell encyclopedias door to door and pumping gas on Route 66.

Still searching for his niche, Parker won a federal grant for post-graduate study at the University of Kansas. He earned a master's degree in American history with an emphasis on the Jacksonian Era of the 1830s.

Andrew Jackson long has fascinated Parker. "He's one of the toughest people who ever lived," the coach says of Old Hickory. "He personifies the American Myth, that any commoner can make it to the top. I believe it's still possible to rise above. But the point is, myths are what keep any society afloat."

Parker suspected that his master's degree would lead to a doctorate and a job as a college professor. But in 1968, with football "in my blood," Parker got a job offer from Phoenix Union High School to be a teacher and assistant football coach.

A year later, Camelback High hired him as head coach. Parker took a team that had finished 1-9 the year before and went to the state playoffs.

"We had a bunch of young, hardheaded cowboys," he recalls. "If they weren't that way, I would have been fired because I was so tough on them. I got a reputation about being an SOB to play for. I was, and am."

Camelback won the state title in 1974. After another season, Mountain View hired Parker. "We needed people who could get us off the dime," says Mountain View principal James Curlett. "We had to show some tangible successes and do some things to show people we were going to be successful. His aggressiveness fit our needs."

That aggressiveness troubled some. A retired football referee told Mesa school board members that Parker would embarrass them with his volatile sideline behavior. They hired him anyway, and the new coach ruffled feathers when he announced his team would practice on Saturdays. "I was asked what was wrong with doing things the way they'd always been done around Mesa," Parker says. "I told them that a Mesa team hadn't won the state championship since 1964, and that's how I judge success."

Cross-town rival Jerry Loper, whose Westwood High teams have split 12 games with Mountain View, says, "He hates to lose and he is always prepared, and that's why he was successful from day one. His kids don't loaf, and you can't throw a formation at him that he can't cope with. From the start, he got into controversies by insulting people. He can do that very, very easily. But he's never insulted us. Maybe that's because we're competitive with him, and that's his type of language."

Just because Parker is an ugly loser doesn't mean he's a sore loser. His answer to a loss is to work his players harder.

"I don't go beat them up every time we lose," he says, "but one night when we got back from Flagstaff, I was so mad at our effort I could have killed one or two of them without much remorse. I made them run up and down the field, I don't know how many times. If we play without that kind of intensity that I think you should be committed to, then they're going to catch hell. The tradition, the expectation at Mountain View that they're going to catch hell is very real."

Mountain View finished a surprising 4-3-1 its first year and was undefeated in 1977. Most pundits predicted, however, that in 1978 the Toros would have trouble with their first big-league schedule. The team went 13-1 and won the state championship.

"We kicked butt and nobody could believe it," Parker says. "The new boys on the block weren't supposed to do something like that." That team typically wore down its opponents with an indefatigable defense and a relentless group of running backs. "He used to be a pile of dust and an old Oklahoma boxcar comin' at you," recalls Parker's former assistant, Joe Pico. "He always was defense-oriented, and I took the offense. I don't buy the line that says Mountain View has better athletes. They don't. Jesse is just a master at molding the material he has into winners."

But in 1981, Mountain View fumbled. During spring practice—a two-week period before the school year ends—someone attending a baseball game at Mountain View saw Toro football players practicing with tackling dummies. That's a no-no in the spring.

The Arizona Interscholastic Association (AIA), which governs high school sports, punished Mountain View harshly, barring it from the 1981 state playoffs. Principal Curlett says he was flabbergasted. "We acknowledged that it was a technical violation and we expected a warning," Curlett says. "They nailed us to the wall. Anytime you're highly successful, people want to subscribe reasons why you win. We're the bad guys."

Parker admits his players were leaping over stationary dummies during agility drills, which is against the rules. But, he adds with venom, "I'll never forgive those idiots for taking the season away from those kids. It was so petty. If we had been so concerned about training in top secret, we sure wouldn't have been near a baseball field doing it in public."

Mountain View lost its first game in 1981, then rolled to nine wins in a row. Two years later, the school won its second state football title, but not without controversy. In the semifinal game against Sierra Vista Buena, Parker called time-out with less than a minute remaining to give his kicker a chance to add three points. The Toros led 33-0 at the time. The Buena coach and southern Arizona sportswriters blasted Parker after the game.

"I wanted him to kick under pressure because we had the final coming up the following week," Parker shrugs. "I did what I thought was best for the team, for my team."

Then, after the title game, someone told Parker an AIA official wanted him for a victory presentation. "I told him to go to hell or something like that," he recalls. "I want to have as little as possible to do with them."

The Toros won their third state title in 1986 and had a shot at a fourth last season. But intracity rival Dobson High beat them in the state final, 35-14.

Each year, Parker takes his defeats harder. When he first became a head coach, his wife says, he left most of his emotions at the stadium. "By the time Jesse came out of his office after the game," she says, "he was OK. We'd always go to someone's house for a while and relax. He wouldn't be happy, of course, but there never was any depression or down periods.

"Now, he puts so much pressure on himself. He's not on a pity party. He just searches and searches his own mind for what he did and didn't do."

These days, in his 13th year at Mountain View, Parker is restless. He says he wanted to accept a coaching offer last summer from a high school in Queen City, Texas, a town of about 1,750 near Louisiana and Arkansas. But his wife talked him out of it.

"This is a touchy subject," he says. "It was a small school, about 500 kids, but I was ready to go. My wife said it wouldn't be right for me. I've had a strong desire to go to Texas—it's almost a mythological place for football. But I also realize this school's been good to me. For a person who always demands that his kids be goal-setters, my goals are surprisingly close range. When one season ends, I just start thinking about next year."

After Parker gets home each year from Mountain View's post-season football banquet, the season's end hits him hard. "I have such a tremendous letdown that I get depressed for weeks on end," he says. "I don't know what to do with myself without football. I live for the season. I thoroughly enjoy the intensity of the game itself and the preparation. That's why I want it to go on and on and on."

The Face Off

by Brian Peterson of the Minneapolis Star Tribune. This faceless Minnesota Viking is Paul Coffman, who unwittingly created this photographic illusion by laying back his head and positioning his helmet on his chest. Copyright © 1988, the Star Tribune.

Coming Down

by Richard T. Conway of the Cleveland Plain Dealer. Cleveland running back Kevin Mack finds himself in the unenviable position of having to make a crash landing after being upended by the Cincinnati line during a 1988 National Football League game. Copyright © 1988, The Plain Dealer.

Soviet Beat Thompson Off Basketball Court, Too

OLYMPICS

By *BARRY LORGE*

From the San Diego Union
Copyright © 1988, the San Diego Union

Alexander Gomelsky, the brains behind the Soviet men's basketball team, not only outcoached American comrade John Thompson in the Olympic Games, he also gave him lessons in good will, media relations and international diplomacy.

Gomelsky outscored his rival from Georgetown University in interviews as surely as his experienced, disciplined team stunned the more physically gifted Americans in the semifinals at Chamshil Gymnasium.

In an upset that shifted the balance of power in basketball, the Soviet Union won the first Olympic summit since the controversial 1972 gold-medal game in Munich, 82-76. In the postgame coaches' forum, the charming, silver-haired Gomelsky was a bigger winner. He speaks fractured, fragmented English with a Russian accent. The testy Thompson speaks fluent English with a Soviet mentality.

Talk about reversal of roles and stereotypes! Gomelsky is *glasnost* personified—open and approachable, his comments liberally laden with wit, wisdom, insight and Western notions. He belongs in the National Basketball Association.

It is NBA alumnus Thompson—6 feet, 10 inches of intimidating glare—who is authoritarian, secretive, suspicious and confrontational. Khrushchev would love him. He closes practices, isolates and gags his players, thinks the press ought to all be like Tass and generally acts as if his idea of Utopia would be preparing his program behind the Kremlin walls.

With a vastly deeper talent pool from which to select, Thompson came to the Olympics with a defense-oriented team flawed for the occasion. He brought only one outside shooter—Hersey Hawkins, who got hurt—to exploit the three-point arc, which in international basketball is barely more than 20 feet from the hoop. The Soviets got a big lead by hitting seven three-pointers, and the Americans had no bomber to retaliate.

Psyched and strategically superior, the Soviets systematically defused Thompson's vaunted press and won on merit. Could this really be the same Soviet squad that looked so bad in losing the first game of the preliminary round to Yugoslavia, which will also be the opponent in the gold-medal game?

"For competition like this, I like win last game, not first game," Gomelsky said. "You see every game, my boys better and better and better. This is my tactic."

The United States, by contrast, came up flat for the medal round and suffered only its second defeat in 87 games since basketball became an Olympic sport. The previous loss was the infamous international incident of '72, when the Soviets won at the buzzer, 51-50, after the final three seconds were replayed. For the first time, the Americans will not be in the final; they were to play Australia for the bronze medal while San Diego slept last night.

The U.S. loss was celebrated by many folks Thompson had alienated by going global with the Georgetown phenomenon known as "Hoya Paranoia."

He had criticized the NBA as unpatriotic for playing pre-Olympic series with the Soviets. He chastised the Portland Trail Blazers for helping 7-2 Arvidas Sabonis—one of several Soviets who likely will play in the NBA soon—to rehabilitate an injured Achilles tendon.

Gomelsky countered by explaining the spirit of cooperation.

"Is my opinion that Mr. Thompson is great coach, but he is not foreign minister," he said. "Today United States and Soviet Union have good contact in politic, in economic, in sport. All people, all countries are very happy for this friendship because world can sleep at night, no problem. Maybe Coach Thompson not understand this position."

While Thompson maintained his Cold War attitudes, Gomelsky extolled the benefits of cultural exchanges on the hardwood.

"United States is a great team," he said. "Good individual players. Strong boys, very quick, very jumping. But every year my boys have nice competition against college basketball teams—minimum 12, 15 games in United States.

"I know Coach Thompson no like it when my boys play Milwaukee Bucks and Atlanta Hawks . . . This is not only friendship, United States and Russia, this is good preparation for my basketball. After Atlanta Hawks visit 1½ months ago, Soviet Union has very basketball boom. Basketball today is number second sport, after soccer football. This make me very happy, and I thank you.

"This I like," Gomelsky said. "The United States, this is fantastic basketball. Many coaches, many players, no problem to make a national team. In Soviet Union, many people play basketball, but start at age 14, 15 years. In United States, children before dribble and shoot; after, learn talking. This is big difference. For 20 years, United States have serious forum. Understand?"

Perfectly.

Gomelsky wants Soviet stars to play in the NBA—"this is good contact"—and supports proposals before the International Basketball Federation (FIBA) to open international competition, including the Olympics, to NBA pros—even though he knows this would again make the United States a prohibitive favorite for the forseeable future.

That is Comrade Gomelsky's capital idea: Basketball lovers of the world, unite; you have nothing to lose but your gold medals.

Building a Better Horse

HORSE RACING

By *DAVID LEVINE* and *JOHN ROLFE*

From Sport Magazine
Copyright © 1988, David Levine

He rises with the sun, his warm breath steaming in the cold mountain air. Both the athlete and the sun awaken to find the beautiful hills of central California's Santa Ynez range glazed with a light February frost. The sun will make short work of that; as it does, he will be hard at work of his own.

His coaches, clutching cups of coffee to warm themselves, lead him to the examination room. A thermograph of his leg is taken to see how it has been recovering from slight injury. The results are good; no heat is evident, indicating that his sore tendons are recovered and ready to go. Some treadmill work follows; a heart pad is strapped around his formidable chest to monitor his conditioning. After his workout on the treadmill, blood is drawn to check his lactic acid level, another indication of how well his training has progressed. If he were not in good shape he would head for the pool, where an underwater treadmill would give him a more strenuous workout without putting excessive pressure on his tendons. But he tests out well; a little rest with some ice for his legs (or maybe some electromagnetic-stimulation boots to further relieve the soreness) and by tomorrow he'll be ready for a full hard workout.

The athlete's name is Ron Bon. He is three years old. He is a horse.

As of this cold sunny February day, there are 49,658 registered three-year-old thoroughbred horses in this country. All of them, including Ron Bon, are technically eligible to compete in the upcoming Triple Crown races. Most of them, like Ron Bon, won't make it.

Ron Bon, then, is typical of his breed. As a horse he is the product of millions of years of heredity and thousands of years of domestication by humans. As a thoroughbred horse he represents about 300 years of further refinement, having been selectively bred for one thing only: speed.

At full run for a distance of from six furlongs (three-fourths of a mile) to a mile and a half, the thoroughbred is the fastest horse on earth, and as such he is the foundation for a multi*billion* dollar international industry of owners, riders, breeders, trainers and—we shouldn't forget—fans who lose the rent money on some plug who looked like a sure thing.

But a funny thing has happened on the way to the finish line recently. Although thoroughbred racing is, as it claims, dedicated "to the improvement of the breed," it seems that the breed isn't improving at all. Unlike humans, who continually set new records in speed, whether running, swimming, skating or dogsled racing, the thoroughbred isn't getting any better at the one thing he is required to do—run fast. Look at the numbers: The record for seven furlongs at Aqueduct was set in 1968; the world record for a mile was also set that year. Perhaps it is more revealing to look at one race, the Kentucky Derby. Times came down regularly—and quickly—from the late 1890s (average winning times were around 2:10) until about the 1940s (times averaged under 2:04). Since then they've leveled off dramatically: Whirlaway's 1941 winning time—a then-record 2:01-2/5—has been topped only six times since, and only twice in the last 14 years. Eight of the last nine winning times were 2:02 or higher. The record time in that race has similarly stagnated. Except for the Gretzky-like 1:59-2/5 performance of Secretariat (a true superhorse, almost freakish in ability) in 1973, Northern Dancer's 1964 record of 2:00 would still be standing.

But don't write off the thoroughbred just yet. While the breed probably can't get any faster through genetic improvements, and you can't reason with a horse to get him to run like the wind ("Just win this race, Swifty, and you'll have a long life of eating and making hay; lose, and it's off to the dog food factory"), a small and disparate band of researchers, trainers and owners, unconnected by anything save a shared desire to serve the horse better, is finding that the breed can be improved if it can be treated more ... well, like humans. Like human athletes, that is.

Ron Bon, then, is also atypical. Here in California, he is being raised and trained under the aegis of the Westerly Training Center with the help of the newest equipment and most radical ideas in the racing business, a stodgy, old-boy industry rooted in the "if it was good enough for my daddy and his daddy, then it's good enough for me" way of thinking. Even if Ron Bon isn't good enough to win a Kentucky Derby, he can still be trained as a athlete, taking advantage of the explosive improvement in equipment and information during the past five years or so. By employing some of the same training principles humans use, trainers can reduce the odds that he'll end up lame and uncompetitive, and increase the chances of his giving his best performance. Maybe even help him set new records.

So meet Ron Bon, Thoroughbred. Where the past meets the future.

★   ★   ★

The domestication of the horse just might be—after the discovery of fire and the invention of the wheel—the most important advance in human history. Horses have been ridden, eaten, sacrificed, mythologized and worshipped since prehistory. Was Pegasus a winged cow? Were unicorns horned sheep? Did Revelations rain down the Four Pigmen of the Apocalypse? Would Richard III trade his kingdom for a cat? Of course not; they were horses all. Men and horses, then, go way back.

Horses go way back farther. About 55 million years back, in fact, to a small, 12-inch-tall beast with four toes on its front feet and three on its hind feet. This creature was so unhorselike that when it was discovered it was given the name *Hyracotherium,* which is from the Greek word for hog. More doglike than hoglike, it is also known as *Eohippus,* the dawn horse.

Over the next few million years—from *Eohippus* up to *Equus caballus,* the modern horse—the fourth front toe disappeared. The middle toe became more prominent, developed the beginnings of a hoof and took over. Eventually the two side toes stopped even reaching the ground. Today these side toes have been reduced to splint bones, vestigial remnants on either side of the cannon, or shin bone, so that, in essence, the horse is running on one finger.

Well, not quite. Running on one finger is a bit simplistic. The horse leg is a complex thing, differing from, say, human legs in a number of ways. For one, the horse's knee is more comparable to our wrist; there are seven joints in the foreleg alone, which are all developed from the middle finger. In the back legs the knee joint or hock is more like our ankle; below that, again, is the middle finger variation.

Further, the horse has no muscles below the knee; the lower leg is controlled by a complex system of bones, tendons and ligaments. These tendons are long and strong (much longer than the Achilles tendon, the longest human tendon) and are the extension arms of the horse's musculature. A horse's speed comes from the huge muscles of its upper leg, back, chest and haunches; this energy is in effect transferred to and stored in the tendons and ligaments of the lower leg, which act something like a set of springs, planting and recoiling against the turf.

What all this means is that the horse's legs—particularly the forelegs, which carry about 60 percent of the horse's weight—are paradoxically strong and delicate mechanisms, quite susceptible to injury. A thoroughbred is designed by nature to run comfortably at about 25 miles per hour, but in a race that speed is pushed to 40 mph or more. The resulting stresses are often more than those brittle legs can bear. "What is limiting the horse," says Dr. George W. Pratt Jr., a professor of electrical engineering and computer sciences at MIT who studies horse biomechanics, "is his ability to keep his wheels on while going full out."

"A racehorse is an athlete putting out maximum effort," adds Dr. Dennis M. Meagher, chief of equine surgery at the University of California at Davis. "When competitive individuals take themselves to the maximum, something may give. Similar to knee injuries in football players, you see leg injuries in horses." In fact, in much the same way that most football players have some degree of knee damage, the majority of racehorses suffer some lameness. Considering that at full gallop a horse's leg is bearing a peak force of nearly twice its body weight—perhaps a ton or more—across relatively small and compact structures, occasional lameness is not surprising.

Nevertheless, running was built into the prehistorical horse. As one of the hunted in the food chain, it had to escape predators. Its defense was speed. Long before men intervened in the selection process, Nature was on the job.

       ★   ★   ★

The first recorded mounted horse race occurred at the 33rd Olympiad in 624 BC. But the creation of the breed thoroughbred was astonishingly recent.

Modern racing began in Great Britain—and specifically around Newmarket, England, which is still the center of British racing—around the 16th century, when royalty took to amusing itself by racing such local breeds as Galloways and Hobbies. By the first half of the 17th century this stock had been diluted, and King Charles II, along with his "Master of the Royal Stud" James D'Arcy, attempted to create a new breed, in effect to build a better racehorse. They knew exactly where to go: Arabia.

The Arab is the oldest domesticated breed of horse, going back to about 2000 BC. Horses have long been crucial in Arabian life; no less than Allah himself, it was believed, created the horse out of a handful of the south wind, saying: "Thy name shall be Arabian, and virtue bound into the hair of thy forelock and plunder on thy back. I have preferred thee above all beasts, in that I have made thy master thy friend. I have given thee the power of flight without wings. I will set men on thy back, that shall honor and praise me, and sing hallelujah to my name."

How's *that* for pressure? And, indeed, if the thoroughbred is the Maserati of horses, the Arab is the Rolls Royce. "The build of the Arab is perfect," wrote one horseman. "All the muscles and limbs of progression are better placed and longer in him than in any other horse. Nature, when she made the Arab, made no mistake." Bred by the Bedouins for strength, beauty and stamina (they have been resonantly called Drinkers of the Wind), with a fine silky mane, a broad chest, strong limbs and clean, well-defined tendons and muscles, the Arab is still crossbred to develop and upgrade other breeds of horses today.

From 1660 to the mid-1700s about 200 horses from the Middle

East were imported to Britain and mated with the best of the racing mares; about half were Arabians, the rest closely related breeds like Turks and Barbs. Among these imports were three studs who stand alone in thoroughbred history: As defined and prescribed by the keepers of the sport, all thoroughbreds must be descended through their sire side from one of those three original founders. (The foundation mares, sadly and sexistly, are mostly anonymous, except for one Arabian mare whose unfortunate name lives on: Old Bald Peg.)

The first of the three sires was the Byerly Turk, a stallion captured in battle in 1686. The Godolphin Barb came to Britain around 1730. These two horses founded significant lines of descent—the Herod line out of the Byerly, and the Matchem line out of the Godolphin—but perhaps the most famous of the three was the Darley Arabian, certified as "of the most esteemed race among the Arabs," who was imported in 1709. Our own Ron Bon traces his ancestry back, 25 generations on his father's side, to the Darley.

This breeding history has everything to do with what the thoroughbred is and can be. This is a closely bred animal coming from a relatively small stock in a very short time (the term thoroughbred wasn't used until 1821). It's quite common to find a single ancestor appear several times in a horse's family tree as close as four generations back. In Ron Bon, for instance, the sire Pharos is both his father's and his mother's great-great-great-grandfather. Old Bald Peg's distinguished name can appear thousands of times in the pedigree of a modern horse. Most breeders and geneticists feel that this isn't close enough to constitute excessive inbreeding, and indeed you don't see thoroughbred equivalents of the banjo-playing kid in *Deliverance*. Still, as Dr. Douglas J. Futuyma, professor of ecology and evolution at the State University of New York at Stony Brook, says, such inbreeding is a "real prescription for deleterious effects. And starting with such a small number of horses can lock in a genetic code that is difficult to break out of. It's similar to certain dog breeds with congenital hip problems." While the thoroughbred has retained the Arabian's speed and beauty, he has perhaps lost that breed's inherent soundness.

The first great modern racehorse was the Darley's son Flying Childers, "the fleetest horse that ever ran at Newmarket or . . . was ever bred in the world." But his brother, Bartlet's Childers, was even more important; his great-grandson, and Ron Bon's 18th great grandfather, was Eclipse.

Foaled during a solar eclipse in 1764, this great champion was never beaten as an athlete and never matched as a sire. A full 90 percent of all thoroughbreds can trace their roots to him. More than simply being the most famous and beloved horse ever, he is also the link between the early great days of racing and today.

Eclipse ran his first race at the age of five, in competitions that were at greater distances than today—four and five miles—and often run in heats. He was more in tune with the Arabian heritage of stamina and strength. In 1797 it was recorded that only eight percent of racing horses were two years old, while 44 percent were five or older. But the kings who controlled the sport of kings quickly decided they preferred speed and precociousness to stamina and maturity; they bred the swift, rather than the strong, and within two generations racehorses were longer in stride and shorter in tooth. Eclipse's grandchildren were running as two- and three-year-olds, and by 1860, 35 percent of racers were two, while only 16 percent were five and up. Those figures pretty much hold today.

Thus, within Eclipse's lifetime, the foundations for all of the thoroughbred's strengths and weaknesses were in place. And while thoroughbreds themselves were fruitful and multiplied, while Eclipse begat Pot-8-O's who begat Waxy, and on to Polymelus who begat Phalaris, and on to Hail To Reason who begat Halo who begat Ron Bon, the gods of racing were painfully slow in improving either the breed or the way it was handled.

★   ★   ★

In July of 1986, Dick Sturgis, an expatriate Arkansan with money from his commercial real estate business and 30 years in the horse trade, put up about $4.5 million to buy the 160-acre Westerly Stud, and another $4 million to renovate the existing facilities and buy the newfangled equipment to make Westerly state-of-the-art. He spent $80,000 for the treadmill, $40,000 for the thermography unit, he-can't-remember-how-much for the blood analyzer. He did it because his trainer, John Fulton, made a commitment to relocate his 55 horses here, away from the racetrack, and to use the new equipment on the horses he trained. Eventually more trainers will move their businesses here and rent space from Sturgis, and there will be 240 horses training at Westerly, and it'll make money. Because the results should prove that it can make a difference.

"What I wanted to do for a number of years," Sturgis says in his office at Westerly, "is take the technology and science that was coming out of the various veterinary colleges and actually apply it to good racehorses.

"I *knew* there were mistakes we were making in the training of our horses that were keeping us from getting them in races as long as they should be there. We were just losing too many horses to injury, unnecessarily. I believed it had to do with the accepted methods of training that we've been doing for 100 years."

Racing observers estimate that only 30 percent of all thoroughbreds born in North America ever make it to the track. Those that do must then overcome the added demands that have been placed on them in the last decade or so: increased year-round racing on tracks that are apt to freeze solid and an increase in purse money that entices trainers to keep horses in competition.

Proponents of training centers confidently predict they will be the wave of the future. Horses now do the bulk of their training at racetracks, where workout schedules are restricted to the hours before 10:00 a.m., to clear the track for the day's races. Off-track centers afford the trainer the luxury of scheduling afternoon workouts and a choice of different courses and terrains on which to train. They van their horses to races and bring them home afterward.

The concept of training centers is not new; in Europe, where all racing is on grass, horses must train off-track to preserve the racing surfaces. What is novel about the handful of U.S. off-track facilities —like Westerly, Fair Hill in Maryland, a very few others—is the technology and training methods. The thoroughly modern thoroughbred can train at the equine equivalent of a health spa; all that's missing are Jazzercize classes.

Take Ron Bon, for instance. Sturgis happens to own Ron Bon; he bought him as a yearling. John Fulton put the colt through his basic training when, one morning, the thermograph showed some heat in the tendons of both front legs. Fulton stopped his training for a while, then ran him with support bandages on his legs. They did some gait analysis—photographing and studying the patterns of leg movement in the horse's various gaits—on the treadmill and noticed that the bandages kept his legs from dropping, adding support and relieving stress on the tendons. Since then, they've seen no more heat.

"In the past I wouldn't have seen anything," Fulton says of the injury. The common practice among trainers is to feel a horse's legs for heat, a diagnostic tool as scientific as your mother feeling your forehead. "The thermograph is sensitive to one-half degree centigrade," Fulton explains. "No trainer could feel that with his hands. We found the problem and corrected it before it was too late. If we hadn't, in his next run or his next, he would have bowed a tendon and possibly ended his career."

An ordinary horse might not be broken—that is, trained to be ridden—until the age of four or more. Thoroughbreds, however, must not only carry men but race with them at the too-early age of two. As we've seen, a horse's legs are delicate structures, and at two they really aren't ready for this kind of stuff. It's like teaching 12-year-olds to throw a curveball: They can do it, but the chances of permanent injury are great. The most common injuries to a young horse are bowed tendons (like sprained tendons in humans) and bucked shins (similar to shin splints or stress fractures, this condition is unique to young thoroughbreds and a direct result of immature bones pounding on hard turf). They can end a promising colt's career before it ever gets started.

The folks at Westerly don't plan to race their horses at two. Rather, their training program is designed to ready the young horses for long careers at the track. As yearlings they are walked on the treadmill and allowed to trot for a mile or so every other day. They are broken at the age of one and a half, then put back on the treadmill, which can run at varying speeds and be raised to an angle for further conditioning. They will also work on the aqua-tred, the underwater treadmill Fulton uses at nearby Flag Is Up Farms that can lessen the weight on the horse's legs by 40 percent while giving him an exhausting aerobic workout. Through the age of two he can work on the track; by then he should have worked through the most dangerous time of his development. "So far," says Fulton, "on our program, we've had no bucked shins."

More than preventing injuries, the new equipment can help trainers and owners find out early just how good a horse might be, whether his potential is as a sprinter or a distance horse, or indeed whether he might be better suited to pulling a milk wagon. "One of our yearlings looked great, had great conformation (body build), he was my favorite," laughs Dr. Kjersten Harvey-Fulton, Westerly's head vet (and John Fulton's new wife). "But he turned out to be a dog. No aerobic ability at all." With that kind of information, says John Fulton, "you know if you should spend $40,000 to train him or just dump him off."

Opinions on the effectiveness of all this gadgetry are sharply divided. Most of this innovation is coming from the younger trainers—John Fulton is 39—and some progressive veterans like Jack Van Berg, Alysheba's trainer, who is planning to build several centers around the country incorporating some of the new training equipment. Racing's old boys—such as Woody Stephens and Charlie Whittingham—are more skeptical. "I'm waiting for more research," says Whittingham. "I'll go along with what looks good, but I'm not going to make a great change. I've done things pretty much the same for 50 years and I've done well." Or, as one trainer scoffs, "No heart monitor is going to make a horse go any faster."

Dr. John Fisher, a veterinarian and trainer for 20 years, has trained horses at the Fair Hill Training Center in Elkton, Maryland; he says his feelings are mixed. "The big challenge with all this new stuff is being able to implement it," he says. "You might buy it if you could be convinced it would do the job, but right now there's no proof these things work. It's great to theorize, but the bottom line is you have to win races."

"A lot of people think it's voodoo," Sturgis says. "The horse business is very traditional. But I visited the Olympic Training Center in Colorado Springs years ago and said this is what we need to do. We need to do motion analysis, heart-rate monitoring, the things that tell us what direction the athlete is moving in and why. We took the Olympic Training Center, moved it to California and made it a horse training center."

Although the object isn't to make a faster horse—you can't teach a horse to lengthen his stride or change his running form—it is to make more horses run at their full potential more often, so the result might be a faster horse. If some budding Secretariat who might previously have been felled by injury can survive the heavy attrition rate and make it to the Derby healthy and in peak condition he might be able to set new records. "Even a one percent improvement," says John Fulton, "can mean a few lengths in a race."

It's too early to tell just how well it's working. It's even too early to tell just *what* is working. "Vets don't get taught sports medicine, there's no curriculum," says Dr. Harvey-Fulton. "The equine sports medicine conference recently had only its second meeting. Basically, we're stealing from human sports medicine and kind of feeling our way along." But the players at Westerly can feel that it *is* working. "I can't say with numbers that it's working," says John Fulton, "but I can see the difference in the horses."

"John has one colt, Torres Vedras, by Conquistador Cielo," Sturgis says. "Sheik Mohammad bought him for $1.1 million. The horse got so screwed up with all the racetrack confusion he wouldn't leave his barn. Real head case. They sent him up here, John took his time with him, worked him on the treadmill. He got so happy he acted like a puppy dog—he'd come up to you looking to get his ears scratched. He lost his first outing by a head, won his second impressively. That's what you can do here that you can't do at Santa Anita. Horses just blossom here. And a happy horse is a productive horse."

Over at Fair Hill, Dr. Fisher says, "I know that since I've been here, my horses have made more starts, suffered less injury and the average earnings per start is up. But as yet, there is very little hard data available on these things." This spring, Fisher is conducting an experiment with the aid of Dr. David Nunamaker, a veterinarian at the University of Pennsylvania's New Bolton Center, a prestigious equine research facility, on preventing bucked shins.

"Bucked shins are related to bone shape changes," explains Dr. Nunamaker. "Horses model and remodel their bones according to their training regimen. When strain is high it will change the outside layer of the bone. We found that running horses at high speed over shorter distances accelerated these bone changes. We produced (the strength of) four-year-old bones in two-and-a-half-year-old horses. We now want to see how the various track surfaces affect this process." Racing's innovators hope that as more research is conducted, more unconventional training methods will be accepted by the old guard.

Since he's footing the bill at Westerly, Sturgis gets the last word. "I can see the enthusiasm in the staff. Our horses are staying in the program, we're not dropping casualties along the way.

"It's fun to be on the cutting edge," he concludes, and then adds with the sense of a man footing the bill, "especially when the theory is, in practice, working."

In movement the thoroughbred is long, free, easy and fast at all paces, near perfect in conformation, balance and symmetry of proportion. He is the aristocrat of the equine."

So wrote the authors of *The Complete Book of the Horse.* Our friend Ron Bon represents the common aristocracy, but he has a cousin (of course, all thoroughbreds are cousins, but we have one particular cousin in mind) of whom it was said, "This is probably the best horse there has ever been. He's what everyone has been trying to breed for the past 100 years." You can probably guess his name: Secretariat.

In Secretariat, the breed created an individual of uncommon spirit, competitiveness and talent. On top of the breed's extraordinary capacity for work—an athletic horse's heart rate can increase tenfold in a hard run, from about 24 to 250 beats per minute—it gave up an individual with an unheard-of stride length of 31 feet, where normal is about 24 feet. It yielded a horse who withstood the rigors of training and racing to set standards that may not ever be matched. As Brian Singleton, director of the Equine Research Center in Newmarket, England, said elsewhere, "You put Secretariat into a biomechanical model on a computer and smoke comes out of the back of the machine. It's just . . . he shouldn't be."

But there's a phrase in this business: A good horse is like a loaded shotgun; any damn fool can pull the trigger. It's the unloaded shotguns—the Ron Bons—who stand to gain most from the new age of thoroughbred training. As pushed by places like Westerly, the breed looks to be improving once again.

Don King's Tight Grip

BOXING

By *GLEN MACNOW*

From the Philadelphia Inquirer
Copyright © 1988, the Philadelphia Inquirer

Boxing strongman Don King portrays himself as a black Horatio Alger. He loves to tell the triumphant tale of how a former Cleveland numbers runner, after spending four years in prison for manslaughter, rose to dominate the cutthroat business of prizefighting.

Don King is today a multimillionaire. He has tasted the food at White House state dinners, been honored by groups such as the NAACP and the B'nai B'rith and beaten the government in a $1 million tax-evasion case.

"I transcend earthly bounds," King recently said in an interview with Playboy magazine. "I never cease to amaze myself, because I haven't yet found my limits. I am quite ready to accept the limits of what I can do, but every time I feel that way—boom!—God touches me and I do something that's even more stupendous than whatever I've done up to then."

The men who fight for him and the promoters and managers who deal with him see Don King as something less than a hallowed phenomenon.

Listen to their words:

Former heavyweight champion Larry Holmes: "Don said to me, 'Why give money to the white man? Don't you want to help your brother?' Well, I wanted to help my brother. But it turned out he (cheated) me. . . . Don King doesn't care about black or white. He just cares about green."

Rival promoter Cedric Kushner: "I used to have two pit bulls. They were too mean, so I had to get rid of them. The only difference between those dogs and Don King is that Don is much more vicious."

Former cruiserweight champion Alfonzo Ratliff: "He's like a spider who pulls you in with his money. . . . Before you know it, you're all caught up in the web and you're at his mercy. And this man has no mercy."

King declined requests to be interviewed for this article. He dismissed his critics in March, telling *The Inquirer*, "All of my fighters should get down on their knees and thank me for what I've done for them."

Since 1974, King has promoted more than 200 title fights, including at least 35 of the last 45 heavyweight championship bouts. Until the recent domination of Mike Tyson and Michael Spinks, he had cornered the market on heavyweights for more than a decade. Even now, as some suggest that his grip over boxing is loosening, King has promotional ties to more than 100 fighters and stands to make up to $3 million as a promoter of tomorrow's Tyson-Spinks title fight. His role in that bout? "He's just setting up the undercard," said co-promoter Butch Lewis. "It's the easiest $3 million anyone ever made."

How has King done it? How has he remained boxing's indisputable kingpin despite persistent lawsuits and government investigations, despite a trail of broken, angry boxers?

The answer lies in King's use of power and self-promotion, of finances and flamboyance. And it lies in King's talent for exploiting boxer's dreams of wealth by drafting his own business rules in a virtually unregulated sport.

Among more than 30 boxers, managers, rival promoters and law enforcement officials interviewed by *The Inquirer*, there is broad agreement that King has maintained control over boxing in recent years by:

• Enticing fighters to sign exclusive promotional contracts with him by promising them quick title shots. The long-term option contracts give King total control over the fighters' careers and leave them with no bargaining power. New York's inspector general termed the contracts "nothing more than legalized extortion."

• Requiring fighters to hire his stepson Carl as their manager—a position that places Carl in the role of negotiating for their wages against his father. Many boxers say that Carl King shows no interest in their careers or finances. In addition, they say, he often takes 50 percent of their earnings. Most states set the maximum manager's fee at 33 percent.

• Mandating that fighters train at his Ohio complex and then charging them up to $1,000 a day. King deducts expenses from fighter's earnings (such as sparring, training and travel costs) that most states require be taken from the total purse.

• Persuading fighters to sign blank contracts (which he fills in later) or last-minute revisions calling for shrunken paychecks. Several fighters say that King bars them from showing the contracts to attorneys or—in some cases—even reading the contracts themselves. As a result, they say, they often receive paychecks for just a fraction of what they were promised.

• Breaking and juggling fight contracts, stealing fighters under contract to other promoters or managers and paying managers to get them to turn against their own fighters.

"Don King buys whoever he has to buy," Holmes said. "He takes a young fighter that doesn't have any money, and he puts $1,000, $1,500 or maybe even $20,000 on the table. Boy, then you do anything. Only later do you realize he bought you, he owns you, and it wasn't the right thing to do."

★   ★   ★

The FBI investigated King and other boxing promoters for several years in the early 1980s. No charges were filed. Current New York State Inspector General Joseph Spinelli, who headed that investigation, said King made boxing his dominion by knowing how to prosper from the sport's incredible chaos.

"There was no criminality," Spinelli said, "because there are no laws that govern this industry. The problem is that there is no regulatory body setting the rules. Don King is playing by the rules—you have to look at how the boxing industry is run. Who is governing it? There are three different organizations, different rankings, three different champions, different rules, all kinds of divisions. It's just a mess, and Don King is smart enough to know how to exploit that mess."

In his recent Playboy interview, King said the perception that boxing was corrupt had helped him advance.

"Society didn't want to get in on it," he said. "They looked at boxing and decided that it was infiltrated with racketeers. So because it's unorganized, it allowed a guy like me to come in."

★   ★   ★

Philadelphia heavyweight Tim Witherspoon came to work for Don King not by choice, but because his former manager, Mark Stewart, sold Witherspoon's contract to King in 1982.

Over the following years, Witherspoon succeeded in the ring— winning a portion of the splintered world championship in 1984—but his finances lagged far behind his professional status. Although his announced purses rose—from $100,000 a fight to $250,000 to $400,000 —Witherspoon said he never received more than a small portion of what King promised him.

In July 1986, Witherspoon defended his World Boxing Association title against England's Frank Bruno. Witherspoon's purse for the fight was publicly announced at $1.7 million. He said he took home $98,000.

"I never knew what I was signing," said Witherspoon. "He wouldn't let me take my contracts to lawyers, wouldn't even let me read them myself. If I argued, King would threaten to cancel the fight or have me suspended. So, mostly I went along.

"Then he'd start deducting this and deducting that . . . and I would end up with nothing."

Witherspoon's former trainer, "Slim Jim" Robinson, backs him up. "Don said, 'Sign this or you won't fight.' Timmy never knew how much he was making."

Witherspoon lost his title in December 1986. He is now boxing club fighters for marginal purses. He is suing Don and Carl King, accusing them of restraint of trade, antitrust violations, fraud, violation of federal racketeering laws, breach of fiduciary duty, conversion and unjust enrichment.

The Kings have denied all allegations and countersued for $2 million each, accusing Witherspoon of breach of contract.

"The suit could take years," said Dennis Richard, one of Witherspoon's attorneys. "Timmy is in a long line of people suing Don and Carl King."

★   ★   ★

Don King's method of attracting boxers is simple: He promises them a quick route to the title and a quick route to riches. Those who perform well usually get their title shot. Many, however, never see the riches.

King insists that his fighters sign long-term contracts that give him tremendous control over their careers. If the fighter wins a title, the contract is extended through the entire length of his championship—with purses to be determined by King. The fighter may work for no other promoter—even one who offers a much larger payday.

"The contracts give the promoter absolute say over what a fighter will get," said Spinelli. "He can't fight if he doesn't fight for King, and there are some fights King doesn't want. If the fighter protests, he doesn't get any more fights."

Spinelli, who also investigated boxing for New York state, called King's contracts "horrible. But in the world of boxing, they're legal. In my mind they are nothing more than legalized extortion."

So why would a fighter sign such a deal?

Consider the case of James "Bonecrusher" Smith, who briefly held part of the heavyweight title until losing it last year to Tyson. Smith, an Army veteran and college graduate, entered professional boxing at the late age of 28.

Because of his age, Smith wanted a fast shot at the title. The day King offered him a chance to fight Witherspoon for the WBA championship in 1986, Smith left his manager, Alan Kornberg, and signed an exclusive contract to have Don King promote his career and Carl King manage it.

"If I didn't go with them, it was a good possibility I never would have gotten a title shot," Smith said. "King kind of controls the division. If Don wants the fight made, the fight gets made."

And if Don King doesn't want the fight made?

"Well, it doesn't get made."

Kornberg sued the Kings, saying they enticed Smith to break a contract with him. The suit was settled with Kornberg and Carl King becoming co-managers—each taking 25 percent of Smith's earnings.

Smith retired shortly after losing to Tyson. He ran unsuccessfully for county commissioner in North Carolina and is pondering a comeback.

If so, he has no qualms about going back to King. "Don was always fair to me," Smith said. "I never felt I got cheated."

In contrast, consider heavyweight Eddie Gregg, a mediocre fighter in King's stable. Gregg was 32 when he tried to break from King in 1986 to fight Gerry Cooney for $50,000—the largest purse of his life.

King sued to stop the fight, saying that Gregg had broken four exclusive contracts with him by signing with another promoter to face Cooney.

Gregg and his manager, Thomas Gallagher, testified that they had never seen the details of those contracts and that they had signed most of them before they were even filled out. Gregg said that King arranged just two fights for him the previous year, even though the contracts mandated a minimum of four.

New York State Supreme Court Justice Martin Stecher ruled against King, letting the fight go on. Stecher cited King with "all-knowing paternalism" and said that King "had no right to fill in the blanks" in the contracts. He called the pacts "unduly harsh" and "one-sided."

"Look at what it has offered Gregg by way of sustenance during the past 10 months," Stecher wrote. "A total of $12,500, a figure little above the poverty level, which presumably, Gregg must share in some proportion with his manager. . . . There is no demonstration of devotion of a single dollar or a single hour to Gregg's career."

In May 1986, Cooney scored a first-round knockout over Gregg.

Don King frequently requires fighters to sign two contracts—one with him to promote their bouts, one with Carl to manage their careers.

The practice is not unique in boxing: The father-son team of Lou and Dan Duva has worked similar arrangements, as has the brother team of Chris and Angelo Dundee. But none has dominated as the Kings have.

★   ★   ★

"Carl became my manager because Don King said the only way he would promote me was to have his son be my manager," said Ratliff, the former cruiserweight champion. "I didn't want anything to do with Carl King, but I had no choice."

King does not argue over allegations that he favors Carl's boxers. "A father wouldn't be worth his salt if he didn't help his son," he told Playboy.

One of a manager's basic roles is to negotiate with the promoter on behalf of his fighter.

"How could Carl go to his father and say I deserved more money?" asked Ratliff. "Who was he working for? Where did his loyalties lie?"

Those interviewed for this article said that the Kings' strategy was to encourage a promising boxer to break his contract with his manager.

Then, if the manager files a lawsuit, they simply offer a cash settlement or a small piece of the boxer's future earnings.

"It's a business expense for them," said rival promoter Butch Lewis.

Lewis accused King of stealing heavyweight Greg Page after, Lewis said, "I took Page from 0-0 to 22-0." Lewis said that King "gave cash to Page's friends and advisers. He gave his dad and mom money—about $25,000 to $50,000. He spread it around to the guys Page hung out with. So the people around Page kept saying what a great guy Don King is and how he should go with King."

Page could not be contacted, but he has previously said that he signed with King because he believed King could make him the most money. King told the *Washington Post* that Page's dying father, Albert Page, "signed his son to me on his deathbed."

Lewis sued King for tortious interference with contract. After a jury ruled for Lewis, he accepted a $200,000 settlement. "It was a good deal for Don," said Lewis. "He made a lot more than that on Greg Page."

Indeed, the Kings control so many careers that Don King has promoted bouts in which men scheduled to fight each other shared Carl King as their manager. The most notable was the December 1986 WBA heavyweight championship bout in which Bonecrusher Smith beat Witherspoon. Smith was a last-minute substitute for the injured Tony Tubbs.

"Timmy did not want to fight Bonecrusher, because he had already beat him," said Robinson, Witherspoon's former trainer. "When he said this to Carl, Carl—in front of me—said, 'Boy, I don't know if my father would like that. I'll have to discuss this with Dad.' A real manager doesn't discuss things with 'Dad.' A real manager looks out for his fighter."

★   ★   ★

After that Madison Square Garden bout, the New York Athletic Commission suspended Carl King's license for violating a rule requiring a manager to get commission approval if he has two fighters on the same card.

Gov. Mario Cuomo ordered Spinelli to investigate apparent irregularities in the Smith-Witherspoon fight. Spinelli wrote a report pushing for rules that would bar a manager from being related to a promoter and ban longterm option contracts in New York state.

New York, as well as New Jersey and Nevada (the nation's other preeminent boxing states), has long had a rule barring a manager from taking more than one-third of a fighter's earnings as his salary.

Carl King has regularly violated those rules, fighters say. For example, Witherspoon's "pay-off sheet" from Don King Productions Inc. for his 1984 fight against Pinklon Thomas in Las Vegas clearly shows $200,000—or half his earnings—going to Monarch Boxing, Carl King's management firm.

In a brief interview this month, Carl King said: "I've had fighters with whom I've had 50-50 deals. Wherever it's been, it's been regulated. I've followed the state rules."

Carl King ended the interview after several questions, saying: "I've gone through this song and dance before. I don't care to do it again."

Witherspoon, Ratliff, Robinson and heavyweight Mitch (Blood) Green all said that Carl King got around the state rules by making boxers sign two management contracts—one paying Carl 33 percent (which was filed with the athletic commissions) and one paying him 50 percent (which was actually enforced).

"I knew the real deal was 50-50," said Green, "but they made me sign another one paying (Carl) one-third so they could give it to the commission."

Why would Green sign the 50-50 contract if he knew it violated state regulations?

"I don't sign with that knucklehead, I don't get to fight," Green said.

Green, a 6-foot-5 former gang leader from Queens, N.Y., fought for the Kings for five years. In 1985, said his attorney Richard Emery, Green agreed to box Mike Tyson for $50,000.

"Just before the fight," Emery said, "Carl and Don King came to him and said, 'You take $30,000 or you don't fight.' There was no explanation."

Green protested the pay cut and initially refused to fight. Then, with reporters in tow, New York Athletic Commission chairman Jose Torres went to Green's dressing room and said, "If you don't fight, I'll suspend you and you'll never fight in this country again."

Given the threat, Green fought. He said his take-home pay was $7,500.

Torres said he had no evidence that Green's purse had been cut when he ordered Green to fight. "I checked the contract and it was a legal contract," Torres said. "I think when Green saw what Tyson was getting ($200,000), he felt he wasn't getting enough himself."

Green sued King after King broke up a December 1986 fight that Green had scheduled with Bonecrusher Smith. Green was so incensed at the time that he tried to physically attack King at a news conference.

His suit accuses King of tortious interference with contract. (King countersued for assault.) King tried to have the suit dismissed, but New York State Supreme Court Justice Beatrice Shainswit denied his motion last year.

Don and Carl King, Shainswit wrote in an opinion, "juggled contractual relationships when it served their economic purposes. (Green's) rights were mocked as defendants charted their respective courses."

*   *   *

The Kings pulled Smith out of the fight with Green because they needed Smith for another fight. Tubbs, who was scheduled to fight Witherspoon for the WBA heavyweight title, sustained a shoulder injury weeks before the bout.

Rather than cancel the fight, Witherspoon's suit alleges, Carl King—without Witherspoon's permission—crossed Tubbs' name off the contract and wrote in Smith's. The Kings deny the allegation.

When Witherspoon balked at fighting Smith, Torres publicly threatened to suspend Witherspoon.

"Torres chose to intervene solely on Don King's behalf," said Nicholas Clemente, one of Witherspoon's attorneys. "It is as if King said, 'Jump,' and Torres asked, 'How far?' "

Torres argued that he was never unduly influenced by King. "In Witherspoon's case, I went to see him before the fight and he refused to tell me what was the beef," Torres said. "I think it had more to do with money than who was the opponent. I would never allow Don King or any other promoter to do the things these fighters are saying."

Torres, reportedly under pressure from Gov. Cuomo, resigned last month.

*   *   *

New York Athletic Commission spokesman Marvin Kohn said that while he had heard nasty rumors about the Kings for years, their record in New York was clean.

"I'm not going to defend King," said Kohn, "but if boxers know they're being cheated, why do they sign these contracts? Why do they do it if they think it's wrong?"

Likewise, New Jersey athletic commissioner Larry Hazzard said that King's record in that state was clean. "I've heard the rumors everyone else has heard," said Hazzard, "but if the fighter doesn't formally complain, there isn't much we can do."

King, 56, has been the power in professional boxing for the last 14 years, earning, according to some estimates, at least $100 million. He lives in a $5 million home on a 190-acre compound near Cleveland (Carl lives on the estate) and also owns a four-story brownstone in Manhattan.

King's entree into boxing came through Muhammad Ali, who recruited King to promote his 1974 heavyweight title fight against George Foreman in Kinshasa, Zaire—a bout King dubbed "The Rumble in the Jungle."

King stayed with Ali to promote the spectacular "Thrilla in Manila," against Joe Frazier in 1975, which many regard as the best heavyweight title fight ever.

Since Ali's retirement, King has emerged as the sport's largest personality.

When Larry Holmes succeeded Ali as heavyweight champion in the late 1970s, the promoter became a passage to the championship—

fighters signed with King because only he could get them a shot at the belt.

Nearly every heavyweight champion and challenger since then carried King's stamp of approval. Since 1984, the jumble of titleholders that included Mike Weaver, Michael Dokes, Gerrie Coetzee, Page, Tubbs, Witherspoon, Thomas, Smith and Trevor Berbick were all under exclusive promotional contracts with King. Each won his title from, and lost it back to, another King fighter—often in the first defense.

Tyson, who was just 13 when he started boxing for Cus D'Amato (who later adopted him and who died in 1985), rose up without King's assistance. But he still has used King to promote his last five bouts.

Holmes recently sued King for more than $300,000, which he said King improperly took as a "consultant's fee" after Holmes' January fight against Tyson. He settled last week for $100,000.

Settling lawsuits has been a longtime practice for King.

"It's his way of doing business," said rival promoter Kushner. "Rather than deal in a straightforward manner, he'll do something underhanded, and then, when he's sued, settle matters for a fraction of what it would have cost him to act properly. For the person suing King, it's a matter of taking some money now, or being caught up for years in an expensive court battle."

Kushner himself sued King in 1986, contending that King had enticed Coetzee to break a contract for a title fight against Dokes. Kushner's suit asked for $750,000 in damages; he settled for $150,000.

Despite another dispute involving a fight this April, Kushner said he would continue to co-promote bouts with King.

"We are not on friendly terms," said Kushner, "but I would do business with Don in 30 seconds if the offer was good. I have to give the devil his due—he hasn't cheated me every time we've done business. And I learn from my mistakes."

One suit King has not settled was filed by former heavyweight Randall (Tex) Cobb. It may be heard this summer in the Texas District Court in El Paso.

Cobb was scheduled to receive the greater amount of $700,000 or 30 percent of all revenues to fight Holmes for the heavyweight title in November 1982. Cobb estimates the 30 percent share would have been more than $1.3 million.

One week before the fight, Cobb said, his manager, Joe Gramby of Philadelphia, told him the fight would be canceled unless Cobb agreed to take a flat $500,000. Cobb said that he received no explanation for the pay cut but that Gramby advised him to sign the new, smaller contract.

"Gramby and King told me that if I didn't do that, (King) wouldn't let me fight," Cobb said. "I'm just a dumb good old boy. I didn't care about the money as much as the championship. So I did it."

*   *   *

Cobb lost a unanimous decision to Holmes at the Houston Astrodome. Only afterward did he conclude that his own manager, Gramby, had apparently received $200,000 from King for "consultant services" on the same day Gramby persuaded Cobb to take a reduced paycheck.

A letter purportedly from King to Gramby is on file in the court. Written and signed by King, it says: "This letter will confirm our understanding that in addition to $500,000 being paid to Randy Cobb as his purse under contract dated August 25, 1982, DKP (Don King Productions) agrees to pay $200,000 to Joe Gramby for consultant services."

At the bottom of the letter, under the words *accepted & agreed* is the signature *Joe Gramby*, which closely matches Gramby's signature on an earlier contract.

Said Cobb: "Gramby screwed me; Don King paid him under the table and bought him off. . . . It would have taken a blithering idiot not to see it. I fight for a living, I'm not the president of GM, but eventually, when it's wet outside, I realize it's raining."

Cobb's suit accuses King and Gramby of fraud, tortious interference with contract and breach of fiduciary duty.

Gramby denied receiving any money from King. Asked about the letter from King, he said: "Look, this letter is unfamiliar to me. I didn't get no $200,000. I heard rumors, but it isn't true."

Gramby said that Cobb's purse was cut $200,000 because Cobb violated a contract provision requiring him to be in Houston 14 days before the fight.

And, Gramby said, he is countersuing Cobb on slander allegations for remarks Cobb made about him last year on *Late Night With David Letterman.*

In his response to the suit, King denied all accusations and said that the statute of limitations had expired.

Cobb is not the only fighter who said his paycheck was improperly cut by King.

Witherspoon said that King required him to train at King's complex outside Cleveland and charged him abnormally high fees. (Ratliff makes the same allegation.) Witherspoon said that King told him he was to pay $100 a day to train at the King facility.

A postfight expense report given to Witherspoon by Carl King for the 1986 fight with Smith was part of the New York state inspector general's investigation. One page of the report titled "Witherspoon expenses," lists "training camp" costs as "28 days @ $100," which would total $2,800.

But the report shows that $28,000 was taken from Witherspoon for training camp expenses—meaning he was charged $1,000 a day, rather than $100. He was also billed $4,000 for four days of training in Florida.

Beyond that, the training expenses (along with about $45,000 in other expenses) appear to have been improperly deducted from Witherspoon's share of the gate.

New York Athletic Commission rules require that a manager receive his share after all expenses are deducted from the gross purse. That would mean that Carl King, in this case, would get one-third of Witherspoon's $400,000 purse after the $75,000 in expenses were deducted.

Carl King, according to financial reports given to Witherspoon by Don King, took his share from the gross—not the net—proceeds. All expenses were charged to Witherspoon, as was the $30,000 payment to trainer Robinson.

Witherspoon received even less money for his 1986 title defense in London against the British champion, Bruno. Witherspoon's attorney, Dennis Richard, said that British promoter Mickey Duff (who organized the fight) and HBO (which televised it) allocated $1.7 million for Witherspoon's purse. Duff would not confirm the $1.7 million figure but said he "would not argue" with it.

King, in several postfight interviews, said Witherspoon was to receive a total purse of $550,000.

Regardless, Witherspoon said, he came home with just $98,000.

The most curious deduction in that fight was $250,000 that King took from Witherspoon to persuade Tubbs—who had a contract to fight Witherspoon—to step aside. King has confirmed paying Tubbs to step aside, but said the money did not come from Witherspoon's share.

"Don said to me, 'We got to pay this boy (Tubbs), so you can have the real payday,' " Witherspoon recalled. ". . . He said it was my responsibility."

But Duff said he, too, gave King money to buy out Tubbs' contract. "I paid an amount that presumably had Don King assume taking care of the Tony Tubbs situation," said Duff. "Witherspoon was never supposed to have paid to take care of Tubbs."

So did King take $250,000 from both Witherspoon and Duff, telling each man it was his sole responsibility to take care of Tubbs?

"Let's say what appears to be obvious must be true," said Duff, who would not elaborate.

Despite all the lawsuits, despite complaints from fighters and rival promoters, King continues to reign over boxing. Some suggest that because his relationship with Tyson and Spinks is cooler than it was with Ali and Holmes, his influence may be diminishing.

But other boxing insiders predict that King will continue to dominate the business long after the current crop of heavyweights has retired.

"Nobody should underestimate Don King," said Kushner. "Nobody should ever think he's out of the picture until you see them put him in his box. When they do that, somebody like myself would then be prepared to say, 'OK, now maybe Don won't have anything to do with this fighter.' "

As Long as Gibson Can, Dodgers Can

BASEBALL

By *THOMAS BOSWELL*

From the Washington Post
Copyright © 1988, the Washington Post

Leadership among ballplayers, as among politicians, is as important as it is indefinable. The gift expresses itself in many styles. But, once it exists, the team bends to the leader and the whole game, in turn, bends toward that team. Kirk Gibson, who is batting .182 in the National League playoffs, is such a leader, perhaps the best in baseball at this moment. What Reggie Jackson and Pete Rose, Willie Stargell and George Brett have shown us in recent Octobers, Gibson is showing now. He's what players call "Big Time." Others play the game. He means to change it.

Oct. 10, 1988 was a big-time day for Gibson and his Los Angeles Dodgers. A few minutes before 1 a.m., he hit a home run over the center-field fence to win Game 4, 5-4, in 12 grueling and amazingly convoluted innings which required four hours and 29 minutes. "About time I did something," growled Gibson, who'd been one for 16.

A few minutes after 1 p.m. on the same day, he hit another monstrous home run to provide three vital runs for L.A. in its 7-4 victory in Game 5. Now, thanks to Gibson's leadership, his example, his demands and his play, the Dodgers are one victory from taking a pennant away from a far more gifted New York Mets team which beat the Dodgers 10 times in 11 meetings this season.

In his final act Monday, Gibson beat out an infield hit in the ninth inning, then stole second base to set up the Dodgers' last insurance run. Before he got to second, he knew he'd aggravated the hamstring pull that has left him gimpy for a fortnight. As he hobbled off the field, waving for a pinch runner, the Shea Stadium crowd gave a momentary, spontaneous cheer of delight that Gibson could bedevil them no more.

Gibson saw it for what it was. "The notion of respect" came to his mind, he said. Of course, he now despises every Mets fan even more. Cheer my injury, will you. "Those are the sort of things that inspire me," he said wolfishly, vowing that he has "a burning desire" to play Game 6 in Chavez Ravine on Tuesday.

This is Gibson's leadership style: a stubble beard, a perpetual limp, a recklessness that borders on deliberate injury and a complete refusal to be embarrassed by the fact that his All-America football physique obviously is not intended for baseball. Nothing about the game looks natural to him. His speed is an explosion, often slightly misdirected, necessitating bizarre last-minute corrections. His spectacular catch in left field on Saturday was a one-man, three-ring circus—part clown, part trapeze artist, part juggler. His slides resemble safety blitzes. His stance and swing are always grim, mechanical, graceless and, when he finally connects, ferociously powerful.

Sparky Anderson did Gibson the injustice a decade ago of comparing him to Mickey Mantle—a natural ballplayer. It's taken a thousand games of sweat and hundreds of games on the disabled list, but Gibson has survived to be Gibson, a sort of laconic punk-cut road warrior. "Sometimes the Man Upstairs tortures me terribly, but then He puts me through wonderful times like these," said Gibson, the Tigers' MVP in the '84 Series. "I guess it's like fishing. You wait 36 hours for one muskie, but it's great when you get him."

On his homers, which made losers of Roger McDowell and Sid Fernandez, Gibson did an almost unique thing in sports. In a moment of joy and vindication, he showed nothing. He jogged the bases —not too fast, not too slow—as though it were spring training. Then, when he reached the dugout, he exchanged hand slaps with a trace of a smile so faint that only his teammates, looking into his eyes, could see it.

Oh, yes, the New York Mets watch Gibson. They see what he does for the Dodgers and what he is doing to them. "That team really seems to revolve around Gibson. He's not a guy to show anybody up. He's not out there to style. He's a gamer," said Wally Backman, aware that some of his Mets are stylers. "Now, all their guys are gamers. On paper, their lineup doesn't (match up) with ours. But they're busting their butts, being aggressive, making things happen. That's the way we should play."

Since Gibson arrived this spring as a free agent, the Dodgers, so often accused of being too mellow, have aped his approach. When Mike Scioscia ripped Dwight Gooden for a two-run homer with nobody out in the ninth inning of Game 4 to rob the Mets of a win and force extra innings, there was Gibson pounding Scioscia when he got to the dugout.

Even the Dodgers pitchers now act a little crazy, with no sensible big-league respect for their bodies. When L.A. ran out of pitchers in

Game 4, who started warming up but Orel Hershiser, the slim super-star with the accountant's face who had pitched seven innings the previous day. Orel, what are you doing, son?

Gibson makes everybody think it's 1908 again and the game is being played for blood and honor. Hershiser came in and got the last out, with the bases loaded, for a save.

Now, the whole Dodgers team has the gung-ho fever. Was it really just six months ago in Vero Beach that a Dodgers prankster put eyeblack inside Gibson's hat rim? Gibson tore the clubhouse up, left camp, criticized his teammates and said that wasn't how he played baseball, like it was some Sunday picnic for laughs. They could be goof-offs. But include him out.

Thanks largely to Gibson, these are different Dodgers. They even amaze Manager Tommy Lasorda. "I looked up in the eighth inning today," said Lasorda, incredulous, "and Hershiser's down in the bull-pen throwing *again.* What have I got to do, throw a lasso around him? Well, hell, he's already hot and we get in a jam, I'd have brought him in."

That's how John McGraw and Pepper Martin talked. And Kirk Gibson. Does the players association know about this?

Beneath everything, the secret of Gibson's effect on the Dodgers is a quality that he has developed only in recent years. Beneath his hard exterior, an emotional, almost sentimental interior has been appearing as his hair line recedes—especially where teammates are concerned.

"I think what happened to Jay Howell inspired some of us," said Gibson. "We don't want him to feel he let us down. We've been saying we want to take the Series back to L.A. and he's going to be the guy to nail down the last game.

"You create these crazy scenarios," added Gibson sheepishly.

To remind his teammates of how much grief Howell would take if they lost, Gibson wore the initials "JH" on his sleeve. After Gibson limped off the field in the last inning, Scioscia told him, "If you don't play tomorrow, I'm going to wear 'KG.' "

It's not hard to figure out why.

Just a case of follow the leader.

Fastest Thief

TRACK AND FIELD

By *LEE BYRD*

From the Associated Press
Copyright © 1988, the Associated Press

Three days ago, a barely literate Jamaican emigrant to Canada, once a rail-thin stripling who raced his chums for pennies, stole the Olympic wind and the fancy of a startled world. Now he has reaped the whirlwind.

Benjamin Sinclair Johnson Jr. was no lank teen-ager when he curled his steely, 5-foot-9 frame into the 100-meter blocks Saturday, pausing for one last cutting glance at his American rival three lanes away. He was the Big Ben of Canada, its post-Gretzky national hero, the Rambo of sprinting and the world's fastest human.

Then, as usual, Ben Johnson took to the starting gun like flash-paper to a match. But his stride was stronger than ever, and he streaked across the finish in 9.79 seconds, a world record, leaving Carl Lewis a step behind. Canada had its first gold medal in the Summer Games since 1968, and Johnson, a vocational school dropout, had a license to print money. Perhaps $10 million to $15 million of it over the next five years, according to his agents.

It all crashed down Tuesday. The hero of these Games had tested positive for steroid use. His gold medal was retrieved, handed back speechlessly by a son who first, shamefully, had to fetch it from his mother. It was his gift to her. Now, from a hotel where he already had registered with a counterfeit name—John Benson—the world's fastest man would leave Seoul in disgrace with a new title as well. World's Fastest Thief. The Canadian government even took away his $650 monthly stipend.

Singlehandedly, he had turned the Games of the XXIVth Olympiad into a model, not of high purpose, but of the dark side of society. Yes, other athletes have been caught, cheating their competitors and their own health by ingesting performance-enhancing drugs at risk of lifelong infirmity, even brain damage and death. But surely not this man, the standard bearer of athletic promise.

The evidence, according to the International Olympic Committee, was indisputable. Canadian officials, stunned and embarrassed beyond belief, agreed. Johnson and his personal agent offered a theory about possible sabotage, perhaps a spiked drink on race day, a refrain heard before from athletes who got caught. The medical people heard that out, looked at the charts, and said Ben Johnson had been taking illegal drugs for some time, and was not the victim of a sudden dirty trick.

There were, especially in retrospect, many signs that something was very, very wrong here. Perhaps Johnson himself was speaking volumes when he said, moments after his glorious victory, "I don't care about winning the gold medal and the world record. The main thing is I beat Carl. I care about beating Carl Lewis." At any price, it appears.

The week of the race, his coach, Charlie Francis, boasted that Johnson, 26, had bench-pressed 396 pounds, a personal high. Johnson weighs only 172. In the preliminaries, Johnson was jittery in the blocks, false starting once, and ran such mediocre heats he almost didn't qualify for the long-awaited confrontation with Lewis. Over the summer, when once he angrily left his coach for a private sabbatical in St. Kitt's, near his native Jamaica, he ran poorly, losing twice to Lewis in tuneup meets. Jamaican Olympic officials, without offering evidence, had told reporters en route to Seoul that they knew Johnson had obtained steroids.

Sports Illustrated magazine reported today that Johnson's personal physician, George M. "Jamie" Astaphan, injected the runner with steroids on St. Kitt's last May. Astaphan, who accompanied Johnson to Seoul, denied it.

There had been whispers about Ben Johnson since 1987. About his unusually muscled body, his phenomenal speed of recovery after brutal workouts, his incredible improvement from one early race to the next. Johnson, in his just-released authorized biography, denied any drug use, and attributed his swift recoveries from practice to the rubdowns of trainer Waldemar Matuszewski.

Lewis, who said Tuesday he is "deeply sorry" about Johnson's fall from grace, has himself trafficked in rumors about drug use by the Canadian, starting at Rome a year ago, when Johnson beat him in the then-world record time of 9.83 seconds.

Lewis didn't name Johnson, but made it clear whom he had in mind when he declared that "some champions in this meet" were using drugs. "I could run 9.83 if I was on drugs, too," Lewis said. The press wrote off Lewis' comments as heresy, hearsay and sour grapes. Meanwhile, the IAAF, track and field's governing body, drug-tested Johnson in Rome. He passed.

Johnson had submitted to drug testing eight times since Feb. 21,

1987, according to Paul Dupre, president and chief executive officer of the CFTA. But the last time, he said, was at the Winternational Indoor Games in Ottawa, in February 1988.

Dupre said Johnson wasn't tested at the Canadian Olympic trials in Ottawa last month because he was the odd man out in a system that tests two of the three top finishers. Johnson's number didn't come up after the national 100-meter final, even though he won.

Anabolic steroids do strange things to body and mind alike. Some athletes believe they're Popeye's spinach come true, for producing lean muscle mass, like sprinter's quads and hamstrings. Medical experts are divided over that. But they are agreed at the sorrowful side effects, including personality change. "Roid rage," they call it. An urge to destroy, if not self-destruct.

Other sprinters noticed there was something different in recent weeks about Johnson's trackside demeanor, as if he had climbed out of the wrong side of bed. When he finished third in a match against Lewis in Zurich last month, he hardly looked and acted like a man ready to run a 9.79 five weeks later.

But he did. What a glorious moment it was. And what an ungrateful pup he was, bleating over the defeated Lewis before Francis shut him up.

Back in the training room there were more signs of trouble. Johnson took nearly two hours to produce the obligatory urine sample, downing several bottles of beer in the meantime. Nothing unusual in that—many athletes have such difficulty after grueling competition—but he was more than irritable about it. There was no glow of victory about the man. "I want my Mom! I want my Mom!" he exploded. The Canadian medical team finally calmed him down.

Nearly 36 hours later, chemists working the night shift at the Doping Control Center in downtown Seoul discovered the "A" sample they were testing contained the banned steroid stanozolol. They had no idea who they had caught, since the vial bore nothing more than a number. In an instant, they reported the finding to the International Olympic Committee, which decoded the number, and, just as quickly, sent a hand-delivered letter to Canadian officials at Olympic Park. By this time Johnson and his teammates were asleep, having celebrated for a second day. After all, Canada hadn't won a gold medal in the Summer Games in 20 years, not even in 1976 at Montreal, and now it had the most prized of all. But not for long.

In colorless, bureaucratic language, the letter informed the horrified officials of the Canadian Olympic Association that Johnson's "A" sample was positive and that the still-sealed "B" sample would be opened and tested at 10 a.m. Monday. They were invited to attend, and bring anybody they chose, including Johnson, along.

At 7 a.m. Monday, chief Canadian medical officer Bill Stanish broke the dreadful news to Dave Lyon, leader of the Canadian track and field team, and Francis. They decided to keep the potential disaster to themselves, pending the outcome of the second test, which all three attended.

That test, following a thorough discussion of the circumstances surrounding the collection and analysis of the first sample, took three more hours. The "B" sample produced exactly the same results as the first.

The three men then went to the Shilla Hotel, at 1:30 p.m. Monday, where they discussed the findings with Roger Jackson, Canadian Olympic Association president, and Canada's chief of mission, Carol Anne Letheren.

Francis, who had coached Johnson for 10 years, dating to his recruitment, as a teen-ager, to an Optimists Club team, finally left for the Olympic village to tell Johnson himself. That conversation remains secret, but Francis says Johnson denied that he deliberately took steroids. The athlete offered the notion that his sarsaparilla, a syrupy Jamaican concoction, was tampered with while at the stadium, according to Francis.

The Canadian team then had exactly eight hours to prepare its defense before the IOC met to decide the case. Johnson was secretly taken to a hotel, and locked in with Stanish and Jackson to tell his side of the story.

Said Jackson: "He claimed he has never taken steroids. He claimed there were many irregularities in the drug-testing procedure, that there were unauthorized people in there, and that he could have been the victim of (a substance) in his beer, or whatever."

Testing of Johnson was also questioned by Larry Heidebrecht, Johnson's personal agent, who would remain in Seoul to repeat the spiking theory. Heidebrecht, incidentally, is the agent chiefly responsible for landing the huge endorsement and commercial contracts which awaited a more successful departure.

Johnson, having said his piece, was ordered to await the outcome at the International Hilton Hotel, where he was registered under the false name. His belongings were fetched from Olympic village. By this time, Johnson's fellow sprinters already knew something was wrong. Johnson was missing from practice for a team relay event, nothing new, but so was their coach, Francis.

At 10 p.m., the Canadian officials met with the IOC medical commission, reported Johnson's explanation, and left. After several hours' discussion and evaluation, the medical experts rejected his story, on grounds that the evidence clearly excludes the possibility that he was innocently doped the day of the race. Their recommendation was passed on to the IOC executive board.

Meanwhile, at 2:15 a.m. Tuesday, Canada's assistant deputy minister of sport, Lyle Makosky, telephoned Sports Minister Jean Charest. "Minister, I regret to tell you that I am the bearer of terrible news," Makosky said. "I've learned tonight that Ben Johnson has tested positive on his A and B sample, and the medical commission has accepted the results of the lab."

Makosky then presented the inevitable consequences: Johnson

would be stripped of his medal and expelled from the Olympics.

Charest was speechless at first. "It's a terrible thing," he finally said, "for Ben Johnson and for Canada."

Letheren was designated for the unhappy task of delivering the coup de grace to Johnson. At 3:30 a.m. she went to his hotel, where he was closeted with his mother, Gloria; his sister, Jean; Francis, and Heidebrecht.

Letheren explained the decision. Then she asked Johnson to hand her his medal. Without a word, he did so.

The deed was done. At 8:30 a.m., the IOC's executive board formally ratified the medical panel's decision. Johnson and Francis were already at Kimpo Airport, boarding a Korean Air Lines flight to New York City. The athlete, who speaks only passable English in the best of circumstances, was still incoherent. Francis, asked for a statement to the people of Canada responded: "What can I say? It's an unfortunate situation."

At 9 a.m., the IOC formally announced its decision to the world:

"The urine sample of Ben Johnson (Canada, athletics, 100 metre) collected on Saturday, Sept. 24, 1988, was found to contain the metabolites of a banned substance namely stanozolol (anabolic steroid).

"The IOC medical commission discussed all arguments presented by the Canadian delegation, especially the statement that the substance in question might have been administered after the competition by a third party.

"The steroid profile, however, is not consistent with such a claim.

"The IOC medical commission recommends the following sanction: disqualification of this competitor from the Games of the XXIVth Olympiad in Seoul.

"The decision remains independent of any sanction which the international federation concerned may wish to apply in accordance with its own regulations."

That federation promptly barred Johnson from competition for at least two years. Two years without running, his only life.

As a child, young Ben raced, barefoot, against the neighborhood kids for pennies and nickels. Sometimes the prize was a ticket to the movies. Young Ben left Jamaica at age 16, four years after his mother settled in Toronto, where she works in an airport kitchen.

Johnson was introduced to Canadian track 10 years ago, when his brother Edward, now a preacher in Texas, ran for Francis' team. He tried a mechanics course at a community college, but dropped out. He has a speech impediment, and speaks English poorly, much less the languages of countries, like Japan and Italy, which have dangled huge endorsement contracts in front of him. But he knew one thing perfectly well, postulated by another Ben long ago: "Time is money." Especially world-record time.

Ben Franklin, by the way, knew another maxim, handed down by his British ancestors. It says a fool and his gold are soon parted.

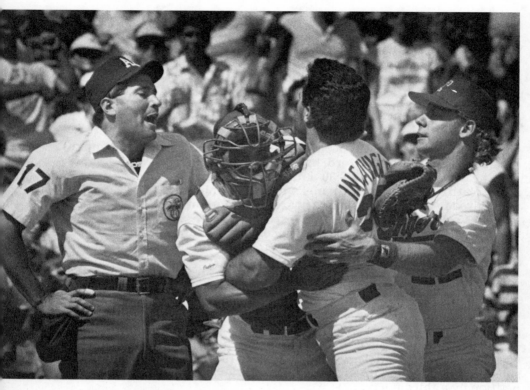

Ump Grump

by free-lancer Robert Bunch for United Press International. Texas Rangers third baseman Steve Buechele (right) and catcher Geno Petralli restrain teammate Pete Incaviglia during an argument with American League umpire John Hirschbeck. Incaviglia eventually was ejected from the game. Copyright © 1988, Robert Bunch.

Neither Rain. . .

by Ed Suba Jr. of the Akron Beacon Journal. Isao Aoki braves light rain and stormy conditions to get in a few practice putts before the start of the World Series of Golf at the Firestone Country Club in Akron. Heavier rains finally came and washed out the first day of action. Copyright © 1988, the Akron Beacon Journal.

Glory to the Gridiron

GENERAL

By *RICK REILLY*

From Sports Illustrated
Copyright © 1988, Linda R. Verigan
Director, Rights and Permissions

Let's play the $25,000 Pyramid. Here are the clues:

Watching hairlines recede ... Reading the dictionary ... Waiting for Godot ... Cross-stitching ... Alphabetizing your canned goods ... Attending a workshop somewhere on sorghum. ...

You holler: "Things More Exciting Than Watching Baseball!"

Ding, ding, ding! You win! You also get the complete audio library of Jim Palmer explaining why Sid Fernandez sometimes throws screwballs on 2-and-1 counts to hitters missing one or more fingers.

Admit it: Baseball is to thrills what beets are to taste buds. If baseball is so exciting, why is there the seventh-inning stretch? You ever heard of the third-quarter stretch in football? Forget it. Nobody gets drowsy watching football.

In this country you're not supposed to say the D word about baseball: dull. Or dumb. Or dreary. If you tell people you would rather be stripped naked, covered in tuna oil and lowered into a tank full of barracuda than watch an entire baseball game on TV, they give you the standard, "Well, you're not *sophisticated* enough to appreciate the *subtleties* of the game."

From what I can tell, "sophisticated" means you don't mind watching a game in which out of 80 at-bats—about 400 pitches—you might see five hits. "Subtleties" means you don't mind paying $12.50 to watch it in person. If baseball is so subtle and graceful, how come the guys in the bullpen never watch it? They're either trying to spit tobacco juice on each other's socks (very subtle) or figuring out how they can get Chinese food delivered.

Football is much too quick-fix for baseball fans. After all, who can find sports sophistication in a 60-yard diving-catch touchdown bomb? And it's true, there's no subtlety in a guy's getting hit so hard that the first thing he says when he comes to is, "Mom, let me sleep 10 more minutes."

Football is so terribly unsubtle that if you're at a game, you're afraid to leave your seat because you think you'll miss something. Baseball is so wonderfully sophisticated that you leave your seat in *hopes* of missing something.

How was the game, Fred?

"Terrific. Had a corn dog in the second, some Jujubees in the fifth and a twist cone in the seventh."

Yeah, but who won?

"It depends on how well you know the balk rule."

The best player in football history was Jim Brown, a granite statue of a man. The best player in baseball history was Babe Ruth, a Jell-O parfait of a man. The best arm in football is John Elway's. The best arm in baseball is John Elway's.

Football has cheerleaders. Baseball has batboys. Football has Joe Montana. Baseball has Bob Knepper. Football has instant replay. Baseball has Don Denkinger. Football has Dan Reeves nattily turned out in a $500 suit. Baseball has Don Zimmer spilling out of an ill-fitting uniform.

In football, an upset means something. The worst team beats the best team maybe one time in 25. In baseball, the worst team beats the best team two out of five times. What's to celebrate?

If you're at a football game, there are 11 different matchups you can watch on every play. Set your binoculars on the wide receiver trying to outjuke the cornerback or the center trying to bull the noseguard. In baseball, try setting your binoculars on anybody other than the pitcher or the batter.

What did the right fielder do that time?

"Well, first he put his glove on his knee, then he bent over, then he stood up straight again. Just like last time."

Baseball lovers say that their game is timeless, that it has kept the traditions that link it to the past. Right. Let's go to the Seattle Kingdome and watch designated hitter Steve Balboni—here's a real athlete—get an AstroTurf double that the outfielder loses in the roof.

Which game is more athletic? Football players come off the practice field looking as if somebody had used their helmets to boil lobsters. Baseball players come off the practice field wearing their hats backward after a grueling game of pepper. Baseball is so taxing that sometimes guys can get in only 18 holes before a game. Put it this way: Nobody's surprised that guys like Charlie Kerfeld, Mickey Lolich and Terry Forster have played baseball. What's surprising is that Dom DeLuise never did.

So let's call baseball what it is—a nap aid. And the next time somebody tries to make you feel guilty about hating baseball, remind him of what ESPN college football commentator Beano Cook said in 1981 when Commissioner Bowie Kuhn announced that U.S. hostages recently released by Iran would all receive free lifetime baseball passes:

"Haven't they suffered enough?"

Nebraska Hardships Ease Each Fall Saturday

COLLEGE FOOTBALL

By *MALCOLM MORAN*

From the New York Times
Copyright © 1988, the New York Times Co.
Reprinted by permission.

Right about 2 o'clock in the morning on those special Saturdays, when the automobile turns southeast onto State Highway 92, Harold and Polly Gentry and Darrel and De Willet, two retired couples who live in nearby Gering, begin another autumn adventure.

For miles and miles, theirs is almost always the only car on the two-lane highway through the middle of the night. They watch out for deer as they pass ranches and leave the darkened sand hills in the Nebraska panhandle.

They turn south onto 385 at Bridgeport, and finally reach Interstate 80 at Sidney. An hour disappears as the car passes from mountain to central time, and soon, about a half-hour before their 8 a.m. breakfast stop in Kearney, a large orange sun appears on the horizon to signal the start of a football Saturday. By then they have joined the others on the interstate, almost all in red, as they point east toward Lincoln, the state capital and emotional focal point.

There is no major league sports franchise to dilute the affection in this state for the University of Nebraska Cornhuskers. It exists from the Iowa line in the east to Wyoming and Colorado to the west. No other major university within the state can divide the passionate loyalties from the South Dakota border to the north to the Kansas line to the south.

Southern California has to deal with U.C.L.A. Penn State copes with Pittsburgh. Michigan contends with Michigan State. Florida State must recruit against Florida and Miami. Texas has challenges throughout the state. Alabama bears the presence of Auburn.

But here, through cattle country, the irrigated fields and the less fortunate farmlands affected by the drought, there is one team, one approved color to wear, and one line that follows the fanfare at the start of the fight song: "There is no place like Nebraska...."

So many Nebraskans face crucial business decisions and time-consuming tasks each autumn, and yet, with the tickets already sold for the six home games at 73,650-seat Memorial Stadium, the streak of sellouts that began in 1962 will this year reach 161. There is important work to complete, but....

"It's also the time you need college football to help you keep your perspective and get through it," said Bill Dicke, a cattle nutrition consultant from McCook. "You just work harder the rest of the week to make time."

"Any other day of the week, if something goes wrong, you stay there and fix it," said Reed McClymont, whose family has been feeding cattle in Holdrege, in the south central part of the state, for more than a century.

"But in the football season," said his brother, Ed, "it's always, 'It can wait until tomorrow.' "

The passion has been more powerful than the hardships that periodically exist in agricultural and ranching communities. "In some places," said Tom Osborne, the head coach and a native of Hastings, "football tickets might be one of the first things to go. But with a lot of people in Nebraska, the football tickets would be one of the last things to go.

"You can do without a lot of other things before you give up football tickets, because you know you may not get another shot at them. People have made a lot of sacrifices to have enough money to see the games and stay overnight."

It does not seem to matter that the quarterback, a wingback and the kicker are from California, the left outside linebacker is from Houston, the cornerbacks are from Kansas City and Colorado Springs, and the New Jersey pipeline remains important. "When they're here," said Allen Swanson, a rancher from Arthur, "they're Nebraskans. That's the way it is."

Generations of followers, up to and including some of the players who will begin the 99th year against Texas A & M in the Kickoff Classic next Saturday night, have memories of listening to the radio as they go about their work on Saturday afternoons. They would wait earnestly, in trucks and barns, grocery stores and hospitals and any room in the house, for the moment that would inspire Lyell Bremser, the voice of the Huskers from 1938 through 1983, to shout his signature exclamation: "Man, woman and child! Look at those Cornhuskers roll!"

The joy produced by such moments pushes the Gentrys and Willets to make their trip. They are back in the car after the final gun, heading west, listening to the interviews, digesting the game, waiting for other scores, wondering about their bearing on the next week's rankings.

They arrive home at 2 a.m., 24 hours and more than 820 miles removed from their departure. "It's not nearly as tiring as you'd think," Harold Gentry said. "But when they lose, it's a long trip home."

There have been few such trips in the past quarter century. Nebraska can break the record of 26 consecutive winning seasons that it now shares with Alabama and Penn State. The Huskers have won no fewer than nine games for 19 years, each of which has ended with a bowl appearance, and they have finished in the top 10 for the last 18.

The devotion can be found across the state. Bernice High, an 87-year-old fan in Bertrand, is legally blind. Legally, selectively blind.

"She somehow sees when they're on TV," said her son-in-law, Keith (Swede) Fastenau, a farmer.

"She can see interest checks and Nebraska football," said her daughter, Miriam (Shorts) Fastenau.

Then there is the case of Byron Hock and Ellie Kleeb, seniors at Kearney State University when they decided to marry in 1974. Their wedding day, the bride and groom learned too late, was the day of the Nebraska-Oklahoma game.

"People didn't come, for that reason," Byron Hock said, "and those that did were bitter."

More than 200 guests were expected, and minutes before the scheduled start of the ceremony, the United Methodist Church in Broken Bow was nearly empty and the bride was becoming frantic. "My wife said, 'Isn't anybody coming?' " he remembered.

Their guests were there. They were just outside, in their cars, listening to Lyell Bremser until the last possible instant. The couple still has a picture taken that afternoon of a crowd of several people, including the groom, staring at a transistor radio on the floor.

The devotion does not necessarily end when death does them part. Byron Hock's uncle Dean died last January. In the lower right corner of the red-granite tombstone he shares with his wife in a three-acre cemetery next to the Hope Lutheran Church, there is a side view of a white football helmet with a red block "N." And there, close to the day Dean Hock was born and the day he died, appears his epitaph:

GO BIG RED.

★   ★   ★

An important factor in the personal attachment between the people and the Huskers came about by accident. More than a decade ago, when the National Collegiate Athletic Association imposed limitations on the number of scholarships major college programs could offer, the Huskers faced the possibility of a serious shortage of talent.

Nebraska ranked 36th in the nation with a population of 1,606,000 in 1984. In an effort to maintain the level of talent, Osborne built an elaborate system to encourage prospects to play without an athletic scholarship. Those players, the walk-ons, have an opportunity to succeed—and possibly earn eventual financial aid—if they are willing to endure years of unrewarded effort.

The system has provided small towns, some so tiny that the high school team has eight players a side instead of 11, with the chance to produce players for the big time.

"They may not be stars," Osborne said. "Maybe he didn't play a lot. But a guy who could come down here and play and letter is of some importance to that community. So they have a little sense of ownership."

Only about one-third of the scholarship recruits are from Nebraska, but about 60 percent of the traveling squad was developed within the state. Recruits from elsewhere may possess the superior physical gifts necessary to compete on a national level, but the effort of the walk-ons provides the physical and emotional backbone of the Nebraska program.

The walk-on system, with its thankless short-term demands and potential long-term benefits for determined prospects, is heavily publicized. It appeals to the farmers and ranchers whose conservative principles are based upon the worth of an honest day's work. "Basically, we get a paycheck once a year," said Allen Swanson, the rancher from Arthur. "The rest of the year, we're at the mercy of the bank." During an era in college athletics in which corrupt administrators and selfish athletes have been publicized and emphasized, the carefully polished image of a program free of scandal, with hardworking, nonscholarship players, intensifies the link between the Huskers and their fans.

Because of the success of the walk-ons and the limited population, nearly everyone, it seems, can boast of some personal involvement. Someone from their high school played for the Huskers. A neighbor became a starter, their teacher's brother made it, or the friend of a friend helped beat Oklahoma. The cycle continues. Small children ask for an autograph, look way up into a player's eyes, and see where they want to go. Huskers look down into the faces of the children, and see where they've been.

The first couple of years you're here, you say, 'what am I doing here?' " said Mark Blazek, a senior safety from Valparaiso who began without a scholarship in 1984. The year before, as a senior in high school, Blazek had sold soft drinks in the south end zone. Recently, Blazek accidentally walked into a family meeting to plan for Oct. 1, Mark Blazek Day, in Lincoln. Townspeople organize trips, work to obtain tickets, and travel by the busload to the capital to honor their player at a dinner or reception following the game. "You feel kind of funny," Blazek said, "to have everybody running around like that."

Blazek has a 3.957 grade-point average in social science education. He was one of two Nebraska players selected as a first-team academic All-American last season, for a total of 29 in the last 25 seasons. He will soon apply to law schools and hope that his athletic identity will help his legal career. "It opens some doors, as big as Big Red is," Blazek said.

Doors have been opened for decades. Bill Mueller (pronounced Miller) was a first-year law student in 1950 and a senior halfback in the Husker backfield that included the All-American Bob Reynolds. To his teammates and the fans, he was Rocky Mueller. "Because I had such great hands," he said, and smiled at his little lie.

After the end of his football career, at the beginning of an interview with an Omaha law firm, he introduced himself as Bill Mueller. The interviewer thought the face was familiar, "He said, 'Don't you go by the name of Rocky?' " Mueller remembered.

The inquiry suddenly created an awkward situation, because Mueller was not familiar with a single successful attorney who had ever been called Rocky. "I said, 'Yes,' " Mueller said. "And he said, 'You just keep the nickname.' "

Thirty-five years later, his business card says William P.

Anyone who has ever worn red on an autumn Saturday seems to know better.

★   ★   ★

The intense loyalty that has kept the football program above those from far richer universities and states may soon be considered insufficient. The little sense of ownership that Tom Osborne talks about may soon come at a higher price. Sometime very soon, as the Nebraska program attempts to sustain its success into the 1990s, decades of devotion will collide with economic realities.

"Someday," said Bob Devaney, Osborne's predecessor and now the athletic director, "if you have a few 6-5 or 7-3 seasons, the interest is going to lag. So we've got to build for what might be a rainy day."

His athletic department raises more than $1.7 million annually, a figure that Devaney and Osborne say is significantly below that of other major schools. Devaney would like to increase that amount to $3 million by persuading season-ticket holders—almost 80 percent of whom do not belong to any booster organization—to make a donation beyond the cost of their tickets.

Devaney describes this need as his top priority. The department is paying off a new $15 million recreation building that includes an indoor practice facility. The state no longer subsidizes the women's program. Those regular and lucrative New Year's Day bowl appearances cannot last forever.

He can also sense the public relations mess that would result if fans are told their years of ticket purchases, and lung power, are not enough. "You take some guy, maybe he has eight good tickets, and he says, 'I had these tickets back when you couldn't give them away. I bought them then. Why should I pay to get these same seats now?' " Devaney said.

"It's not a real bad argument," he added. "We've just got to go ahead and try to do the best we can in appealing to each season-ticket holder that he should contribute to the best of his financial abilities."

Solicitations for mass booster memberships could forever change the relationship between team and fans. Would longtime fans in an already financially strained region begin to disappear? Would their well-to-do replacements send the already high expectations even higher? Would a much bigger sense of ownership lead to more bitter and frequent complaints about the lack of a national championship in the 15 years of the Osborne era?

Less than a week from the start of a season, as the fans stock up on their red outerwear, those questions seem as far away as the Orange Bowl. Soon, Memorial Stadium will again become the third-largest city in the state, and the voice of Kent Pavelka, Lyell Bremser's successor, will carry for miles to wherever work is being done.

"I think Nebraska football is one of those rays of hope," said David Edeal, a thick-necked sophomore, a third-team walk-on center from Loomis, and the valedictorian of a high school class of seven. "A lot of people in the area, they forget their problems for four hours. They get so wrapped up that fourth-and-goal is as much an exciting time in their lives as knowing when to sell the beans."

So that is how the demanding thousands in red are so good at play-calling. They must study the competition. They must draw upon moves that have succeeded or failed in the past. They must commit themselves to a decision that will determine the outcome of a group effort, and this summer, of all summers, they can't afford to punt. And when their work is done, man, woman and child, they can turn their attention to the truly important issue of their time: Tom Osborne's harvest, and Nebraska's championship drought.

Say Hey! Great Moments In Minnesota Baseball

BASEBALL

By *DANIEL KELLY*

From Minnesota Monthly
Copyright © 1988, Minnesota Monthly

You'd need a book.

No. You'd need a bookcase heavy with big, fat, handsome books —leather-bound books with thousands of photographs, sepia-toned and technicolor, and page upon page of lovely statistics—to hold the great moments in the long history of baseball in Minnesota.

No. No number of books could do the job even passably well. Because the joy of baseball, that greatest game of all, is something which can be contained in only one vessel on the planet: the human mind. And because, for the faithful lover of the game—that poor soul who, no matter how sour his countenance, how desperate his circumstances, how deep his discontent, feels the juices flow with the word that the spring-training camps have opened; who rises each morning from April to October and dives into the agate type of the box scores; who, whenever he drives past a Little League playground, all summer long, itches to stop, and watch a bit, and remember how it was; who would rather sit on a splintery bleacher plank than almost anywhere else in the world—for such a person, every baseball moment is a great moment.

So much of the rest of life so often seems pale. Never baseball. Not for an instant. Not when you know how good it can be.

But no word, and no picture, can capture that mysterious whatever it is that bewitches us baseball nuts, claiming our young souls, never letting go. Words and pictures are stand-ins for the real thing, overmatched by the moments that were and the memories that are.

Armed with only words and pictures, I am helpless to make you feel baseball deeply unless you have felt baseball deeply. Unless the music of baseball names—The Splendid Splinter, Willie, Harmon,

Tony-O—grabs at your gut. Unless, for you, the glories of Earth include a backhand stab in the hole and a bullet throw to first (*"just got 'im"*); a banana-shaped curveball, aimed at the eyes, the batter bailing out, red-faced as the ball nips the black; a drag bunt dumped deftly into no-man's land; a whistling line drive through the box; a flying pivot on the 6-4-3; a hot dog and a beer under starlit skies.

Unless you can remember what begs to be remembered.

★   ★   ★

Let us remember Ted Williams. The Splendid Splinter, straight in from California, long and tall and handsome as all get-out in the uniform of the Minneapolis Millers. Nineteen years old. Europe was at the edge of war in 1938; in Minneapolis, Ted Williams was hitting .366. And then he was gone—to Boston. To the majors. To the Hall of Fame. To myth.

Let us remember Willie Mays. Ten years before Calvin Griffith moved his Washington Senators to Minnesota, and 36 long years before an easy toss from Gary Gaetti to Kent Hrbek spiked the Cardinals' hopes and brought us the championship of the world, the baseball fans of Minnesota saw what perfection looked like. His name was Willie Howard Mays. He came from Westfield, Alabama.

Willie Mays, the Say Hey Kid, was five days shy of his 20th birthday on May 1, 1951, when the Minneapolis Millers of the American Association, after an Eastern road trip, opened their home season at Nicollet Park. A Norwest bank stands there now, where Willie stood.

The next day's lead story in the *Minneapolis Morning Tribune* was "Allied Planes Blast Korea Dam to Flood Path of Red Attack." But the news most worth remembering was on the sports pages: "Miller 'Mudders' Overwhelm Columbus 11-0." The *Tribune's* reporter that day was the man who, as time went by, would become the grand old man of Minnesota baseball—the man who would spend so many years in the radio and television booths of the Minnesota Twins, smoking cigars and chewing raw onions, laughing wheezily, infectiously, uncontrollably. His name was Halsey Hall.

The Minneapolis Millers captured the first Black Mush Bowl game in Association opening history Tuesday.

Before 6,477 soaked but happy customers, they downed the Columbus Red Birds 11-0 in 6⅔ innings of cavorting on a diamond that nearly required two successive triples to score a run. The Whitewasher was Hoyt Wilhelm.

Willie Mays said howdy-do as bombastically as any newcomer in history. He got three hits, made a sparkling catch against the flagpole, unfurled a typical throw.

After the game, a young reporter named Sid Hartman asked Millers Manager Tommy Heath about the kid in center field, whom columnist Joe Hendrickson labeled "the new Negro flash." Heath said:

"That's the way Mays has played all year. You think the boy isn't that good, but he comes up with impossible plays every day. He does something to help us win every game. He can hit, throw and run. What more can you ask? The boy is the greatest prospect I have ever seen!"

And then Willie, too, left us—so soon. Too soon. After just 35 games. After 71 hits in 149 at-bats: a nifty .477, with 18 doubles, three triples, eight home runs, 39 runs, and 31 runs batted in. Leo "The Lip" Durocher, manager of the New York Giants, needed Willie to fill the vast emptiness of center field in the Polo Grounds. Before May was out, Mays was gone. Joe Hendrickson wasn't happy:

There's only one thing to write about today. For better or for worse, the New York Giants have taken the big gamble of possibly ruining baseball's greatest prospect in hopes he can furnish the extra something needed to get Leo Durocher into the National League race.

Twenty-year-old Willie Mays is prematurely on his way to the big town, to the big leagues because greedy Lippy asked for him.

In 121 games for the Giants that first year, Mays hit .274, with 22 doubles, five triples, 20 home runs, and 68 runs batted in. Greedy Lippy's Giants won the National League pennant. Willie Mays won a nation's love that year, and he never let go of it.

Willie Mays came back to Minnesota in July of 1965, to play for the National League All-Stars. He led off the game. He hit a home run.

Let us remember Harmon Killebrew, the Idaho Strongboy, the balding Bonus Baby. Number 3. The Killer, round and muscled, smiling. Lumbering toward the batter's box. Stepping in, eyes fixed on the mound. Tapping his bat on home plate. Three deliberate half-swings, menacing and powerful. The bat at rest on his collarbone. The Killer, relaxed. Crouching as the windup unfolds, bat raised to strike. And then the pitch, screaming in, down the middle, and Harmon uncoils, and the ball soars high and deep—going, going, gone, over the chain-link fence into the left-field pavilion at Metropolitan Stadium. Home run! Twins win! In the memory, that's how it happened every day.

Take a drive out to where the Met was. Find the street called Killebrew Drive. Get out of your car, face to the north, and hear the distant echo of the crowd. Harmon Killebrew owned this place.

Let us remember Bob Allison, sliding toward the left-field corner at the Met, in the fifth inning of the second game of the 1965 World Series. The Dodgers' Ron Fairly is on first. There's nobody out. The score is 0-0. Jim Lefebvre's line drive is headed for the left-field corner, for extra bases. Allison hasn't got a prayer. Sandy Koufax watches from the dugout; this is the break he needs. Allison runs like the wind, dives, tumbles, slides, *makes the catch!* Killebrew says, "It was the greatest catch I've ever seen." Red Smith of the *New York Herald Tribune* writes:

> *The Twins racked up the incomparable Sandy Koufax Thursday, creamed the Dodgers 5-1 to make it two victories to none, and the froggy voice of tin horns croaked hallelujahs as the demigods of the prairies departed for the California smogland.*

Smogland is unkind to the Twins; they lose three straight. Then, back home, the ace of the Twins' pitching staff, Mudcat Grant, smashes a three-run, 392-foot home run in the sixth inning of Game 6, to tie the Series 3-3. But the Dodgers have Koufax rested and ready for Game 7, and nobody beats Koufax twice in a week. Lou Johnson's fourth-inning drive to left hits the foul pole: home run. Koufax is invincible. He has struck out nine Twins and allowed only three hits when, with two outs in the bottom of the ninth and the Dodgers leading 2-0, Red Smith picks up the action:

> *Like a fussy householder, Sandy Koufax raked the earth in front of the pitching rubber with his spikes. He lifted his cap, exposing dark hair wet with sweat, fitted it back carefully and stooped for the resin bag. Gloved right hand on his right thigh while his left fist held the ball behind his hip, he craned forward in a bellyache crouch, staring past Bob Allison and his bat to read the catcher's sign.*
>
> *Again he reached for the resin bag as though reluctant to throw the last pitch. When he straightened, his eyes were on Harmon Killebrew, a baserunner at first. Without looking toward the plate, he fired.*
>
> *Allison swung and missed for the 360th putout of baseball's 62nd World Series. Koufax took one little schoolboy hop of glee, then settled into the leisurely stride of a gentleman of distinction who is better at what he does than anybody else in the world.*
>
> *From playing field and dugout, his flanneled playmates rushed for him but they put on the brakes as they drew near. Ball players are intensely physical critters and when a man has pitched a three-hit shutout to win the championship of creation, he isn't even money to reach the showerbath alive, but the Dodgers might have been artisans moving Michelangelo's Pieta out of Flushing Meadow or handmaidens bearing a Ming vase.*
>
> *Gently, tenderly, they convoyed the most precious objet d'art in their small world down the dugout steps.*

We got to see Koufax at work. He beat us. A great moment.

Let us remember Tony Oliva, the last of the fabulous Cuban exports. Tony-O, stinging the ball from foul line to foul line. Tony-O, diving for the ball in right field, destroying his knee, limping away from Cooperstown.

Let us remember Cesar Tovar. Pepe. Playing every position, one inning apiece, in the final home game of 1968—a nine-ring Calvin Griffith circus to lure reluctant fans. Eleven thousand three hundred and forty showed up to see the Twins and the Oakland A's, to watch Tovar start the game on the mound, to see him double- and triple-pumping as he got Bert Campaneris and Sal Bando to pop out, as he walked Danny Cater, as he fired a screwball—a *screwball!*—to strike out Oakland's whiz-kid cleanup hitter, Reggie Jackson. Dave Mona reported for the *Minneapolis Tribune*: "His fancy motion cost him a balk call with a man on base, but his earned-run average of 0.00 is the lowest in Twins history." Tovar's Twins won the game, 2-1.

Let us remember Rod Carew, that pure and flawless hitter of a baseball, his cheek round and full with a tobacco-and-gum concoction designed to produce the proper "squinch"—which, he explained, kept his lead eye open wide. Rod Carew, his wrists strong and supple, flicking the bat like a flyswatter. Rod Carew, ambling off third, with the green light from Billy Martin, flying toward home once again. Safe! Seven thefts of the plate in one year. Record-book stuff. Amazing.

Let us remember Joe Hauser, of the 1933 Millers, clouting home run after home run all through the summer—69 in all. Pedro Ramos, on April 11, 1961, shaking hands with Earl Battey after the Twins' first game ever—a 6-0 defeat of the Yankees, in Yankee Stadium. Jim Kaat, bounding off the mound, pouncing on a bunt toward third, wheeling and firing to Vic Power at first. Power stretching, one-handing it with his big, floppy glove. Out! Bert Blyleven, 18 years old, turning everyone's head with the scariest curveball since Camilo Pascual. Tim Laudner, firing down to Gary Gaetti to pick off Darrell Evans and break the Tigers' backs. Kirby Puckett being Kirby Puckett.

And let us remember, if we can, August 24, 1981, the day when hope returned to Minnesota. Baseball's first players' strike had just ended; the Twins were 3-10 and falling fast in the season's "second half." A man named Ed Hrbek, of Bloomington, Minnesota, was dying of Lou Gehrig's disease—but, on that night, he might have considered himself the luckiest man on the face of the earth. His boy Kent was in New York to play first base for the Minnesota Twins. At Yankee Stadium. Against the New York Yankees—for whom Lou Gehrig, the Iron Horse, played 2,130 consecutive games at first base. Jay Weiner reported for the *Minneapolis Tribune*:

Kent Hrbek, a pretty normal kid from Bloomington, did something no one is supposed to Monday night.

He hit a home run in his first major league game. He mashed a high fastball in the 12th inning and, in his fifth big league plate appearance, single-battedly defeated the New York Yankees 3-2 for his new club, the Minnesota Twins.

Less than 36 hours from life as a $650-a-month Class A Califor-

nia League first baseman, Hrbek, 21, swung a pretty swing, raced from home plate, past first base, watched as a George Frazier 2-2 pitch exited Yankee Stadium, slapped his big hands and circled the same basepaths that Babe Ruth, Joe DiMaggio, Mickey Mantle and Reggie Jackson have trod.

"It hasn't sunk in yet," said Hrbek, holding court with the New York press corps after helping to snap a two-game Twins losing streak. "I had won a few games out there in Visalia, but nothing like this. It was my first game . . . I did good."

It would have been a homer in Visalia, too. It flew over Yankee Stadium's right-center-field fence to the left of the 353-foot sign. It was Hrbek's second hit of the night—he had knocked in the Twins' first run with an infield single in the fifth inning—and it gave a struggling ball club a deserved fairy tale sort of night. . . .

When Hrbek, a Tony Oliva fan as a kid, arrived at his cubicle last night, there was a bright new shirt with No. 26 waiting for him, with his name sewn above it, but no pants.

"You don't get to wear pants the first day, rook," infielder Chuck Baker, his new road roommate and locker room neighbor remarked.

"The first day," Hrbek said later. "That's what's weird about all this. It's the first day.". . .

In Bloomington, Hrbek's parents, Ed and Tina, were watching on the tube and some beer-drinking buddies were going bonkers at a Bloomington bar.

They saw what Hrbek saw. "I knew they were going to throw me fastballs," he said. "And he got the ball up, a little bit. It went . . . and here I am . . . I guess."

Hrbek shook his head, stared at his feet. "Here I am," he said. "Hopefully, to stay."

★   ★   ★

Let us drink deep of baseball memories, rich and fragrant, forever ripening, unspeakably sweet.

Olympic Farewell

OLYMPICS

By *LEE BYRD*

From the Associated Press
Copyright © 1988, the Associated Press

To the doleful toll of the Emille Bell, South Korea bade a magnificently sad farewell to the XXIVth Olympiad Sunday night. The sadder thing is that neither the warm sorrow nor the glory of this parting was altogether shared.

Legend has it that the bell, a national treasure, has the most melancholy tone of any in the world, echoing the ancient wail of a Korean daughter separated from her mother. Koreans take partings especially hard. But for the world, the most pitiable thing separated in Seoul was not the host nation and its guests, but a few individuals from the best in themselves.

Canada's Ben Johnson lost himself in steroids, seeking a cheater's edge. Bulgaria's entire weightlifting team left in shame, for the same reason. Two American swimmers got to keep their gold medals but disgraced themselves and their team by celebrating with another drug of choice, alcohol, and turning into petty thieves.

An American boxing coach couldn't read a bus schedule, printed in plain English, and cost a good kid from the slums of Detroit the chance to honor his murdered brother with Olympic gold. A South Korean boxing coach attacked a referee and delivered the lowest possible blow to his nation's pride and hospitality. The list of boxing debacles, from outrageous officiating to ugly crowds, goes on and on, all too typical of the sport's legacy.

An American sprint relay team flew 8,000 miles to mishandle its baton 100 meters short of the finish. An individual sprinter delivered his only finishing kick to a Korean's taxicab. Members of an NBC television unit, with later apologies, tried to walk around with the words "We're Bad," on their backs, as if Koreans were supposed to understand that American street colloquialism.

The American basketball team came to play defense and found it couldn't shoot. A massive swimming team produced just two individual gold medalists, and watched the East Germans win 18 events. Overall, the United States, for the first time ever, finished third in the medal count.

Ah, but these things happen. Like Korea's plum wine, the sour comes with the sweet, the yin with the yan. And the Games of Seoul did have their sweet moments. Soaring moments, as wondrous as the closing ceremony itself, when Hodori and Cobi, the mascots of Seoul and Barcelona '92, floated arm-and-arm into a crystal night.

There was Greg Louganis, on the verge of defeat, his head once bloodied in a sickening crash on the board, summoning pure resolve on his final dive in a glorious Olympic career, to retire a champion. And Ulf Timmerman, the East German shot-putter, who mustered the might for one last golden heave.

Or the youthful Janet Evans, a California mall rat and junk-food addict, whose blithe spirit and awkward stroke propelled her past all the nutrition-conscious, method-drilled East Germans in sight.

Or the aging champions, marathoner Rosa Mota of Portugal, sprinter Evelyn Ashford of the United States, who showed the youngsters that determination counts above age.

There were the sisters-in-law, Florence Griffith-Joyner and Jackie Joyner-Kersee, who distanced their fields in contrails of joy and, with feminine grace, etched a new sporting dimension to the meaning of sexual equality.

That list goes on and on, too. It is a longer one, in fact, than the account of Seoul's sins, for all the horrid judging, drug revelations, and sadly common displays of nationalism, racism, cultural intolerance and an assortment of other manifestations of human pettiness.

One hundred sixty nations came, the most ever, to an Olympics virtually free of political boycott. Only Cuba was missed. And Juan Antonio Samaranch, the august chief of the Olympic movement, could say, in a stadium filled with behaved fans and exuberant athletes, that these were "the best and most successful games in our history."

That said, no Olympics have ever delivered entirely on their promise. And the 24th Games were no exception, even as Seoul's motto, "Harmony and Progress" was repeated so solemnly at Chamsil Stadium 22 days ago. It is impossible. A simple wave of the Olympic flag, with its five interlocking rings, cannot erase the political and cultural differences of the world. A motto cannot end enmity, cure stupidity, temper arrogance.

Sporting contests, after all, neither mandate nor control social values. They reflect them. So it came as no surprise, really, that the Games of Seoul had moments darker than Chamsil Stadium when the Flame was extinguished. That is the way of the world.

Americans, and not a few others, arrived here with the specter of terrorism lurking in their minds. As measured by that fear, the Games were a spectacular success. South Korea, and all the nations who poured unprecedented cooperation into guaranteeing the safety of their athletes and guests, accomplished that mission with a generally unobtrusive effort that may never be truly measured or appreciated.

What Americans did not count upon was the havoc that could be created, not by terrorists or radical students, but with their own insensitivity. They got off on the wrong foot, literally, when U.S. athletes broke ranks at the opening ceremonies. The decorum-conscious Koreans were not amused at seeing the greatest event in their national history being turned into a California beach party.

That was followed very shortly by a series of ugly episodes at the boxing venue, where the national pride of both countries took senseless turns. Some Americans couldn't understand why Koreans, too, made such a federal case of the youthful rowdiness of the two U.S. swimmers, who tore a plaster lion's head off a hotel wall and took it to a hooch palace. Westerners called it a mere prank. But theft is no prank in Korea, which is virtually free of that crime. And stealing something just for laughs, to the Koreans, is particularly reprehensible.

Politics and athletics have often clashed at the Olympics. But Korea and the United States were supposed to be the best of friends. At times, it didn't seem that way. The Korean press played up the rift as if the Americans were trying to ruin the proudest moment of a little brother grown of age, a sense of betrayal within the family.

But the family survives. Lost in the headlines were the thousands of kindnesses mutually shared. The Korean hosts provided Americans and all their guests with first-class accommodation and assistance to the end. Rooms were cleaned spotless, the buses were on time, food was fast and plentiful, the phones worked, prices were reasonable and often cheap, and nearly all that service came with a smile.

For all the flag-waving battles at the Olympic venues, there was this scene, too: at 1:30 a.m., Friday at the press bar in Olympic Park. The television is tuned to live coverage of the launch of Discovery. At liftoff, a huge cheer and applause fill the room. Reporters turned to find it is coming from the Korean waitresses and busboys.

It was a shining moment. Even, like so many others in Seoul, a truly Olympic one.

Watch Kenny Jump

BASKETBALL

By *LEWIS FREEDMAN*

From the Anchorage Daily News
Copyright © 1988, the Anchorage Daily News

The man who invented the jump shot stood behind the foul line in the gym of the Angoon School, cradling a basketball in his sturdy hands.

He dribbled the ball, shifting it right, shifting it left, and abruptly jumped. His shoulders square to the basket, his legs straight, right arm extended, the man who invented the jump shot let the ball roll off his fingers. The ball swished through the net.

"I bet I scored a thousand points off this one shot alone," he said.

A thousand more than anyone would have dreamed.

Kenny Sailors, the man who invented the jump shot playing one-on-one against his big brother on a Wyoming ranch during the Depression, is the Thomas Edison of basketball. His invention lifted the sport out of the dark ages.

The basketball of Sailors' adolescence was a tamer game. In the 1930s, a jumper was a dress, not a basketball weapon; downtown was the place you went on Saturday for a movie, not a place you shot from; and a one-hander was the president waving to a crowd.

Coaches thought shooting a basketball was like driving a car—two hands on the wheel for safety—and that jumping was something you did into a lake.

That was before Oscar Robertson. Before Elgin Baylor. Before Jerry West. Before Magic, Isiah and Bird. They did not learn how to fly from Kenny Sailors, but in a sense they learned how to shoot from him. The jump shot made them famous, but Kenny Sailors made the jump shot famous.

They don't even know who he is, but they owe Kenny Sailors.

★   ★   ★

They love their basketball in Southeast Alaska. On game nights towns shut down and fill gymnasiums. Angoon, an Admiralty Island Tlingit Indian village of some 600 people, is such a town.

Kenny Sailors, 68, coaches high school girls basketball here. In a school with 37 kids in grades 9-12, there are 15 girls on the basketball team.

The man who invented the jump shot has seen brighter lights: playing for Wyoming, he was the Most Valuable Player of the 1943 NCAA tournament and was a star guard the first five years the NBA existed.

But he has also seen smaller towns: as a kid in Hillsdale, Wyo. the closest neighbor was a half mile away. Kenny Sailors probably knew better what to expect from Angoon when he moved here in September, 1987 after 22 years as a big-game hunting and fishing guide in Gakona, than Angoon knew what to expect from him.

"At first it was 'A Boston Celtics player? Here? What?'" said senior Michelle Howard. "But he doesn't talk about it. Only when you ask. It was kind of neat to see. Last year when we got to different towns people asked for his autograph."

Alaskans' favorite kind of big shots are the kind who don't know that they are. That's Kenny Sailors. There's no swagger in his walk, no braggadocio in his speech. He's 5-foot-11, got a gray-haired brush cut, wears glasses, sweaters and white socks with his shoes, and he doesn't make a big deal out of very much—especially himself.

The only time Sailors wants kids living in the past is in his social studies class. He wants them to walk out knowing the history of the US of A, not the NBA.

Sailors felt he was rusty after 14 years out of the classroom. But last spring the students voted him teacher of the year.

"He's considered a treasure," said Angoon Principal Ronald Gleason.

Just back from a 16½-hour ferry ride from Kake, where his team lost two games, Sailors sat in his classroom bantering with Athletic Director Rick Anderson and boys basketball coach Bill Noonkesser.

It's all teasing.

"He's the ugliest coach I've ever worked with," said Noonkesser. Sailors laughed.

"It's a good place to coach," said Sailors, his voice soft and tinged with a western twang. "Everybody's gung-ho about basketball. The parents, the teachers."

"But they don't know the rules," said Anderson. "That's how Sailors can buffalo everyone."

Sailors laughed again and spread his hands as if to ask "Why me?"

Gleason makes Sailors sound like someone who's earned every Boy Scout merit badge.

"Occasionally, you're exposed to genius," said Gleason. "If you're lucky enough you can share in that genius. He's a role model. He embodies what you want athletes to do. He's a self-made athlete. He embodies discipline, initiative, dedication, perseverance, sportsmanship and citizenship."

People ask what Sailors is doing in Angoon, but it really isn't that mysterious. The biggest loves of his life, besides Marilynne, his wife of 45 years, are basketball and the outdoors. Here he has a basketball team and more bears than people in his neighborhood.

When he and Marilynne moved to Admiralty Island last year, Sailors said it was to scout new bear hunting grounds. But he also said this about staying active: "As you get older, it's like whisky. You either mellow or go sour."

After 23 years in Alaska, Sailors is a sourdough, not a sourpuss. A sourpuss doesn't make it in a small town. On a windy and rainy night Sailors was 10 minutes late for the 6 p.m. practice. His team huddled in the doorway of the gym and when he climbed out of his truck one player said, "You're late." Someone else said, "Coach, we're freezing."

"You'll never know what I go through," Sailors said to a visitor.

The man who invented the jump shot put his key in the lock, held the door open for the players, then entered the gym, groped for the lights, and rolled the balls out of a closet. He has no assistant coach, no team manager. Sailors does it all. There aren't even any cheerleaders: Sailors' 20-5 team had so much fun last year that word spread and the cheerleaders became players.

For the next two hours in a gym lined with banners proclaiming Eaglette supremacy and pennants announcing victories in Alaska AA tournaments, Sailors ran the team through a brisk workout. They ran layups and sprints, scrappy, scramble drills and defensive sets.

"Get that ball!" Sailors shouted. "Thatta girl. No easy ones."

Sailors is a pretty good cheerleader himself.

The players split into teams and shot free throws and layups in a race to 21 points.

"I make everything competition," said Sailors. "Sometimes I buy the winning team a Coke."

To the players, Sailors' background gives weight to the plays he diagrams, and they like his manner.

"He doesn't get mad," said player Denise Starr. "He doesn't ever yell. Unless we don't pay attention."

When practice ended Sailors kept one basketball out and demonstrated his own jump shot. Sailors still plays for a team in the local recreational league.

As the girls emerged from the locker room they saw Sailors shooting. "There's Sailors showing off," said Howard, the 6-2 center Sailors calls "Big Girl."

Sailors grinned. "They laugh at me," he said. "They think I'm too old to play."

Then the old man sank a 15-footer.

★   ★   ★

It began in the backyard in Hillsdale, 25 miles east of Cheyenne. Kenny and Bud nailed the hoop up themselves, tacked it onto the windmill. They shot at it for hours with the cows the only witnesses for miles in the flat country.

Bud was three years older and about eight inches taller then, so he won all the time. Kenny dribbled to the basket on the hard-packed gravel court, stopped and shot. Wham! Bud slapped the ball back in his face. Every time.

Sailors idolized his brother, a high school star who later played a season for the University of Wyoming, but it got on his nerves.

One day, trying to elude the big paw of his big brother, Sailors left his feet to take his shot. The jump shot was born.

"It was just a weapon that came naturally," Sailors said some 55 years later as he thought back to his junior high days. "He was big, but he was fast enough to stop my drive. I just did it out of necessity."

Bud, 71, a retired Air Force colonel living in Wickenburg, Ariz., said his brother's dribbling quickness gave him the mobility for the new one-handed jumper.

"We played quite a bit before he figured out he could dribble and get that one-handed shot on me," said Bud. "That was the first time I'd run into it. I was almost 6-5 already. I don't care how tall you are, you're either going to foul him or he's going to make it. He was real accurate with it."

Shooting a one-handed jump shot is as natural as breathing for the basketball player of the 1980s, but in the 1930s and 1940s, it was outrageous.

"If your feet left the floor," said Sailors, "you were a freak. You were on the bench. It's hard for people to believe."

Coaches didn't bench Sailors. He was too good. He was all-state in high school and a two-time All-America at Wyoming, in 1943 as a junior, and in 1946. In between, he spent three years as a captain in the Marines.

Curt Gowdy, the famous sportscaster, was Sailors' backcourt partner two years, though not the championship year. Gowdy, who has seen uncounted thousands of players, insists that Sailors is one of the best.

"He was a great dribbler and very, very quick—like a rattlesnake," said Gowdy, who lives in Florida. "His quickness was the main thing I remember about him. He was a good shot. He was a spectacular player to watch."

With a spectacular shot. All through high school, all through college, Sailors never saw anyone else leave his feet to shoot.

In a section called Inventions That Changed the History of Sports in the "1988 Old Farmer's Almanac," there is a passage about Sailors. It reads, in part "...though the style of the 1930s was to shoot with both feet firmly on the ground, Sailors jumped in the air and released a one-handed shot to get over his taller brother." Also, "Joe Lapchick called Sailors one of the most influential players of the century."

Now deceased, Lapchick, a member of the Original Celtics of the 1920s, was quoted in 1965 as saying "Sailors started the one-hand jumper, which is probably the shot of the present and the future."

The pedigree of Sailors' jumper is well-established, but it is hard to prove he invented it. It couldn't be patented or copyrighted.

Sailors never staked a claim himself. He said he rarely thought much about it until basketball historians and sportswriters began contacting him with increasing frequency.

"I don't say that I'm the first guy who ever shot a jump shot," said Sailors. "I'm sure there must be some kid somewhere who jumped in the air and shot a ball somewhere. But the old-timers credit me with it."

Ray Meyer is one of those old-timers. The retired DePaul University coach knew Sailors in the 1940s and remains a friend.

"There's a lot of people who say they shot it before him," said Meyer. "There's one right here in Chicago who says he shot it in 1925. But if he did jump he didn't jump over two inches. Kenny went up in the air.

"Kenny was the jump shooter that we know today. He got off the floor."

One reason for disputes is Hank Luisetti. Luisetti, from Stanford, was the first to popularize the one-handed shot. But it wasn't a jumper. Luisetti took the game from the two-handed set shot to the one-handed set shot. Yet somehow over the years, the two developments —one-hander and jumper—blurred in the public mind.

"He kind of got overshadowed by Hank Luisetti," said Wayne Patterson, research director of the Basketball Hall of Fame in Springfield, Mass., of Sailors. "You think of a change in the way of scoring and you think of Luisetti. He's credited with the one-hand shot. The average fan is not going to know the difference between the two.

"But we put out what's called an honorable events list every year and we credit him (Sailors) with being the first one to use the jump shot in competition."

Strange that Sailors should be overshadowed by anyone. He glittered on Broadway in 1943.

Sailors was a sensation when he brought his jump shot east to Madison Square Garden and scored 16 points as Wyoming won the NCAA title over Georgetown, 46-34.

The *New York Times* game description read this way: "Sailors was the key man. His ability to dribble through and around any type of defense was uncanny, just as was his electrifying one-handed shot."

In Laramie, Wyo., where Sailors' MVP trophy resides, there is instant recognition of Sailors' name in the athletic department 42 years after his final game for the Cowboys.

Sailors averaged 15 points a game in the 31-2 championship season and in 1946 he was the Helms Foundation College Basketball Player of the Year. This year USA Today selected an all-time NCAA team. Sailors was picked for the team of 1939-49.

"He's considered one of our two or three all-timers," said Sports Information Director Kevin McKinney. "He was our first great player. A lot of people say he got us in the big-time."

McKinney, who has worked at the university for 21 years, was too young to watch Sailors take jump shots, but he knows his Cowboys' history.

"I know everybody was just stunned around here when he did it," said McKinney. "He's an historical figure around here."

Larry Birleffi, who has written about or broadcast Wyoming basketball for nearly 50 years, went to school with Sailors. He said Sailors was always in the gym practicing that crazy new shot.

"We thought it was a little radical really," said Birleffi.

By the time Sailors finished at Wyoming, said Birleffi, "he was a household name."

Enough of one to later become a two-term state legislator.

★　　★　　★

The National Basketball Association was founded in 1946, the year Sailors left college. Televised games are now shown in some 75 countries. Then the league wasn't even known in 75 cities.

Sailors played most of the Cleveland Rebels' games during the 1946-47 season and averaged 9.9 points per game. The Cleveland Rebels? You bet. Plus the Chicago Stags, the Providence Steamrollers, the St. Louis Bombers, the Sheboygan Redskins, the Anderson Packers, and Tri-Cities Blackhawks. All soon-to-be defunct teams.

"It was a strange league," said Sailors. "Teams came in for a couple of months."

This was also the NBA before the 24-second clock, three-second lane violation and 10-second half-court rule.

Floyd Volker, the only other member of the 1943 Wyoming starting five still alive, and who played a season with Sailors in the NBA, likened Sailors' dribbling prowess to the Harlem Globetrotters' Marques Haynes.

"Two men couldn't take the ball away from him," said Volker.

Sailors loved the no-backcourt rule.

"I dribbled out the clock," he said. "If there were more than two guys on me I'd look for the open man. You had the backcourt, you see, and it was tough to corner a guy."

Scores were much lower and only one man, Joe Fulks of Philadelphia, scored more than 20 points a game in the league's first season. Fulks shot one-handed, but didn't use a jump shot. Sailors played with and against the NBA's other earliest stars such as Max Zaslofsky, Bob Davies, Jim Pollard, and George Mikan, the first great big man.

"He could play," said Sailors of the 6-10 Mikan, who starred for the then-Minneapolis Lakers. "He used to say, 'If your wife's counting on this playoff money, throw the ball to George.' "

Sailors, who was 26 when he turned pro, played five seasons for Cleveland, Providence, the original Denver Nuggets, the Boston Celtics and Baltimore Bullets. He was a second-team all-pro, averaged in double figures, and had a career high 17.3 points a game with Denver in the 1949-50 season.

Sailors never planned to play professionally, but was steered to Cleveland by Otto Graham, the Hall of Fame football quarterback for the Cleveland Browns, who had played college basketball at Northwestern.

"They took me on my reputation," said Sailors.

Only Sailors' reputation was not so special with Cleveland Coach Dutch Dehnert. Dehnert, like Lapchick, was a member of the Original Celtics. But he didn't have Lapchick's vision. When Dehnert saw Sailors' jump shot he scoffed.

"You'll never go in this league with that kind of shot."

Of course Dehnert was wrong and Sailors outlasted him in the NBA.

In 1950-51, his last season, Sailors roomed with Charles Cooper of the Celtics, the NBA's first black player.

"It was pitiful," said Sailors. "They wouldn't let him stay in the same places as us. When I'd say something he'd say 'Ah, Sailors, it'll shape up. Give it time.' "

In the NBA of the 1980s, even benchwarmers have six-figure contracts. Sailors made about $7,000 a year. He had endorsements for Bennett's Prune Juice and bubble gum—and the team got the profits.

In his whole pro career, said Sailors, he only saw one other man shoot a jumper. Belus Smawley, who played for St. Louis, shot a fallaway jumper with two hands. Sometimes he fell so far away he landed flat on the floor, said Sailors.

The true jump shot was still in the NBA's future.

★   ★   ★

From the window of the Sailors' cozy apartment facing Chatham Strait, whales, eagles and grizzly bear can be seen. This is why they live in Alaska.

After leaving the NBA, Sailors, Marilynne and their three children lived on a dude ranch in Jackson Hole, Wyo. It was appropriate that Sailors played college basketball for a team called the Cowboys. In his heart, he was one. He hunted big horn sheep and rode horses in Wyoming's vast open spaces. It was only much later, when the kids graduated from high school, and the open spaces filled up, that the family moved to Alaska.

Sailors taught school and coached in Glenallen. He roughnecked in the Copper River Valley. He hunted and fished, caught kings and killed bears. Once, while riding a horse, a grizzly straightened up in front of him. The horse broke into a cold sweat and began shaking, said Sailors.

Sailors probably could have dribbled around the bear, but the horse didn't have the same presence of mind.

"He nearly had a heart attack," he said.

Sailors is still lean and vigorous. Marilynne is too. For them, basketball in Southeast is just one of a series of adventures. Some day they will leave Angoon. But not to retire.

"We're going to Arizona to hunt rattlesnakes," said Marilynne.

She means it, too.

The Sailors' have scrapbooks in Angoon and they have trophies and other memorabilia in safe-keeping at their old house in Gakona. But Marilynne thinks there's one more basketball honor her husband should get.

"I'd like to see Coach in the Hall of Fame," she said. "I think he deserves it."

People don't think of Edison every time they flick a light switch. And they don't remember basketball's dark ages every time they pop the jumper. Still, it could happen. A Hall of Fame committee screens nominations every year. It doesn't matter how long a player's been out of the game.

And, of course, Sailors has never left the game.

The man who invented the jump shot is still taking them. The man who invented the jump shot still puts points on the board in the rec league. At age 68.

"I've got two or three good jumps left in me," said Sailors.

Two or three? Sure. Retirement hasn't yet crossed the mind of the man who invented the jump shot in a windswept prairie a half century ago.

Beheaded

by Curt Chandler of the Cleveland Plain Dealer. Indianapolis quarterback Jack Trudeau seems to be missing something important, courtesy of Cleveland defensive end Al (Bubba) Baker in a 1988 National Football League game. Copyright © 1988, The Plain Dealer.

Bat Eyes

by Greg Trott of the Vacaville (Calif.) Reporter. This airborne bat is almost perfectly centered on the face of San Francisco first baseman Will Clark during a 1988 National League game. Copyright © 1988, Greg Trott, the Vacaville Reporter.

The Missing Links

GOLF

By *RICK REILLY*

From Sports Illustrated
Copyright © 1988, Linda R. Verigan
Director, Rights and Permissions

The most important man in golf has a ball retriever in his bag, a score counter on his belt and a loop in his backswing. He buys three balls for a dollar and shows up at the course in jeans, Reeboks and a golf shirt that's so old it has no emblem. He's the foot soldier of the game, the guy who's up at four in the morning to pay $12 to wait three hours to play a six-hour round to lose $6 in bets.

No company wants him to wear its name on his visor, and nobody shines his cleats. Yet he's the guy who keeps the sport alive. He's the guy who lines up three deep to hit a bucket of almost-round balls off AstroTurf mats, which stain his irons an unnatural green. That's him in the back of the clubhouse, lying about his round and playing gin rummy on a white Formica table that hasn't seen a busboy's rag since Easter.

Lately he's been forgotten. Lately people have thought of golf as some kind of 18-karat Aaron Spelling production, people driving up in expense-account Cadillacs wearing La Mode du Golf shirts and tipping doormen 10-spots. Every new course is more glamorous and exotic than the last. And "greens fees" mean you have to buy a Jack Nicklaus lot overlooking the 18th green.

But golf can't change neighborhoods on us. Truth is, underneath all that, the heart of the game is still the shot-and-a-beer hacker, the golf guerilla, the guy playing courses that move about as fast as a Moscow meat line, and smiling about it. Fuzzy Zoeller may shoot 66 at Augusta and then gripe about the greens, but the essence of golf is still the 14 handicapper who doesn't mind if the tees are rough, the fairways look like the aftermath of a tractor-pull and the greens aren't. He loves the game *for* the game. It's Saturday. He's playing golf. He's gonna gripe?

At Bethpage State Park on Long Island, golfers arrive at 2:30 in the morning in hopes of getting on the first tee by 6:30. Golfers who arrive at 7:30 are lucky to be planting a tee in the ground by noon. At Forest Preserve National in Oak Forest, Ill., players begin lining up at 3 p.m. *the day before* for a 6 a.m. tee time. They sleep in their cars. In Los Angeles, if you haven't called by 6:30 a.m. on a Monday for tee time the next Saturday, you're usually shut out for that day on all 13 public courses. The switchboard opens at 6 a.m.

It's not uncommon for a round of golf to take almost seven hours. If you get around at all, that is. At Pelham Golf Course in the Bronx a few years ago, youths hiding in nearby woods robbed a man on a green of $65 and his credit cards. It is not known whether he then made the putt. When American Golf, a course management company, took over at Pelham, employees were surprised at what they found—dead bodies. Because of that, Kimble Knowlden of American Golf told *The New York Times,* "I try not to be the first one out on the course in the morning."

But warm bodies, too, keep flooding the Bronx's public links. Same as they do in Chicago and L.A. The country is four quarts low on reasonably priced golf courses for John Q. Public to play. The National Golf Foundation estimates that the number of golfers has grown 24%, to 20.2 million, over the last two years. To keep up with that pace, the foundation says a course a day would have to be built between now and the turn of the century. Last year only 110 opened, and more than a third of those were private.

Still, for all of that—the ordeal of getting a tee time, the 20-minute waits between shots and the ungroomed greens—the public course golfer, one of the most abused sportsmen in America, pursues the game loyally and lovingly, as if he had invented it. And nobody's more loyal than the regulars at Ponkapoag Golf Club in Canton, Mass., known, for better or worse, as Ponky. Overheard at a Ponky lunch table:

Ralphie: "You know what my problem is?"

Pete: "No, what?"

Ralphie: "With you fishes, I need a bigger wallet."

Pete: "Slob."

Herbie: "What'd everybody make on that last hole?"

Ralphie: "Four."

Brooklyn: "Five."

Pete: "Other."

Herbie: "Whaddya mean, 'other' ? "

Pete: "Other. Like on TV, when they put up what all the pros have been making on the hole, right?"

Herbie: "So?"

Pete: "So it says something like, '181 birdies, 300-something pars, 98 bogeys, 42 double bogeys and seven others.' Well, I had an 'other,'

O.K.?"

Juice: "I'll guarantee you, tomorrow I'm not shootin' any 'others.' Tomorrow, I'm throwin' a 72 at you slobs."

Tommy: "Right. And I'm Seve."

Juice: "Bet me?"

Tommy: "Sawbuck?"

Juice: "You got it."

Tommy: "So, how do you guarantee it?"

Juice: "After I hit 72 times, I'm pickin' it up."

★   ★   ★

For the third time in history, the U.S. Open, which begins June 16, will be held this year at The Country Club in Brookline, Mass. For the 88th time in history, the U.S. Open will not be held at Ponky. Still, the two courses are only 20 minutes apart in Greater Boston, and it's easy to get them confused.

At The Country Club, for instance, you drive up to the clubhouse, where the boy meets you and takes your bag. At Ponky, you give a boy your bag only at gunpoint. At The Country Club, you change shoes in the locker room. At Ponky, most people don't change shoes. At The Country Club, the men's room is stocked with colognes, hair dryers and jars full of combs rinsing in blue disinfectant. At Ponky, you comb your hair looking into the metal on the front of the paper towel dispenser. At The Country Club, the greens are truer than any love. At Ponky, the greens look like barber-school haircuts. At The Country Club, lunch in the Men's Grille might begin with vichyssoise, followed by an avocado stuffed with salmon salad. At Ponky, you can get a fried-egg sandwich for a buck and a quarter.

At The Country Club, the most esteemed tournament is The Country Club Gold Medal. At Ponky, it's the TV Open. (Each member of the winning foursome gets a TV—color, no less.) At The Country Club, the names are Wigglesworth, Peabody and Coolidge. At Ponky, they're Papoulias, Sullivan and Tomasini. At The Country Club, the members peruse *The Wall Street Journal*. At Ponky, they read the *Racing Form*. At The Country Club, most of the families came over on the *Mayflower*. At Ponky, most of the guys came over on the bus.

Ponkapoag endures 120,000 rounds a year over its two courses, and a whole lot of these are played by the regulars. Among them are Bluto, a construction worker with a high resemblance to Olive Oyl's suitor; Ziggy, who looks like the doorman in *The Wizard of Oz*; Little Eddie, a slightly pudgy accountant; Jimmy, a postal worker; Cementhead, a cement-truck driver; Socks, a contractor; Pappy, a high-tech engineer; and the Can Man, a retired cop who collects plastic garbage bags full of aluminum cans during rounds and hauls them saddlebag-style over his golf cart.

Then there is Bob DePopolo. If The Country Club has Francis Ouimet, winner of the 1913 U.S. Open, then Ponky has DePopolo, 57, inventor of the Triple Tripod Leg-Log putting stroke. To do the Triple Tripod, you get a five-foot putter that reaches up to your sternum (DePopolo insists he invented this extra-long putter, now popular on the Senior tour), stand with legs crossed, use a cross-handed grip and whack away.

DePopolo was a master of all things technical about golf, but he was most obsessive about the wind. In fact, the only ball he would play was a Titleist 8. He said the symmetry of the 8 caused less wind friction than other numbers. "For years," says Paul Bersani, a Ponky regular, "you could not buy a Titleist 8 in the pro shop. DePopolo had 'em all."

DePopolo gave up golf to tend to an ailing mother, but he had long since become a legend. One year he played the Catholic Youth Organization tournament, still held annually at Ponky. After winning his semifinal match on a Friday, he was eating a cheeseburger when a priest admonished him. "Son, what do you think you're doing?"

"Having a cheeseburger, Father," said DePopolo.

"Don't you know it's Friday?"

"So what?" said DePopolo. "It's a free country, ain't it?"

DePopolo, thus rooted out as a Protestant, was immediately disqualified.

★   ★   ★

Ziggy, a short, sturdy man in his mid-50's, gets constant abuse at Ponky for: 1) his toupee, and 2) the fact that in 25 years, he has never gotten the clubhead past his waist on the backswing.

Socks: "O.K., Ziggy, this is the one, Baby. Get those hands way up high this time. Way up!"

Bluto: "Wait, Ziggy, wait! There's a divot on your head." (Despite making a perfect practice swing, Ziggy still strikes the ball with his usual foreshortened style.) "Beautiful, Ziggy. You did it that time."

Socks: "Ziggy, you could make a swing in a phone booth."

Pauli: "Without opening the door."

Rudy: "Remember that time Ziggy made that great shot out of the woods?"

Pauli: "Remember! I was *there.*"

Rudy: "Absolutely great shot. He was all bashed in there, in with the trees. Had no shot. Only he makes a great shot and he comes running out to watch it. Only his toupee is still hanging on one of the branches."

Pauli: "The Parks Department came. They thought it was a wombat."

Ziggy: "Rot, you slobs."

Golf isn't the sport of choice at Ponky. The sport of choice is betting. Golf is just a convenient vehicle for it. At Ponky, they bet on whether the pro on TV will sink his next putt. They bet on how long it will take Russ, the cook, to make a two-minute egg. They bet with their partners, and they bet against their partners. They bet with guys playing two groups ahead and with guys three counties over. They bet while they're waiting on the tees. They bet on whether they can chip into the garbage can or off the ball washer. On a rainy day at Ponky, Pappy the Edgeman (so named because he always wants the betting edge) will take bets on a hole that consists of hitting a ball off the locker room floor, over a bank of lockers, out a door, onto the practice green and into a designated cup. Par is 3.

They'll bet you can't make a 4 on the next hole. They'll bet you can't turn the front nine in 42. Little Eddie will bet you that he can stack two golf balls, one on top of the other, ricochet the bottom one off a wall and catch the top one in his back pocket. (Don't take the bet.) Pappy, the snake, has bet people he can beat them putting with his wedge. (Don't take that one, either.)

Then there was the time Pappy bet Socks 10 bucks that Socks couldn't make a 4 on the next hole. Socks made a 3. "Pay up, Edgeman," said Socks.

"What for?"

"You know what for. I made a 4."

"No you didn't. You made a 3." Took a while for Socks to get over that one.

They bet for 27 holes on weekends, and they bet on their regular nine-hole game after work. They bet "sandies" (up and down out of the sand), "greenies" (closest to the pin on par-3s), "barkies" (hit a tree and still make par) and "Arnies" (make a par without ever being on the fairway). Afterward, they'll bet on hearts, gin, whist and poker until it gets dark, and then go outside, turn the car headlights on the putting green and have putting contests until somebody has won all the money or the Diehards start to wear out. In the winter, when the course is closed, they'll get a pound of bologna, some roast beef, a loaf of bread and some tonic and play cards in the clubhouse, although they're not supposed to have a key. Loser has to vacuum.

Golf is so much fun at Ponky that guys who are members at country clubs come over for a most un-clubby kind of golf game. Rudy Tomasini has been a member of Plymouth Country Club for years, yet every afternoon Rudy shows up to play a 5 o'clock round with the boys, and every day the boys give him the business.

Bluto: "Hey, Ziggy, what's Mr. Country Club doing here, anyway? Why does he want to play Ponky when he could be at the country club?"

Ziggy: "I'll tell you what he's doing. He's slumming, that's what he's doing. He's favoring us with his presence."

Bluto: "Must've run out of hors d'oeuvres over there or something."

Most of the gambling is $5 stuff, but some of it isn't. Herbie lost $18,000 one day at Ponky. Another gambler—we'll call him Nicky— plays golf, the puppies, the ponies, the games, the lottery, anything. "You can always tell whether Nicky's had a good week," says Bluto.

"If he's ahead, he's playing golf. If he's down, he's mowing greens."
Today, Nicky is mowing greens.

Bluto: "Whaddya think Nicky made last year?"

Jimmy: "I don't know. Hundred grand?"

Bluto: "Yeah. And he lost 110."

Sometimes the betting gets complicated. One day Georgie
Conroy, a regular, was playing in a sevensome and had bets going
with everybody. After madly scribbling down all his bets, he headed
for the first fairway, where everyone found his ball. Everyone except Georgie, that is. They were just about to give up looking when
somebody pointed back to the tee and yelled, "Georgie! There it is!"
He had forgotten to tee off.

★   ★   ★

The boys have just found out that qualifying for this year's state
amateur championship will take place at Ponkapoag.

Little Eddie: "Can you imagine a guy from The Country Club
coming here to qualify?"

Bluto: "Man, wouldn't you love to get a three handicap from The
Country Club out there for a little $50 Nassau?"

Jimmy: "I get a game with somebody from The Country Club, I
start refinishing my basement."

Andy: "I'd just like to see the guy at the first tee. He's probably
not used to guys yelling at him on his backswing."

Jimmy: "Yeah, I played at Brae Burn (Country Club) one time,
and I couldn't concentrate on the tee. Too quiet."

Socks: "Wouldn't you love to see a guy from The Country Club
try to get out of our rough? He'd come back into the pro shop with his
attorney."

Cementhead: "I dunno. They got some pretty mean rough out
there for the Open, you know."

Little Eddie: "How do you know, slob?"

Cementhead: "Didn't I tell you? I *played* The Country Club the
other day. Played it even par."

Socks: "Get out! You never."

Cementhead: "I did. I was working on a job on some property
that's next to it. And, you know, I always carry that four-iron and
some shag balls in the truck with me, right?"

Socks: "So?"

Cementhead: "So I realize I'm standing right next to No. 2. It's a
par-3, like 185 yards away. I look around and I see that nobody's
watching me, so I hop the fence. I tee it up and I just couldn't believe
it. Their tees are better than our greens, Eddie! So I hit it and I hit it
pretty good, but it catches up on the left fringe. Still nobody's looking, so I figure, what the hell, I'll go putt out. Their greens, you can't
believe. I felt bad just walking on 'em. So I make a par putting with
the four-iron, and I guess I could've kept going because nobody was
out there, but I decided not to. So that means I'm par for The Country Club, right? Take that, you muni hacks."

Bluto: "Geez. Where do you play next week? Winged Foot?"

★   ★   ★

Sometimes the boys at Ponky hustle visitors, and sometimes the boys get hustled. One day Jimmy Sullivan, a 12-time club champ, and Pappy the Edgeman lined up a game with two guys from Franklin Park in the Roxbury section of Boston. One of the guys from Franklin Park walked with a limp and hit all his shots cross-handed. The Edgeman tried to keep from drooling. They upped the bet to $50 Nassau, with plenty of presses.

As they approached the 9th tee, Pappy was losing his bet, and Jimmy was two under par but still two holes down to his man. Pappy and Jimmy lost big. Jimmy's opponent turned out to be Charlie Owens, now a star on the PGA Senior tour, a lifetime cross-handed player and a man who has walked with a limp for 36 years.

The latest hero of the publinks player is Tour pro Jodie Mudd, who won the 1980 and '81 U.S. Public Links championships. (To enter the Publinks, you can't have had privileges at any private club during that year.) But public courses are more famous for forging the great minority players—guys like Lee Elder, Lee Trevino and current Tour star Jim Thorpe—players who, in their amateur days, could not afford a country club and who probably would not have been afforded membership in one even if they could. But on municipal courses, these guys were *good*. In 1967, Charlie Sifford, a former Tour player, came to Palmer Park in Detroit, a famous hustlers' track, and lost four days in a row. He then left and won the $100,000 Greater Hartford Open.

Thorpe's legendary days were at East Potomac Park in Washington, D.C., when he was in his early 20's. He was unbeatable at Potomac and, therefore, unbettable. So Thorpe had to take his game on the road. Wherever he went, he would show up late, with his clubs falling out of his dilapidated bag and his tennis shoes untied and wearing a shirt with a hole in it. "But I was ready to play," he says. "I could play *anywhere.*"

Except at a country club. "I just didn't feel comfortable at a club," says Thorpe. "Everybody's shoes all spit and shined, clubs sparkling clean, everybody being so polite. Everybody saying 'Good shot.' I wouldn't say 'Good shot' to a guy if he holed out from 300 yards. I might say 'So what?' But I'd never say 'Good shot.' "

One time Thorpe set up a match with the best player in Flint, Mich. On the first day they played a public course, and Thorpe took him for $16,000. "I figured I'd catch a flight out that night," recalls Thorpe, "but at the end of the day, the guy says to me, 'What time we playing tomorrow?' " So the next day he took Thorpe to the Toledo Country Club. Thorpe's game wasn't the same. "Chandeliers hanging everywhere, real thick carpet," he says. "I just wasn't dressed for the part." Thrown off, Thorpe got him for only $1,000.

Thorpe is convinced that, all things being equal, a public course player can whip a country club player every time. "You take a 15 (handicapper) from a public course and a 15 from a country club,'' says Thorpe, ''and that public course 15 is going to walk out with that guy's ass. A public course golfer learns to play all the shots. He has to roll his putts true just to give them a chance to go in. When he gets on nice greens he can make everything.''

On a public course almost any kind of, uh, gamesmanship is fair play. ''I'll jangle the keys, rip the Velcro on my glove,'' says Thorpe. ''Anything to distract the guy.''

Thorpe tells a story about a match in Tampa between the best local hustler and the famous Atlanta-based hustler George (Potato Pie) Wallace. The two men came to the 18th hole with about $20,000 on the line. Potato Pie had driven safely, but his opponent had hooked his ball into the rough, and even the 20 or so spectators following the twosome were having trouble finding it. ''They'll never find it,'' Potato Pie whispered.

''Why not?'' Thorpe said.

''Because I've got it in my pocket.''

Just then, the opponent, standing 50 yards ahead of the search party, hollered, ''Found it!''

Thorpe looked at Potato Pie and Potato Pie looked at Thorpe. ''Well, Potato Pie whispered. ''Looks like the man has got me this time.''

Ponky etiquette: Jimmy is about to hit his drive on No. 10. The bets are flowing. The usual 10th-hole logjam crowd is hanging around. Just as he takes the club back, Socks, standing 20 feet behind him, interrupts.

Socks: ''Hey, Jimmy. Am I safe back here?''

Jimmy: ''Not if you keep that up.'' (Jimmy hits and now it's Wally's turn.)

Little Eddie: ''Excuse me, Wally, but I just wanted to remind you—you haven't come over the top with your swing yet today.''

Wally: ''Thanks, Bum.''

Little Eddie: ''You're welcome, Wally.'' (Wally hits without incident and Socks steps up.)

Bluto: ''O.K., everybody, pay attention. The pro from Dover is on the tee.'' (Socks hits it dead left into the woods.)

Little Eddie: ''Now you got it, Socks. Those lessons helped.'' (Socks hits his provisional ball dead right into the woods.)

Cementhead: ''Atta way to correct it, Socko.''

Bluto: ''Hey, Socks, ever thought of taking up boccie?'' (Cementhead steps up and splits the fairway.)

Cementhead: ''I'm hitting it so straight, all I need is one pass of the mower and I'm in the fairway.''

Socks: ''Hey, Cementhead, this is Ponkapoag. All you get is one pass of the mower.''

Jimmy: ''Yeah, unless it's a weekend or holiday. Then you get no pass of the mower.'' (Lee steps up and hits a perfect drive.)

Freddy: ''What is it with this guy? Every time I bet against him, he swings like he's the poorest man in Boston. You need money that bad, you got to swing like Gene Littler, for Chrissakes?" (Now Little Eddie is up. He is partners with Socks today and has made two straight bogeys.)

Socks: "You're getting heavy, Eddie, you know what I mean? I'm not a frigging camel. I can't carry you forever." (Eddie shrugs, and then hits his drive into the trees.)

Socks: "Eddie, what the hell are you doing?"

Eddie: "I'm screwing up, what's it look like I'm doing?"

Socks: "Eddie, do you understand the term 'fairway'?"

Eddie: "Do you understand the term 'slob'?"

Playing Ponkapoag, says Bluto, is a distinct experience. "It's like you died and went to hell," he says.

Almost half the tees have no grass on them. Only a few sand traps have sand; the rest are overgrown with weeds. The 150-yard markers aren't 150 yards from anything in particular. The greens are a quilt of dirt patches, weeds and long grass, all of which can make a straight putt do a 90-degree turn. "I had one putt today actually back up on me," said Bob Stone, who has been playing Ponky for 25 years. And there's no such thing as a putt dying in the cup at Ponky. The crew members are so inexperienced that when they yank a hole out of the green, they don't flatten the ground around it back down, so every hole has a crown. Only regulars know that to make a putt at Ponky, you've got to allow for the hump of the hole.

All of this is not how it was meant to be. The first 18 holes at Ponky were designed by the famous golf architect Donald Ross in 1933. Ponky now has 36 holes, which require at least 12 crew members to maintain them properly. Ponky has only five.

Problem is, Ponkapoag is run by the Metropolitan District Commission, an archaic arm of the Commonwealth of Massachusetts that operates in 46 towns, patrolling beaches, skating rinks, swimming ponds and pools, and two golf courses. Why the towns can't maintain these facilities themselves is anyone's guess. The MDC hires employees for the courses from within the MDC. As a result, most Ponky staffers have about as much expertise in golf-course maintenance as they do in 747 repair.

Ponkapoag's greens fees are cheap as dirt: $7 on weekends, $6 on weekdays, $3 for seniors on weekdays and $3 for anybody after 3 p.m. Given those rates and the course's overall condition, Ponky is crying out to be leased to a private management company like American Golf, which would raise the prices a little and improve the playing conditions a lot. But the MDC won't do it.

"If there are 25 jobs in a year at Ponkapoag," says former pro Ken Campbell, "then 25 different politicians can give the jobs out. They don't want to give that up." So Ponky becomes, as one Ponkian put it, "a summer drop-off spot for every politician's son, brother-in-law, cousin and niece."

Ponky's members are left, more or less, to take care of the course themselves. Many of them spend their off-hours repainting 150-yard markers, digging weeds out of traps and using their own chain saws to cut down overgrown limbs and trees. They went so far as to buy flags for the pins and rakes for the traps. The rakes were stolen.

Even in the face of such ratty conditions, an act of sheer will is still needed to get a tee time. Unless you're a member of the Inner Club, whose members, for $30 a year, get guaranteed starting times, you must put a golf ball in a long green pipe to establish your position in the tee-off order for that day. Dropping a ball in the pipe at 6:30 a.m., when the pipe is first brought out, will get you a tee-off time at about 11. The only way to beat the pipe is to arrive at the course at 5 o'clock in the morning, sign in with the starter and wait for dawn. On some mornings the fog is so thick at sunrise that groups on the fairway must holler back when it is safe to hit.

So why put up with it all: the shabby conditions, the starting-time masochism, the six-hour rounds? Boston has public courses with shorter waits and better greens. Why do it?

Pete Peters, a dyed-in-the-polyester Ponkian, knows why. "If somebody came up to me right now," says Peters, "and told me, 'Pete, you can become a member of The Country Club today, free of charge. But if you do, you can't ever come back to Ponky,' I wouldn't hesitate a second. I'd stay right here. I'd stay here where I can get some action, have a lot of laughs, relax and be with my friends."

In fact, not only do hardly any of the guys leave Ponky once they become entrenched, they even aspire to what Al Robbins did. Al was a Ponky lifer, a man who played there on weekends when he worked and seven days a week when he retired. But for all his playing, he was still an ordinary hack. Then one day Al parred the 1st hole, picked his ball out of the cup, walked over to the 2nd tee, had a massive heart attack and died on the spot.

Nobody at Ponky grieved much for Al. If anything, the guys thought of him as a lucky stiff. Former pro Campbell remembers why.

"He always said if he ever shot even par on Ponky, he'd like to drop dead then and there," says Campbell. "He finally got his wish."

Barkley Puts Fierce Move on the Game

PRO BASKETBALL

By *SALLY JENKINS*

From the Washington Post
Copyright © 1988, the Washington Post

There is an element of style to Charles Barkley's excess, even if it's the same sort that made Henry VIII do in a few wives. Barkley and his close personal friend, Dom Perignon, once ran up a thousand-dollar nightclub bill in just four hours. Barkley and another freely flowing companion, his mouth, not long ago incurred a $3,000 tab in the shape of a fine from the Philadelphia 76ers for a momentary indiscretion.

Barkley has five sports cars and is planning to buy a sixth this week to go along with his recently purchased, five-bedroom, remote-controlled townhouse. The number of his cars almost equals his place in the NBA; he's among the top four in the league in scoring, rebounding, shooting percentage—and ejections. This is a somewhat unusual development for a 6-foot-4¾, 245-pound man who appears constructed for either more violent sport or sloth, but not the NBA.

An immovable object who is shouldering his way to 28.5 points a game and 11.8 rebounds and shooting 57.9 percent, Barkley is now mentioned as belonging to that handful of all-time upstoppable players in the game. It is well documented that he once moved the 2,000-pound basket and struts six inches to the right with a slam. He has also been tossed from four games this season for his tempestuousness, fined for his comments about his team, kicked chairs and sprayed his money liberally across whole communities.

What makes him think he can get away with this? He's rich. Barkley has a very specific philosophy for spending both his money and his talent.

"You thank God for everything you've got," he said. "And then you enjoy it as much as you can."

Barkley's friend "The Dom" ("I love The Dom,' " he said) is not to be confused with another frequent companion, Domino's Pizza, and Barkley is not nearly as close to either of them as he is to his dearest acquaintance, Snickers. As a 300-pound undergraduate at Auburn, Barkley once went through an entire bag of those bite-sized bars during one 30-minute television show. When he had finished and gone, college friend and teammate Mark Cahill stared aghast at the remains.

"There was nothing left but this little pile of wrappers," Cahill said. "It was inconceivable."

Since then, Barkley has learned the value of jogging and moderation and has turned to spending instead of eating. Since he is in the first season of an eight-year contract worth roughly $12 million (renegotiated last season when he emerged as the heaviest invention since industrial machinery), he is allowed. For the second straight year, he is a potential All-NBA choice and perhaps even an MVP. Clearly, he is going to remain a powerful fixture in the game for which he seems so unsuited.

His cars include a Mercedes, BMW, jeep and a pair of Porsches. His townhouse features a large whirlpool bath with a waterfall, a custom interior decorating job and a television that rises out of a console. His generosity with others is also legend; he once took a $100 bill out of his sock and handed it to a young fan for his birthday.

"I think you have to live as if tomorrow isn't promised to you," he said. "If I'm going to run that floor and if my legs are going to kill me every day of my life, then I'm going to have some fun."

Barkley's view of both life and basketball as limited engagements explains behavior others might find inappropriate. One recent ejection came for pointing out irately and unprintably to an official that he makes 10 times that referee's salary. The $3,000 fine was a result of his remark, after a loss to the Los Angeles Lakers and another ejection, that the 76ers "are just a bad (expletive) team." In a burst of frustration last season, he said some of his teammates were "wimps and whiners."

On those occasions, the question becomes, what prevents some of Barkley's teammates from wanting to kill him? "I'm not sure anything," 76ers Coach Jimmy Lynam said.

Barkley can utter these things, he says, "because they're true. And because I don't use anybody's name." He can also say them because everyone knows that, in the NBA, nobody does more than Charles Barkley.

At a little under 6-feet-5, as opposed to the 6-6 he tries to pass himself off as, Barkley is forced to tangle with the bodies of centers and power forwards much taller than his, if not broader. Moses Malone has gone to the Washington Bullets, Julius Erving is retired and Barkley has been asked to carry the 76ers, who are 29-37 and have won four of their last six. With little in the way of a supporting cast, he has kept them in playoff contention.

He has done it with a game that defies logic. While one of the most physical players in the league, he is also surprisingly nimble. He has only a serviceable jump shot, deriving most of his points from barreling through the middle for tap-ins. Yet with a 37½-inch vertical leap, he has a multidimensional, sometimes guardlike quality and he was named the NBA player of the week last week for shooting 69 percent and averaging 28.8 points and 12.5 rebounds.

"You're asking him to do an awful lot of things," said Hubie Brown, the former New York Knicks coach who is currently a radio analyst for the 76ers. Barkley has had to average almost 30 points just to keep the 76ers from slipping too far below .500. That's an awful lot of energy to expend not to make the playoffs, and thus he is sometimes resentful.

But when Barkley has an outburst, it is generally mere frustration. He is notoriously one of the worst losers in the NBA, or at any other game, including friendly golf or tennis matches with Cahill. His temper is as much the mark of a perfectionist as of a loudmouth.

"Losing is the worst thing I feel can happen to someone," he said. "I realize I'm never going to be perfect. But as long as you strive to, at least you're going to get better. I don't ever want to make a mistake and say, 'That's all right.' Because then it becomes a part of you. I don't want mistakes to become a part of my life."

That Barkley gives himself as bad a time as he gives his teammates keeps them on his side, and his commitment is unquestioned by the 76ers. Any outsiders with questions should consider that he is the shortest player to ever lead the league in rebounding, an accomplishment achieved through desire as much as anything.

The 76ers are aware that Barkley is a fascinating mass of contradictions. His imposing form and behavior on the court are offset by an oddly sweet nature and a sound intelligence away from basketball. He prefers his hometown of Leeds, Ala., to big cities despite his manner of living. On one day, he will say he only plays for money; on another, he tells Cahill, "I want to be the best player on the planet." He has few close friends, and he prefers children to adults; most grownups are too judgmental.

"Children enjoy life," he said. "They don't worry or harass you all the time. They're not into color. They're just there."

He prefers Leeds to Philadelphia because in Leeds he can eat barbecue and converse like a local, rather than an NBA star. He was raised by his mother, Charcey Glenn, and his grandmother, Johnnie Edwards and he says, "They're everything to me. They stick by me and they criticize me. They taught me to work hard and stay out of trouble; nothing is easy, nothing is free."

His grandmother is pressing him to get a degree and Barkley, who left Auburn after his junior season to join the 76ers, is still a year short. His coach at Auburn, Sonny Smith, calls him "brilliant. Had he wanted it, college would've been a breeze."

But Barkley, being rich, handsome and talented, has different priorities. He wants a championship deeply, and something more. "I'm desperate to have a child," he said.

It might be said of Charles Barkley that he has everything except what he really wants. But one thing Barkley doesn't seem to want is adulation. Nor does he want to be anyone's idol.

"I want to be a regular person," he said. "I don't want to be God or a king . . . I want to act my age, like a 25-year-old."

The result is Barkley's candor and a definite lack of interest in what others think of him. Cahill thinks Barkley has concluded there is liberation in not caring about opinions. Aware of his temper and his flaws, he does not set himself up as a paragon of virtue.

"Charles knows he has shortcomings," Cahill said. "He wants to be himself and sometimes that self is a 250-pound man ranting and raving on a basketball court. Charles knows he's not perfect. He's going to cuss people out and go crazy once in a while."

Observers like Lynam contend that with on-court maturity added to his game, Barkley could become one of the NBA's greatest ever rather than just someone's leading scorer. Perhaps part of the problem is that Barkley has not yet discovered the full range of his talent. He admits he never expected to mount the numbers that he has this season, and shuns this MVP talk. He maintains he has no interest in posterity.

Barkley's ambitions are more humble. "Just say I worked hard and was a hell of a player," he said. Once his contract is up, he says he will quit, and his plan is to save $5 million over the next few years, then retire on the yearly interest.

"I think I have two, maybe three more years before I peak out," he said. "I'll just hang in there for seven more years and then live happily ever after."

When he quits, he will do what his frame seems destined for. Absolutely nothing. "I'm not the physical type," he said.

Graf Deposes Navratilova For Wimbledon Title

TENNIS

By *JOHN FEINSTEIN*

From the Washington Post
Copyright © 1988, the Washington Post

It was exactly 6 p.m. on a warm, cloudy Saturday afternoon when the torch was officially passed. It was a moment Martina Navratilova and Steffi Graf knew would come but neither had known when.

Both had always known it would be here, on Wimbledon's Centre Court, and they had known that, at least in a tangible sense, the torch would take the form of the Wimbledon challenge trophy, the plate the Duchess of Kent regally hands to the women's champion each July. It happened today and, although tears were shed, it happened joyously. In a match worthy of its historical importance, Graf beat Navratilova, 5-7, 6-2, 6-1, winning 12 of the last 13 games.

She now has won three legs of the 1988 Grand Slam, the Australian and French Opens before today, and will come to the U.S. Open seeking to become the first person since Margaret Court in 1970 to win a Grand Slam. Graf was everything a successor should be today.

She was behind and didn't waver. She raised her game when she had to. She raised it even further when she sensed the kill.

"After I lost that first set I was really mad at myself," Graf said. "I lost my serve right away and I said to myself, 'Not like last year. You are better than that.' After that, I started to play better."

Navratilova had not lost in eight previous Wimbledon finals, including last year when she beat Graf in straight sets. She had won the last six, had won 47 matches in a row and needed only one more victory to break the record of eight singles titles she shares with Helen Wills Moody. When she jumped in front, 2-0, in the second set, it looked as if she would achieve all that.

"I really played well that first set," Navratilova said. "I thought

I was in good shape but she starting hitting her returns much harder and serving better. She was running everything down. I hit a lot of balls that other people wouldn't even get to and she not only got them, but hit winners off them. I didn't succumb to any pressure today, I succumbed to a better player."

Navratilova wanted this championship perhaps as much as any in her long career. At 31, she is 12 years older than Graf and knows that Graf's time has come and hers is slipping away. She was stretched to three sets in the quarterfinals and semifinals, but said she was not nervous today: "To a large degree the pressure is off. You're in the last match. That's where you want to be. You just go out and play."

A year ago, in Graf's first Wimbledon final, Navratilova used her experience and guile to beat her, serving again and again to her backhand, keeping her deep and volleying sharply.

"I knew she would serve to my backhand, but I thought I had improved a lot because I had practiced for a couple of days with a lefty," Graf said. "In the beginning, I was hitting it well, but then I just started playing badly."

Graf had gone up a break at 3-2 on a scorching backhand return but, up 5-3, went into a brief trance. Navratilova held, broke her 5-all, held again and then quickly broke again with a backhand chip shot at set point and had the first set. She leaped into the air, shaking her fist towards the friends box where her entourage sat.

"I felt really good right then," she said. "It reminded me of last year."

Last year, Navratilova won the first set, 7-5, got the one break she needed and served out the match in the second. When she quickly broke to 2-0 today, it looked like deja vu. Then came the game that turned around the match. Serving at 15-all, Navratilova decided to cross up Graf by going to her forehand. That was a mistake. She blasted one past Navratilova for 15-30.

On the next point Graf used her other great weapon, her speed, racing to Navratilova's drop shot and slapping a cross-court winner for 15-40. Navratilova had saved five break points in the first set. This time, though, she served to the forehand again and paid for it again, another missile whizzing by her.

"I really don't remember that game very well," Navratilova said. "I do remember a lot of second serves, I just don't remember where I served them. It was an important game, though. If I had gotten to 3-0, things might have been different."

Having broken Navratilova's six-game spell, Graf went on a tear. She held quickly for 2-all and then broke again with another great set on a short ball from Navratilova and a backhand down the line. She was flying by now. "She has a real spring in her step when she's rolling," Navratilova said. "She seems to get to everything."

By this time, Navratilova sensed she was in trouble. Graf had not lost a set in 20 Grand Slam matches before today, had not really been pushed. Now, she had been pushed and was pushing back. Graf always plays as if she has a plane to catch, practically running to the baseline to serve or receive. It can be unnerving, especially when the points themselves are over quickly.

With Graf serving at 3-2, a very light rain started, not heavy enough to stop play, but just enough to give Navratilova trouble with her glasses. At 40-15, she walked to her chair for a tissue and began working to dry the glasses. It was not easy. "I would get one dry and while I was doing the other one, the first one would get wet," she said. "I wasn't stalling. I was just trying to see the ball."

With all her titles, Navratilova never truly has been appreciated by the Wimbledon crowd. As she worked with her glasses, some in the crowd began to slow-clap her. Navratilova gestured angrily with her left arm, clearly furious.

"That was a really low thing they did," she said. "How dare they. That really, really upset me. I couldn't believe they would do that. It wasn't fair."

Graf didn't think it was fair, either. "Other girls have tried to stall me," she said. "But I never felt like Martina did."

Graf served out that game, then broke quickly for 5-2, chasing down an overhead from Navratilova and nailing a forehand winner off it. She ended the set with an ace, and it was all even.

Not for long. Navratilova saved two break points in the opening game of the last set, but Graf got the break with a backhand return and another blistering forehand. It was all going too quickly for Navratilova now. Graf quickly led, 3-1, when another light rain started, causing a 44-minute delay.

What the women did during the break was telling: Navratilova went for treatment on her aching body; Graf watched TV. Graf said to herself, "If I don't win this match, I'll break all my rackets."

She won it quickly when the skies cleared again. "I thought if I held that first game back I might have a chance," Navratilova said. "But she returned too well."

Graf broke on another forehand down the line. Navratilova walked to her chair and threw her racket down angrily. Graf held at love. Navratilova led, 40-0, in the next game but Graf won the last five games, finishing it with an emphatic backhand return. In all, it had taken 93 minutes.

Publicly at least, Navratilova refused to cry. She put an arm around Graf as she congratulated her, saying, "You played a great match." Graf did cry. She tossed her racket into the stands and joined in the applause for Navratilova.

Then it was Graf's turn. As the Duchess handed her the silver plate, the person leading the applause was Navratilova. One of the marks of a great champion is the way they respond to defeat. Navratilova was never better than today.

"I wanted to win the ninth one badly," she said. "If my body holds up I'll come back and try again. But if I don't get it, well, eight ain't so bad."

She smiled. "I didn't feel as disappointed as I thought I would," she said. "If I had had a lot of chances or hadn't played well it might have been different, but I just got beat by a better player. In a way, I was happy for Steffi because she played so well and during the victory ceremony I could feel what she was feeling because I had been through it. There was no sense feeling sad. I just got blown out."

She was blown out by a woman clearly touched by the same kind of magic that Navratilova has brought to the game for so many years. To be a worthy successor to Navratilova is a major task. Today, Graf was equal to it.

"It happened the way it should happen," Navratilova said. "It happened in the final on Centre Court against a great player. I don't know if this is the end of an era, but it is the end of a chapter."

There is nothing in tennis quite so simply eloquent as a Wimbledon victory ceremony. There are no speeches, just joy and warmth. Today's ceremony was a memorable one. The new champion, fighting tears of joy, held the trophy while the old one stood a few feet away applauding her.

Some moments need no words. This was certainly one of them.

No Time to Lose

VOLLEYBALL

By *CURT HOLBREICH*

From the Los Angeles Times
Copyright © 1988, the Los Angeles Times

The story of Karch Kiraly begins with his father, whose own story is even better.

That's not to say there is little interesting about the life of Karch Kiraly, acknowledged as the world's best volleyball player on the world's best volleyball team. It's just that even the younger Kiraly can't top the old man's journey.

Becoming the best in the world at what you do is remarkable, but what Kiraly's father did in escaping the failed Hungarian revolt of 1956 at least bordered on the heroic.

And those who know them say that the son is a lot like his dad—an intense, driven perfectionist who doesn't like to lose, at anything.

"Nobody who has ever coached Karch is going to tell you his dad didn't influence him," said Doug Beal, the former Olympic coach who led Kiraly and his U.S. teammates to the 1984 gold medal. "It's just ridiculous to think anything else."

Laszlo Kiraly, 53, was a university student when he took up arms in the 10-day revolt of October, 1956. When Soviet troops and tanks crushed the uprising, he fled Budapest, leaving behind his parents and sister. He hid out for a month, then crossed the border into Austria, carrying nothing but a duffel bag and his rifle strapped across his chest.

Once safely in a refugee camp, he found the West "so ridden with guilt for not having done anything to help the (revolt), they wined and dined us, and gave us the royal treatment."

That led to passage to the United States, where he received one of the scholarships set aside by the University of Michigan for Hungarian refugees.

He earned degrees in engineering and medicine at Ann Arbor—and fell in love. He married his college sweetheart, Toni Iffland, a graduate student in library science from the New York suburb of White Plains. They had three children, a boy and two girls, and eventually moved to Santa Barbara, where Laszlo opened a practice specializing in rehabilitative medicine and Toni started selling real estate.

There, on the beach, he taught the intricacies of volleyball to the oldest of their children, Charles Frederick, nicknamed Karch, a rough version of Karcsi, which is Hungarian for Charles. Las, who had played the game as a member of the junior national team in Hungary, drilled and prodded and even sometimes berated his son, all in hopes of making him a better volleyball player.

Toni Kiraly says she sometimes wondered if her husband didn't push their son too hard, but Karch never seemed to complain.

From those early lessons and parental drive developed a player who has been called by Ruben Acosta of Mexico, president of the international volleyball federation, "the prototype of what a volleyball player should be."

Or as Beal described Kiraly: "He is a hell of an athlete and even more than an athlete, he is a hell of a volleyball player. I don't know if Wayne Gretzky is the greatest athlete who ever skated, but I bet he is the best player. That's the way I view Karch. He combines all the skills better than anyone else. When you put the total package together, he is the best."

Volleyball was invented in this country, yet for years the United States was one of the sport's international doormats. Handicapped by inadequate training facilities and a restrictive budget that made the game a part-time sport for national team members, the United States had sunk to 19th by the 1978 World Championships.

When Kiraly—pronounced Keer-EYE—joined the team in 1981 as a UCLA junior, a new era was dawning for U.S. volleyball. Beal and the U.S. Volleyball Association had just moved their training center from Dayton, Ohio, to San Diego, nearer to the Southern California schools and beaches where the game flourishes.

The switch attracted players such as Kiraly and Steve Timmons of USC, who became the most valuable player of the 1984 Olympics. They helped form the holdover nucleus of a team that has revived the sport in this country and lifted the United States to a sweep of volleyball's triple crown—the 1984 Olympic, 1985 World Cup and 1986 World Championship titles.

In doing so, Kiraly, 27, achieved something his father couldn't gain with a rifle in his hand. He beat the Soviets. And next month at the Olympics in Seoul, he wants to do it again. This time with the world, including his grandparents in Budapest, watching on television.

"It's always good to beat the team that is on top," Laszlo Kiraly said. "The fact that it had been the Soviets made it a lot more fun for me."

To call this an expatriate's sweet revenge, though, to equate winning a volleyball match with losing an armed revolt, would not only trivialize the cause but fail to acknowledge that little, even in the world of sport, is that simple.

Politics, satellite transmissions, marketing strategies and friendship mix in international sport, forming a strange coalition.

It is in this world of contrast, and sometimes contradictions, that Kiraly not only lives but thrives.

Why else would the son of a Hungarian refugee, whose father once shot at Soviet troops, grow up to party with the Soviet volleyball team in a Tokyo hotel room? But there, in a photograph on his refrigerator door, are Kiraly, his U.S. teammates and their Soviet opponents toasting one another.

Why else would Las Kiraly, fervent anti-communist, turn his satellite dish to the Cuban feed to watch his son help beat the Cubans in the Pan American Games in Indianapolis last August?

How else could Kiraly, who before a recent match with Sweden stood quietly singing the "Star Spangled Banner" while his teammates were fidgeting, explain stepping out of his house and into his company car, the official car of the U.S. volleyball team—a red, white and blue Yugo, a car made in communist Yugoslavia?

The irony of it all is hard to ignore. So are the elements that make the tale of the Kiralys a great American success story.

But the new chapters are being written by Karch.

As a senior, he helped lead the Santa Barbara High School volleyball team to an unbeaten record and state championship before graduating third in a class of 800.

At UCLA, he again distinguished himself as both an athlete and a scholar. The Bruins won three consecutive National Collegiate Athletic Association titles during Kiraly's stay and he earned a 3.55 grade-point average as a biochemistry major.

Since joining the U.S. volleyball squad, he has helped push the team into world prominence for the first time since World Championship play began in 1949. He also has three world beach championships to his credit, even though he plays only part time.

Such success has turned Kiraly into a one-person cottage industry for the sport.

He writes articles for volleyball magazines in Italy, Japan and the United States. He is working on an instructional book for publication in Japan. He endorses sunglasses, watches and volleyball wear. He plays on the potentially lucrative beach circuit when his schedule permits. And last year received more than $65,000 from the U.S. Volleyball Association.

All of this, Kiraly estimates, should bring him between $150,000 and $200,000 this year. All is supervised by his agent, Jerry Solomon, chief operating officer of Washington-based ProServ, the same organization that advises Michael Jordan.

Volleyball is moving up in the world and so are the Kiralys.

Karch lives here with the former Janna Miller, his wife of nearly two years, in a modest ranch home on a corner lot on a quiet street in Pacific Beach. The neighborhood is a family oriented beach community bordered by the bay, the beach and La Jolla. They share their home with Timmons, Kiraly's longtime housemate.

"I've lived with Steve longer than I've lived with Janna," Kiraly said. "We've gone through a lot together. He lived with us before we got married, and saw no reason to change that when we did get married. Janna gets along great with Steve. We love having him around."

But after the Olympics, that will change. Karch and Janna will move into an ocean-view home under construction in San Clemente, Janna's hometown. The new location will make for a long commute to practice in San Diego, except for those days when Kiraly can shorten the trip by staying overnight at Timmons' new condominium in Del Mar.

Plans are for both places to be finished in time to rent out the old house in the fall. "We're keeping it for an investment," Kiraly said.

Careful financial planning is the Kiraly way.

"I wouldn't call him miserly," said Aldis Berzins, a former U.S. team roommate of Kiraly. "But he is a careful spender."

When some of his teammates, including Timmons, rushed out to buy expensive new cars with the bonus money they received from the U.S. Volleyball Association for winning the Olympics, Kiraly carefully shopped for his current car—a more modest subcompact.

"He took his time," Janna Kiraly said. "And we had to drive 100 miles to get the best deal."

Still, Kiraly has come a long way from the days when he and several of his U.S. volleyball teammates spent their early nights in San Diego sleeping on the floor of an unfurnished condominium.

"It was a different mentality then," Kiraly said. "We were just into being at the beach all the time. (After practice) we'd play games until dusk and drink a few beers.

"We would have parties in the condo because it was unfurnished, and there was nothing to break. Or we would just throw a ball around the apartment. It was pretty much a no-brainer existence."

For all their good memories, though, those days also had their moments of conflict. Once again, his father played a central role.

Upset with the living and training conditions at the newly established San Diego base in late 1981, Las Kiraly helped organize a group to oust Beal as coach.

"I saw kids living on peanut-butter-and-jelly sandwiches, sleeping on mattresses on the floor," Las Kiraly said. "I didn't see it as Olympic-level training. That really got my ire up."

Conditions soon improved, though, and after a few tense months, the movement to dump Beal died. The attempt strained Las Kiraly's relations with Beal, but that did not stop Beal from calling Las a few months later when he became concerned about what he considered Karch's unadvisable drinking habits.

"A couple of mornings he would come to practice looking as if he hardly slept, hung over, his eyes blurry," Beal said. "Or after a match, we'd go to a restaurant and he would set up a little gaggle of beer bottles and down them all.

"It was never a serious drinking problem, and it never affected the way he played, but it was inappropriate behavior."

Beal said that Kiraly never argued the point with him and that after a discussion with his father, such behavior ceased.

"Each guy on the team had to make a decision about what life-style he was going to live down the road," Kiraly said. "I made the choice to get better and more responsible. Now it has paid off."

What's more, Kiraly could be doing even much better financially if he would quit the U.S. team to play on the beach and in the Italian indoor league.

When the Italians last came bidding in 1986, they offered him $125,000 for six months' work. Combine that with the endorsements and the six-figure income Kiraly said he could earn playing on the beach circuit the rest of the year, and he said he could nearly double his earnings. But that would mean quitting the U.S. team—a choice Kiraly has rejected for now by agreeing to stay with the team through 1989.

He chose to stay despite family advice that his interests might be better served abroad. Janna said that she argued strongly for Italy after becoming upset with the tense contract negotiations with the U.S. Volleyball Association.

"I was so mad, so insulted, so depressed about the way it was handled, I was for getting out of here," she said. "When Karch made the decision to stay, I was a little disappointed. I get a mean streak in me. I wanted to let them see how they would do without Karch. Luckily, Karch doesn't get that way. He's real level-headed."

Since Kiraly made his decision, his price has only gone up. He estimates a current offer could approach $180,000 a season.

"I'm losing money by being here," he said. "But in the long run, we're happy we chose to stay. I would not be helping American volleyball if I was over in Italy."

Making volleyball a popular spectator game is important to Kiraly. With the prospect of another Olympic gold medal a month away, this is a crucial time in the possible development of the sport. Kiraly and his agent figure that by staying in the United States, he can be a more effective spokesman for the game. To that end, he plans to eventually get a master's degree in business administration.

"Karch has the opportunity to be instrumental in taking volleyball from one level to a much higher level," Solomon said. "It is an important time for the sport historically. (Popularizing volleyball) is something he could go down in history for, and that is a lot more important than the difference in dollars, even though the difference was substantial.

"In his heart, he wanted to stay. He just needed someone to tell him that."

This is not to say that volleyball, especially the six-player indoor game, has been an easy sell. In fact, there are many reasons to be discouraged. The team regularly tours the country, playing in sparsely attended events. For example, the June final of the USA Cup against the Soviets drew only 4,881 at the Forum in Los Angeles.

Even here, the team's home base, the support can be less than overwhelming. A recent match with Sweden, the team's last in San Diego before the Olympics, drew an announced crowd of 3,479 to San Diego State's Peterson Gymnasium.

"At times, I feel there is little hope to go beyond the small pockets," said Dave Saunders, a top reserve on the U.S. team and Kiraly's teammate since their days at UCLA. "I look up in the stands and see the same people year in and year out."

Kiraly has his doubts, too. Although he is enthusiastic about trying to make volleyball a mainstream sport, he is not blind to the obstacles.

"I had four people come up to me after the game at San Diego and ask, 'How long have you guys been in town?' " Kiraly recalled. "Well, it just so happens we've lived here for seven years and most people don't know that we're one of San Diego's teams."

Although such experiences cast doubt on the potential success of Kiraly's mission, the growth of the beach game—with its corporate sponsorship support and ESPN contract—has helped fuel his optimism.

Volleyball can be an exciting sport, with its 100-mph serves and crushing play at the net. It would also help to sell the game if everyone could play the game with the intensity and the skill of Kiraly.

"He is a role model in a sport that needs visibility," said Marv Dunphy, the Olympic coach who will return to coaching at Pepperdine University after the Seoul Games. "Every sport needs someone to look up to and, in volleyball, that man is Karch."

Dunphy said that young volleyball players can be seen clutching the hems of their shorts while awaiting serve, just as Kiraly does. Or going without kneepads, just as Kiraly does. He has even noticed the most sincere form of imitation, players who won't give up, no matter what.

That unflagging determination is Kiraly's true mark on the game. There is nothing fancy about it or about him.

At 6 feet 2 inches, he might often be the shortest player on the court. But his well-toned 190-pound body and his 41½-inch vertical leap let him play much taller, and his impact on the game is undisputed. When Kiraly went in against Sweden last month, the Swedish coach immediately called a timeout. It didn't help. After losing the first game with Kiraly on the bench, the United States won the next three, and the match.

Kiraly is animated on the court. He screams and cusses and yells, often at himself, sometimes at his teammates.

He has names for his antics, all slight variations of a self-inflicted smack upside the head. There are the head splitter and the head rattler. Against the Swedes, he preferred what one might call the chest thumper.

"He is almost computer-like in the way he approaches volleyball," said Saunders, his longtime teammate. "He is like a machine. Sometimes he gets too much that way, and we have to loosen him up."

Even for Janna, that can be a difficult assignment. She finds Kiraly wanting to win at everything.

Janna, a nutrition major, played volleyball at Pepperdine and occasionally used to team with Karch in co-ed beach tournaments. Janna said the partnership ended when she realized Karch did not enjoy losing and preferred to avoid co-ed tournaments.

"We'd finish third or something and I'd be all happy," she said. "But Karch wanted to win. I'd love to play as partners again, but we decided to stop. It just didn't work out."

Playing volleyball at the beach used to be how Kiraly relaxed. But now he finds the demands on his time more restrictive.

"I sit at the beach and I keep thinking there is something more I could be doing," he said.

Getting her husband to relax is even difficult for Janna. "He wants to learn all the time," she said. "I'll be giving him a massage, and he will reach for a *Scientific American* to read. I'll grab it and make him put it down: 'You can't read and enjoy this massage. Now just relax.' "

But none of Janna's efforts to humanize the Computer, as his teammates call him, had the impact of a recent family crisis.

After 29 years of marriage, Las and Toni Kiraly separated last fall. The breakup lasted only a few months, and they are back together again, but it deeply affected Kiraly.

"I had been on Karch to relax, then that all came to a head with his parents," Janna said. "Toni just couldn't live with Las anymore. He was too intense. It made Karch realize, 'Hey, there is this other side to my personality that I have to develop or I'm not going to be able to communicate with another person.' "

Janna said she saw a change in Karch. He became closer to his younger sisters—Kati, 20, and Kristi, 14. And he began to more fully express the role his mother played in his development—a contribution so often missed in the recounting of how his father launched his volleyball career. Today, Kiraly talks about being a mix of his parents.

"I have been lucky enough to inherit the patient, loving and nurturing side from my mother, and the organizational and productive side from my dad," he said.

The other side of Kiraly hit home when Las saw his son in a recent television interview. Kiraly talked on camera about the importance of his marriage.

Janna was with Las when he watched the show.

"He started crying," she said. "He wondered, 'How did my son get all this emotion, and I didn't?' "

Las Kiraly was so moved that when a subsequent interviewer failed to raise the question with him, he telephoned the reporter to make the point.

"That show was so special," Las Kiraly said. "Karch talked about how volleyball used to be his life, but now if he plays poorly that day, he comes home to Janna. Hearing that, I felt something in my heart."

Finally, the father who had taught so much to his son, was able to learn from that son.

Is There No Going Back for Houston?

TRACK AND FIELD

By *DAVE JOSEPH*

From the Fort Lauderdale News/Sun-Sentinel
Copyright © 1988, the News and Sun-Sentinel Co.

The restless night has ended, and the homeless here abandon their sandy retreats.

Stirred by the tide, the runners and cyclists, they walk or stagger along Ocean Avenue in search of scraps and handouts, bottles and cans.

A half-full shopping cart of returnables will get a drink at the Wind & Sea bar or a greasy burger at one of the food stands past the small carny on Santa Monica Pier.

"A lot of people probably want to know what happened to me."

Houston McTear, 31, squints to the south as he sits on a bench streaked with bird dung at the end of the pier. Smog has forced the tourists to strain for a glimpse of Palos Verdos to the south. Behind McTear, to the north, the hills of Malibu are brilliant and clear.

"I guess I kind of disappeared for a few years."

Trip past the tourists, past nautical-theme restaurants, and find Houston McTear, who tied the 100-yard world record of 9.0 when just a high school junior in Florida.

Skip by the cheap, oceanfront hotels, stumble by the body Nazis whose Reeboks pound the palm-filled parks, and find Olympian Houston McTear, ranked second in the world in the 100 meters in 1977.

"Maybe I came before my time," he says, rubbing the scraggly growth on his chin. "Maybe I was just a kid out of high school. Maybe everyone threw everything at me at once."

Or maybe it was the way he fell through the cracks of cocaine, or the way he spent parts of 2½ years as one of 8,000 homeless wandering half-etherized around Santa Monica and Venice. Or maybe it was the way he spent a month the past summer in a county jail, allegedly for selling drugs.

Is that what brought Houston McTear from the top of the track-and-field world to this guano-streaked bench?

Is that it, Houston McTear is asked.

Giggles and screams come from the bench beneath the pier and mix with the waves washing in.

Is that what happened, Houston McTear is asked again.

"You know. I was just fast."

★   ★   ★

The kid ran like a gazelle, those in the track world say. He'd step to the line without even stretching and reel off a 9.3 in the 100 meters, having put out a cigarette seconds earlier.

"He was poetry," said Max Bruner, the Okaloosa school superintendent when McTear attended Baker High School in Milligan, Fla.

A living work of e e cummings. No stops no periods no pauses no commas.

"I remember Houston being a ninth grader and running a 60 meters so fast that I thought my stopwatch had broken," Bruner said. "I made him go back and run it again. I couldn't believe a ninth grader could be doing this."

A ninth grader who ran a 100-yard dash in 9.4. A sophomore who ran it in 9.2. A kid who stunned the track world on May 9, 1975, when he tied Ivory Crockett's world record in the 100-yard dash by running a 9.0 in a high school meet in Winter Park, Fla.

"I think about that every once in a while," McTear said.

Sports Illustrated writes about the kid from a poor family in Florida's Panhandle, calling him "the most promising young sprinter in the U.S."

The school system raises money to send McTear to meets around the country. He goes to Richmond, Va., and wins the 60-yard dash in the U.S.-U.S.S.R. meet. He finishes second in the Olympic Trials in 1976.

"He was, I reckon, a celebrity," says his high school coach, Will Willoughby. "He had the talent to break world records."

"He was marvelous," says Al Franken, chairman of the Sunkist Track Meet in Beverly Hills, Calif. "One of the great highlights of this 30-year meet was McTear coming here as a senior in high school and running against the best in the country. The crowd went crazy for him."

There was no stopping the kid with the Hollywood name. Muhammad Ali reads about McTear's poverty-stricken family in *Ebony* magazine and writes a check for $50,000 to McTear's parents, Margree and Eddie—the father makes $3 an hour working in a sawmill—and their eight children. There will be the Olympics in Montreal, endorsements in New York, appearances in Europe.

"It was all pretty dramatic," said McTear's younger brother Charles, manager of a Santa Monica McDonald's. "It was unreal."

But McTear is replaced on the Olympic team because of a pulled hamstring—"Actually it was no big deal," he says—and leaves Montreal for Florida. A letter of intent is signed to play football at the University of Florida but quickly scrapped when Harold Smith offers McTear the starring role in the fledging Muhammad Ali Track Club.

"Harold Smith came along the week after the Olympics and asked Houston if he'd like to come to California," Charles McTear recalled. "One week later Houston was gone."

★   ★   ★

"It broke my heart that Houston couldn't run in the Olympics," said Leroy Walker, chancellor at North Carolina Central University. "He hurts his hamstring at the end of the (Olympics) Trials, though, and there was nothing else I could do."

Walker, the 1976 Olympic track coach and former president of The Athletics Congress (TAC), still laments that he couldn't keep McTear in Montreal through the Games.

"I told him to come out and help me with the practices, that he would have all the rights any other athlete would, and he would get treatment for his injury," Walker said, "but this Smith guy kept pulling at him."

The pull was magnetic, and McTear packed his bags and left with Smith.

"At that time," Walker said, "Ali's name was magic."

And Smith, an acquaintance of Ali and an aide to millionaire plastics manufacturer Philip Fairchild, had the magic to start the track club and its companion boxing club with Ali's blessing.

From 1976 to '81, athletes in the Ali Track Club were pampered by Smith. Despite dropping out of Santa Monica and Cerritos junior colleges, McTear, a poor student, felt no need to continue his education. His times in the 100 meters were good—fourth in the world and third in the country in 1979 with a 10.17—and his life couldn't have been better.

"Harold Smith took care of everything for me," McTear said. "He put me up, took care of all my expenses, set up my meets and made sure I was taken care of. I was in a position I never thought I'd be in in my life, and I enjoyed it. I was pretty much making my money competing. You know, I was just a country kid."

For being a member of the club, Smith rewarded McTear with a condominium in Clover City, cars and cash. Always cash.

"I could never figure out where the money was coming from," said John Smith, an Ali club member in 1980. "I especially couldn't figure it out because it was always cash."

McTear never asked Smith about the money, only about the possibility of acquiring assorted gifts.

"If I saw something I liked, it didn't matter what it was, I got it," said McTear, who was married and in 1978 had a child. "I was into cars, late models at that time. I'd be out riding, go by a (car) lot that

I saw something I liked, and go back and tell (Smith) about it. He'd get something arranged, and he would pay cash for it."

For five years McTear lived his life like a song, "and at that time," McTear said, "I had around $400,000 in the bank."

The joy ride ended in 1981, when Smith was arrested for embezzling millions from a Wells Fargo Bank. Smith, through his case manager at the Boron Federal Prison Camp, said he did not wish to be interviewed.

"All of a sudden," McTear said, "everyone disappeared from the club. I didn't know what went on until two weeks after things went down. All of a sudden the FBI and the police were coming around. I didn't know what was going on. I thought we had a good thing going."

McTear glances ahead, where two older couples are posing for pictures. He shakes his head and laughs in disgust.

"I even had money in Wells Fargo."

McTear's slide began almost immediately. He continued training, "hung around the house" and was introduced to cocaine.

"I guess it was around the time the club broke up," McTear said. "I and a lot of athletes started doing it then, and it basically became my thing."

After being ranked ninth nationally in the 100 meters in 1980 and setting a world indoor best of 6.38 in the 60 meters, there were no reports on McTear in 1981. In 1982 his best 100-meter mark was 10.40, and rumors were that he was too ill to compete in the U.S. Indoor Championships. In 1984, McTear ran a 10.63, "and that wouldn't even have made the top 50 high school times," said Pete Cava, public relations director for TAC.

McTear is vague about 1981-85. He does admit slipping down the cocaine drain.

"I had a problem. Cocaine was pretty much my drug. I had a nice apartment in Westwood, and there were leeches all around me. Basically, I'd go to a meet or train in the morning and afternoon for about four or five hours, and then I had the rest of the evening to myself. I'd do my own thing."

McTear said, "The leeches supplied the drugs, and I supplied the money."

John Smith, now UCLA's assistant track coach, remembers McTear's lost weekend.

"He was living in Westwood around those years and we began working together. I thought he needed a friend at the time, but he was disloyal to me. He'd come to practice and I'd say, 'Houston, you're not straight,' and I kept calling him on it. I'd say, 'Houston, you're loaded, go find someone else. When you come back, you have to be straight.'

"At that time it still hadn't sunk into him to end his habitual need. He can't be around alcohol or drugs at all. He didn't think it was a problem. After track and field he found a substitution in a joint, a pipe, the nose. It was a battle."

McTear, eyes bright today, says he lost his wife because of his problem. "It led to a separation." McTear's wife, Jeanne, left to go back to her hometown of London with their two children in 1982. While McTear's dependence grew, his bank account shriveled. "I was pulling it out twice as fast as I had put it in," he said. "I probably went through more than $200,000 on cocaine."

Did McTear, the boy wonder, fly on cocaine all night? "Yeah," he says, "sometimes."

"I never snorted coke." McTear, bowing his head, speaks softly. "I was on the rock, crack. I would smoke it. I knew how to whip it up, buy my own coke and change it over from powder to rock."

In 1985, McTear realized he had to fix the problem.

"I told (John Smith), 'I want to get rid of my problem, will you guys help me out?' (Smith) paid for it."

Smith says he didn't pay for the six-week rehabilitation McTear received in a center in Tustin. "I set it up," Smith said, "but I couldn't afford it. Let's say that it was paid for by friends of Houston McTear."

McTear says he has forgotten how to convert the cocaine to crack. "But it's probably because I want to."

★   ★   ★

There may be up to 10,000 homeless in this city, according to Suzanne Thompson of the Ocean Park Community Center. "In all, there are 50,000 people on skid row."

Despite the numbers, there are those who take an interest in the straying souls of Santa Monica. Places such as the Clare Foundation, Thompson's community center and the Westside Food Bank provide food and some shelter.

Thompson's center has eight programs, including a 35-bed shelter in the First Christian Church. Doughnuts in the morning. At 11 a.m., sandwiches at the Clare Foundation. Agencies like the Westside Food Bank chip in, "as well as a lot of individuals who come down and feed the people in the park," Thompson said.

Said McTear: "There's really plenty of places around here for food. They even have some places that supply housing."

After completing rehab in Tustin, McTear spent some time with a girlfriend in Venice, Sue, whom he had met years earlier in a Christmas tree lot. But after a falling out, and money running out, McTear took to the streets, the Santa Monica Pier, and a small park above the Pacific, Cactus Park.

Shortly after, he struck up a friendship with Arlene Francis, a registered nurse and evening supervisor at Westwood Hospital.

"He looked so lonely," said Francis, who parked her mobile home some evenings in an open parking lot below Cactus Park. "He came over and said, 'Do you mind if I sit on your blanket?' Even then he had this air about him that he knew who he was, so I had no idea he was homeless."

On Christmas 1985, McTear had dinner with Francis at the hospital. When he was leaving he ran into Dr. Paul Burns, the director of the L.A. Doctors Medical Group and a sports enthusiast. They had met in the late 1970s when McTear was running in Europe.

Burns took an immediate interest and began working with him. Burns, who did not wish to be interviewed, had McTear give lectures on winning at the Beverly Hills YMCA, help set up 5K and 10K runs and do charity work.

But Burns, McTear said, "was trying to put too much on me too fast. He wanted me to train, to talk."

Too much too soon. McTear left.

After spending a couple months in the Flamingo Motel on Ocean Avenue, McTear checked out after quitting his part-time job as a cook. He spent some time with brother Charles in Inglewood, some time again with Sue in Venice, and most of his time on the beach.

"From what he told me," said Ed Francis, Arlene's son and the brother of New England Patriots tight end Russ Francis, "for three years he spent the majority of his time down there (on the beach)."

"It wasn't scary," McTear said, "but you never really knew who was harassing you. Sometimes I'd worry that they'd catch me in my sleep. I pretty much stayed to myself, though, and I'd have guys tell me where to get food."

Said Walker: "About two or three years ago I heard he was on hard times and I tried to get in touch with him, but I never could locate him."

Charles McTear, who worked a block from the Santa Monica Pier and less than a mile from Cactus Park, was one of the few who saw his brother regularly. "I worried about him. I checked on him every other day. He'd come by where I worked or I'd bring him some money. But that was Houston's decision to be there. A lot of people thought when I came out here (in 1982) I could change him, but I can't tell him what to do."

McTear admits that he "slipped two or three times" and used cocaine after 1985.

"It was always a long period of time in between, too," he says. "It was something I had to work out on my own, though. I got the craving. It was a psychological thing."

He also explains away the decision to stay on the streets.

"I guess it was my way of disappearing. I really didn't have a choice, but I was pretty much hiding out. I didn't go inland, so that way people wouldn't recognize me. I was a little embarrassed about everything."

★   ★   ★

From under a small wooden shelter in Cactus Park that the locals have christened the Pagoda, Arlene Francis produces a bail slip from her purse.

Paid in full: $2,500. The date: 9-14-88.

After 29 days in the Santa Monica County Jail, Francis bailed out McTear, who was charged with selling cocaine.

"They tried to give me a drug-dealing charge," McTear said. "The cops down here are like the Gestapo. A lot of drug deals go down in Cactus Park. I'm there just talking to a friend. They produce coke off the guy and they say I supposedly sold it to him."

A Santa Monica Police spokesman would not discuss the case or release the arresting report. Francis thought the police were harassing McTear and invited him off the streets to stay with her and her son.

Ed Francis, who met McTear through his mother in July, said the idea of sheltering McTear "was to give him a platform he could operate from; a place he could get into shape."

With the Francises' help, McTear is training for the first time in nearly four years.

"Ed has done a lot for me," McTear said. "He's got me lifting weights for the first time in my life. On Monday and Tuesday we run, on Wednesday we go to the track at Santa Monica City College, and on Thursday we do some light work, and on the weekends we go back to the weight room."

McTear is talking about a comeback. He called Franken Tuesday for a schedule of indoor events in winter. On Wednesday, he went to UCLA and saw John Smith.

Can McTear, at 31, make a comeback?

"It would be interesting," Franken said.

Said Cava: "It would be like a former fastball pitcher saying that he hasn't pitched in five years but is going to come back."

John Smith says, "I think he can get into shape. I've always been optimistic, but if he's lifting weights, which is something he never did, he could get into race shape.

"He still has a magical name. He would draw interest."

★   ★   ★

There are some who think that the poor kid from Florida was used. Setup, then knocked down, like a bowling pin.

"Too many people used Houston McTear as a springboard for themselves," Walker said. "He needed people who were interested in him as a human being."

Smith agrees with Walker. "Houston is a sensitive young man, but it was a misfortune what happened to him in high school. He wasn't educated, yet he was intelligent. He just wasn't polished."

Franken feels that while McTear came from "a harsh background, I don't think people took advantage of him.

"He was put up, he was fed. I think when it stopped, he was shocked. He thought it was all normal."

McTear feels a lot of people "made money for themselves and used me to get it. They had me sign contracts that I had no control over. I signed all my rights to people, but I admit the money got my attention."

McTear is now focused on writing a book, and, yes, the indoor season.

"If they thought I was the fastest human being back then. . ." McTear doesn't finish. He takes off down a hill next to Cactus Park and runs back up with Ed Francis.

"That's now known as Houston's Hill," Arlene says.

McTear runs up the 10th-of-a-mile hill, stops to catch his breath, begins the walk back to the bottom.

"I've got to put the bad experiences behind me," he says. "The '80s happened, and it was wrong, but I'm not going down that road again."

McTear turns around and begins running up the hill in front of him. Again.

Out of Sight

by Bernard Brault of La Presse newspaper. Undaunted, this truck driver, competing in the Supermotocross at Olympic Stadium in Montreal, finished the race, despite having his vision blocked by an uncooperative hood. Copyright © 1988, Bernard Brault, La Presse.

Mugged

by free-lancer Gary Weber for Milwaukee Bucks magazine. Diminutive Washington guard Tyrone (Muggsy) Bogues lets out a yell as he is grabbed from behind by disguised Milwaukee player Larry Krystkowiak during a 1988 National Basketball Association game. Krystkowiak was actually keeping Bogues from falling out of bounds. Copyright © 1988, Gary Weber.

PRIZE-WINNING WRITERS IN BEST SPORTS STORIES 1989

Beth Barrett (co-author of Recruiting of L.A. Prep Star Probed) is a reporter for the *Los Angeles Daily News* assigned to the Metro desk. She joined the newspaper from the staff of the *Anchorage Times*. She is making her first appearance in *Best Sports Stories*.

Ron Borges (The Boxing Degeneration), a sportswriter for the *Boston Globe*, has spent the last 14 years in pursuit of professional athletes from coast to coast. He began his career at one of the smallest weekly newspapers in Massachusetts, the now defunct *Martha's Vineyard Grapevine*. He worked for the *Sacramento Union*, the *Oakland Tribune* and the *Baltimore News-American* before joining the Globe staff in 1983. Borges was the 1984 winner of the Associated Press Sports Editors award for best feature story and is appearing in *Best Sports Stories* for the fifth time.

Doug Cress (co-author of Recruiting of L.A. Prep Star Probed) is a sportswriter for the *Los Angeles Daily News* and covers the National Basketball Association's Lakers. He previously worked for the *Pasadena Star News* and *Washington Post*. He is making his first appearance in *Best Sports Stories*.

Sam Heys (Hills of Coal, Feats of Clay) has been writing sports and general-assignment feature stories for the *Atlanta Journal-Constitution* for the past 11 years. A former sports editor of the *Columbus* (Ga.) *Enquirer*, the 38-year-old Heys is married, the father of three children and making his second appearance in *Best Sports Stories*.

Howard Sinker (The Elements of Baseball) is a reporter for the *Minneapolis Star Tribune* whose stories have appeared in newspapers and magazines throughout the United States and Canada. The 31-year-old Sinker covered major-league baseball for four years at the *Star Tribune* and currently writes about higher education. A 1978 graduate of Macalester College in St. Paul, Minn., Sinker has also worked for newspapers in Indianapolis, Grand Forks, N.D., and Brainerd, Minn. He is a contributing writer at *Minnesota Monthly* and is making his second appearance in *Best Sports Stories*.

Eric Sondheimer (co-author of Recruiting of L.A. Prep Star Probed) is assistant sports editor/local at the *Los Angeles Daily News*, where he has worked full-time as a sports writer and editor since graduating from California State-Northridge in 1980. He writes a twice-weekly column on high school sports and is making his first appearance in *Best Sports Stories*.

OTHER WRITERS IN BEST SPORTS STORIES 1989

Doug Bedell (Sherrill Paid 'Hush Money') is currently assigned to cover social issues in sports and conducts investigations of possible NCAA rules infractions for the *Dallas Morning News*. He began his work in sports three years ago after working for 10 years as a news reporter for the *News, Louisville Courier Journal and Times, Dallas Times Herald* and *Beaumont* (Tex.) *Enterprise and Journal*. The 37-year-old New York City native is making his second appearance in Best Sports Stories.

Filip Bondy (No Majority Rule) has been a sportswriter with the *New York Daily News* for six years, primarily covering basketball, tennis and soccer. A New York City native, Bondy graduated from the School of Journalism at the University of Wisconsin in 1973 and earned a master's degree in communications from the University of Pennsylvania in 1975. He previously worked for the *Paterson* (N.J.) *News* and *Bergen* (N.J.) *Record* and is making his first appearance in Best Sports Stories.

Thomas Boswell (As Long as Gibson Can, Dodgers Can and Strange Wins U.S. Open) is a sports columnist for the *Washington Post* and a contributing editor and monthly columnist for Golf Magazine. The 1969 Amherst College graduate is one of the most respected baseball writers in the country and has written three books on the sport: *How Life Imitates the World Series, Time Begins on Opening Day* and *The Heart of the Order*. Boswell has won numerous sportswriting awards and is a three-time winner in *Best Sports Stories* competition. He is making his 10th appearance in the anthology.

Lee Byrd (Fastest Thief and Olympic Farewell) has been a writer and editor for The Associated Press since joining the news service in 1966. He covered state government and politics in the Kansas City, Mo., Jefferson City, Mo., Topeka, Kan., and Salt Lake City bureaus before moving to Washington, D.C., in 1970. His reporting assignments in the capital have included the White House, Congress, several Cabinet departments and the presidential campaigns and conventions since 1972. Though never a full-time sports reporter, Byrd has contrived to get many sports assignments over the years, including the 1988 Summer Olympic Games in Seoul, South Korea. The Salina, Kan., native is making his first appearance in *Best Sports Stories*.

Bud Collins (The Queen Finally Falls) has been writing sports and general columns for the *Boston Globe* since 1963. An Ohio native, Collins is probably best-known as a commentator for tennis tournaments televised on NBC-TV. He is a graduate of Baldwin-Wallace College in Berea, O., and also served as the tennis coach at Brandeis University in Waltham, Mass., for five years, where he coached former 60s activist Abbie Hoffman. Collins is making his first appearance in *Best Sports Stories*.

Dave Dorr (A Chip of Pure Diamond) is a member of the sports staff at the *St. Louis Post-Dispatch*. He was born in Colorado, reared in Iowa and was a 1962 graduate of the University of Missouri. His writing career began at the *Des Moines Register*, where he worked before joining the *Post-Dispatch* in 1966. Dorr's specialties are college sports, with an emphasis on football, basketball and track and field. He is a former president of the U.S. Basketball Writers Association and has covered seven Olympic Games. Dorr is the author of a non-fiction book, *Running Back*, and is making his fourth appearance in *Best Sports Stories*.

Mike D'Orso (Beyond "Bull Durham") is a feature writer for the *Virginian-Pilot and Ledger-Star* newspapers in Norfolk, Va. He previously was a senior staff writer at *Commonwealth* magazine, sports editor of the *Virginia Beach Sun* and a sports columnist for the *Virginia Gazette*. D'Orso, who holds a bachelor's degree in philosophy and a master's degree in English from the College of William and Mary in Williamsburg, Va., won a 1988 National Headliner Award for feature writing and was named 1987 Writer of the Year by the Virginia Press Association. His first book, *Somerset Homecoming*, was published by Doubleday in September. D'Orso is making his third appearance in *Best Sports Stories*.

Mike Downey (Kimball Faces Silent Protest) is a nationally syndicated sports columnist for the *Los Angeles Times* who also writes a weekly column for *The Sporting News*. The 37-year-old Steger, Ill., native began his career as a sportswriter in Chicago for both the *Chicago Daily News* and *Chicago Sun-Times*. He also wrote about show-business personalities for the entertainment pages and authored a one-hour NBC-TV special on Comiskey Park and Wrigley Field. He became a columnist for the *Detroit Free Press* in 1982 and twice was voted Michigan Sportswriter of the Year by the National Sportscasters and Sportswriters Association. Downey is making his second appearance in *Best Sports Stories*.

Larry Eldridge (Too Many 10s in Gym) has been sports editor of the *Christian Science Monitor* since 1975. He was a *Monitor* columnist for four years before becoming editor and also worked five years with the *Philadelphia Inquirer* and 11 with the *Associated Press*. He has covered major sporting events like the Olympics and World Series as well as such unusual activities as playing chess in Moscow and Iceland, surfing in Hawaii and skiing in the Alps and the Caucasus Mountains. Eldridge's work has appeared in numerous publications and he is making his second appearance in *Best Sports Stories*.

John Feinstein (Graf Deposes Navratilova for Wimbledon Title) grew up in New York City and received a history degree from Duke University in 1977. After working as a summer intern at the *Washington Post*, he was hired as a metro staff reporter before moving to the sports department. During his 11 years in Washington, he has covered police, courts and state politics on the news side and pro soccer, college football and basketball, major league baseball and tennis on the sports side. He currently covers college basketball and tennis for the *Post* and is a special contributor to *Sports Illustrated*. Feinstein, who won the 1987 commentary category in *Best Sports Stories* and is making his sixth appearance overall in the anthology, has written two books on college basketball and is completing work on a third. His first, *A Season on the Brink—One Year With Bob Knight and the Indiana Hoosiers,* was published in the fall of 1986 and his second, *A Season Inside—One Year in College Basketball,* was published in late 1988.

Tom Fitzpatrick (Champion of the Counting House) is a columnist for *New Times* in Phoenix, Ariz. He previously wrote a column for the *Chicago Sun-Times* and won the Pulitzer Prize for deadline reporting in 1970 for his coverage of the Weatherman Riots. Fitzpatrick was a runner-up in the Pulitzer competition for commentary in 1971 and is making his first appearance in *Best Sports Stories*.

Lewis Freedman (Watch Kenny Jump) is sports editor of the *Anchorage Daily News*. A 1973 graduate of the Boston University School of Public Communication, he is currently finishing his master's in international affairs at Alaska Pacific University in Anchorage. Freedman worked for the *Philadelphia Inquirer, Florida Times-Union* and *Syracuse Herald-Journal* before joining the *Daily News* five years ago. He is making his second appearance in *Best Sports Stories*.

Lee Green (co-author of Road Warrior) is a free-lance writer from Ventura, Calif., whose work has appeared in such publications as *Playboy, Esquire* and the *Los Angeles Times Magazine*. He also is a former contributing editor and columnist for *Outside* magazine. Green, a 1972 UCLA graduate who worked as publicity director for women's athletics at the university from 1974 to '78 after a stint as a television news and sportswriter for Metromedia in Los Angeles, has written one book, *Sportswit,* and is currently working on a novel. He is making his third appearance in *Best Sports Stories*.

Curt Holbreich (No Time to Lose) covers San Diego State University sports for the *Los Angeles Times*. The 30-year-old Holbreich is a graduate of Wesleyan University and the Columbia University School of Journalism. Prior to joining the *Times,* he worked for the *Pittsburgh Press, USA Today* and the *Camden (N.J.) Courier-Post*. He is making his second appearance in *Best Sports Stories*.

Sally Jenkins (Barkley Puts Fierce Move on the Game) is a staff writer for the *Washington Post*. A 1982 Stanford graduate, Jenkins primarily covers college football, golf and boxing. She was born in Fort Worth, Tex., reared in New York City and worked at the *San Francisco Chronicle, San Francisco Examiner* and *Los Angeles Herald* before joining the *Post* in 1985. Jenkins is making her first appearance in *Best Sports Stories*.

Dave Joseph (Is There No Going Back for Houston?) has been a sports writer for the *Fort Lauderdale* (Fla.) *News/Sun-Sentinel* since March 1983. He was reared in South Boston, Mass., and graduated from Northeastern University in 1981. Joseph worked at the *Patriot-Ledger* in Quincy, Mass., from 1978-83 before joining the *News/Sun-Sentinel*. He covered University of Miami sports for a year and a half before moving to the horse racing beat. The 30-year-old Joseph is making his first appearance in *Best Sports Stories*.

Tom Junod (Run, Lindsay, Run) has been a staff writer for *Atlanta Magazine* since July 1987. He worked as a medical writer at Emory University in Atlanta and contributed free-lance stories to the magazine before joining the staff full-time. Junod is a native of Long Island, N.Y., and is making his first appearance in *Best Sports Stories*.

Daniel Kelly (Say Hey! Great Moments in Minnesota Baseball) is the editor of *Minnesota Monthly* magazine. His memoir of his father, "Love, Bill," was cited as a Notable Essay of 1987 in the most recent anthology of *The Best American Essays*. Kelly is making his first appearance in *Best Sports Stories*.

Mark Kram (Making a Killing) has been a projects writer in the sports department of the *Philadelphia Daily News* since March 1987. Before joining the *News,* he worked as a sportswriter for the *Detroit Free Press* and *Baltimore News-American*. A native of Baltimore, Kram is making his second appearance in *Best Sports Stories*.

David Levine (co-author of Building a Better Horse) is a former senior editor of *Sport* magazine. He is currently a free-lance writer whose work has appeared in such publications as *Sports Illustrated, TV Guide, Seventeen, Elle,* the *New York Daily News* and *Special Reports*. Levine is making his second appearance in *Best Sports Stories*.

Barry Lorge (Soviet Beat Thompson Off Court, Too) is sports editor of the *San Diego Union* and a contributing editor to *Tennis* magazine. The 1970 Harvard College graduate moved to San Diego in 1981 after five years as a staff writer for the *Washington Post*. Lorge is making his sixth appearance in *Best Sports Stories*.

Bruce Lowitt (The John Thompson Way) has been a sports feature writer and national baseball writer with the *St. Petersburg* (Fla.) *Times* since 1986. The Brooklyn, N.Y., native began his journalism career with the *Port Chester* (N.Y.) *Daily Item* in 1965 before working as a newsman, political writer and sportswriter with the *Associated Press* for 19 years. Lowitt, who is married and the father of two children, is making his first appearance in *Best Sports Stories*.

Glen Macnow (Don King's Tight Grip) has been with the *Philadelphia Inquirer* since 1986, writing primarily about the financial, legal and marketing aspects of sports. A former writer with the *Detroit Free Press* and *Fort Lauderdale* (Fla.) *News and Sun-Sentinel,* Macnow is making his first appearance in *Best Sports Stories*.

Fred Mann (Steroids: The Deadly Obsession) has been a sports columnist with the *Wichita Eagle-Beacon* for four years. A graduate of the University of Washington, he has written feature stories for the sports, metro and state desks and has also covered the police beat. Mann has twice earned honorable mention in feature writing from the Associated Press Sports Editors. He is making his first appearance in *Best Sports Stories.*

Hubert Mizell (Dan Jansen's Sorrow) has been a sports columnist with the *St. Petersburg* (Fla.) *Times* since 1974. Mizell, who began writing about sports in the *Florida Times-Union* in Jacksonville while still a teen-ager, worked for the *Associated Press* in Miami and New York before accepting his current position. In 1980, he took first place in the column-writing category among the nation's largest newspapers in a competition conducted by the Associated Press Sports Editors association. He is making his first appearance in *Best Sports Stories.*

Malcolm Moran (Nebraska Hardships Ease Each Fall Saturday) has been a reporter with the *New York Times* since 1979. A native of New York and a 1975 Fordham University graduate, he worked for three years at Long Island-based *Newsday* before joining the *Times.* Moran, who served as president of the United States Basketball Writers Association during the 1988-89 season, lives in Stamford, Conn., with his wife Karla. He is making his third appearance in *Best Sports Stories.*

Ken Murray (A Season of Futility) covers college basketball and professional football for the *Baltimore Evening Sun.* He joined the *Sun* in 1983 as a beat writer for the Baltimore Colts and covered the club for one season before the National Football League franchise moved to Indianapolis. He also has worked for the *Baltimore News-American,* the *Fort Worth* (Tex.) *Star-Telegram,* the *Austin* (Tex.) *American-Statesman* and the *Pottstown* (Pa.) *Mercury.* He is making his first appearance in *Best Sports Stories.*

Bill Plaschke (Ready Now Family's Rock) covers the San Diego Padres baseball team for the *Los Angeles Times.* A 1980 graduate of Southern Illinois University at Edwardsville, Plaschke joined the *Times* in 1987 after 3½ years as a baseball and national features writer for the *Seattle Post-Intelligencer.* He has won five Associated Press Sports Editors national awards and collaborated with Seattle Seahawks Coach Chuck Knox on the book, "Hard Knox, the Life of an NFL Coach." Plaschke is making his first appearance in *Best Sports Stories.*

Rick Reilly (Glory to the Gridiron, The Missing Links and The Mourning Anchor) has been writing about sports for 11 years, the last four with *Sports Illustrated.* The Boulder, Colo., native began his career with the *Boulder Daily Camera* after graduation from the University of Colorado and later worked for the *Denver Post* and *Los Angeles Times.* Reilly won two national awards at the Associated Press Sports Editors convention in 1984 and won the top feature award at the Associated Press Editors convention the same year. Reilly, who lives in Littleton, Colo., was the winner of the *Best Sports Stories* magazine competition in 1988 and is making his fifth appearance in the anthology.

John Rolfe (co-author of Building a Better Horse) is a former associate editor of *Sport* magazine and is currently on the staff of *Sports Illustrated for Kids.* He is making his first appearance in *Best Sports Stories.*

Paul Rubin (Tyrant on Field, Populist in Classroom) has worked for *New Times* since 1985. A native of New Haven, Conn., he graduated from the University of Arizona in 1977 and worked for newspapers in southeastern Arizona for four years before joining the *Times.* The 37-year-old Rubin is making his first appearance in *Best Sports Stories.*

Malcolm Smith (co-author of Road Warrior) is making his first appearance in *Best Sports Stories.*

PRIZE-WINNING PHOTOGRAPHERS IN BEST SPORTS STORIES 1989

Bernard Brault (Speedboat Breakup and Out of Sight) is a staff photographer for *La Presse* newspaper who also does free-lance work out of Canada. Brault, who lives in Longueuil, Quebec, began his career in 1976 as a staff photographer for a local newspaper before taking the free-lance route four years later. His work has appeared in several Quebec sports magazines and he has contributed to such wire services as *United Press Canada, Reuters* and *Canadian Press.* Brault, who began contributing to *La Presse* in 1984, has earned numerous citations for his work and gives seminars on sports photography a couple times a year. He is making his fourth consecutive appearance in *Best Sports Stories.*

Dave Einsel (Land of the Giants) is a staff photographer for the *Houston Chronicle.* A native of Abilene, Tex., he studied marine biology at Texas A & M University before taking a job as a photographer with the *Bryan/College Station* (Tex.) *Eagle.* The 29-year-old Einsel worked for the *Eagle* nearly five years before joining the *Chronicle.* He is making his first appearance in *Best Sports Stories.*

Jerry Lodriguss (Victory Ride and On the Ropes) is a staff sports photographer for the *Philadelphia Inquirer.* A New Orleans native, Lodriguss worked for newspapers in the New Orleans area after graduating from the University of New Orleans with a degree in communications. He also has free-lanced for publications such as *Sports Illustrated, Time, U.S. News and World Report* and *USA Today.* A former Louisiana Newspictures Bureau Manager for *United Press International,* Lodriguss is making his second appearance in *Best Sports Stories.*

OTHER PHOTOGRAPHERS IN BEST SPORTS STORIES 1989

Bruce A. Bennett (Crash Landing) specializes in feature articles and photos that deal primarily with the technical aspects of auto racing. He is currently a contributing editor for *Open Wheel* and *Stock Car Racing* magazines. Bennett, an award-winning photographer who holds degrees in engineering and business, is making his first appearance in *Best Sports Stories.*

Robert Bunch (Ump Grump) is a staff photographer for the *Corpus Christi* (Tex.) *Caller-Times* who did a lot of free-lance work in the Dallas area for four years before joining the *Caller-Times* in December 1988. A 1974 East Texas State University graduate, he previously worked at the *Tyler* (Tex.) *Morning Telegraph* and *Bryan/College Station* (Tex.) *Eagle* before going free-lance. A photojournalist with 11 years experience, Bunch is making his second appearance in *Best Sports Stories.*

Curt Chandler (Beheaded) is a staff photographer for the *Cleveland Plain Dealer.* He has been with the *Plain Dealer* since February 1986 and formerly worked at the *Standard-Examiner* in Ogden, Utah, and *The Chieftain* in Pueblo, Colo., after doing free-lance work in Chicago. The 31-year-old Chandler is a 1978 graduate of the Medill School of Journalism at Northwestern University and was the 1987 National Press Photographers Association Region Four (Ohio, Indiana, Michigan, Kentucky) Photographer of the Year. He is making his first appearance in *Best Sports Stories.*

Richard T. Conway (Coming Down) is a staff photographer for the *Cleveland Plain Dealer*, a publication he has worked for the last 28 years. He is currently a general assignment photographer who was a sports photographer for 10 years and the paper's Graphics Editor for 10 years before that. A Cleveland native, the 47-year-old Conway is making his first appearance in *Best Sports Stories*.

Louis DeLuca (Head Start) has been a staff photographer for the *Dallas Times Herald* for the past five years. He began his career with the *Shreveport* (La.) *Journal*, moved to the *Chicago Sun-Times* in 1983 and to Dallas a year later. DeLuca has won in *Best Sports Stories* competition on four occasions: in 1987 and 1988 for best black and white feature photo, and in 1984 and 1986 for best black and white action photo. He was the 1982 Photographer of the Year in Louisiana, Texas and New Mexico and was runner-up for that honor in 1985 and 1987.

Jeff Guenther (Down But Not Out) has been a staff photographer for the *Chattanooga* (Tenn.) *Times* for the last 6½ years. He attended the University of Tennessee for three years before accepting a summer internship with the *Times* in his last year of college. Guenther is making his first appearance in *Best Sports Stories*.

Brian Peterson (Heavy Hitters and The Face Off) has been a staff photographer for the *Minneapolis Star Tribune* since April 1987. Prior to joining the *Star Tribune*, Peterson worked for the *St. Paul Pioneer Press Dispatch*, the *Colorado Springs Sun* and the *Faribault* (Minn.) *Daily News*. He was selected the Minnesota Press Photographer of the Year in 1984, 1986 and 1987. A 1981 graduate of Bemidji State (Minn.) University with a degree in mass communications, Peterson is making his first appearance in *Best Sports Stories*.

Christopher Smith (That Rainy Day Feeling) has worked in the photography department at the *Brantford* (Ont.) *Expositor* for the past two years. A graduate of McMaster University in Hamilton, Ont., Smith began working for the newspaper as head proofreader in 1971 before moving into the composing room for a 10-year stay. He is making his first appearance in *Best Sports Stories*.

Ed Suba Jr. (Neither Rain. . .) is a staff photographer for the *Akron Beacon Journal*. A Bowling Green State University graduate, Suba has been a news photographer for 13 years and has worked at numerous papers in Ohio, Indiana and West Virginia. He is a Cleveland native who has had several short stories published and the author of several screenplays. Suba is making his first appearance in *Best Sports Stories*.

Greg Trott (Bat Eyes) is a staff photographer with the *Vacaville* (Calif.) *Reporter*. A 1981 Fresno State University graduate with a degree in photojournalism, Trott worked as an intern for two years with the *Redding* (Calif.) *Record-Searchlight* before joining the *Reporter*. Trott, who has sold some of his work to *The Sporting News* and the National Football League, is making his first appearance in *Best Sports Stories*.

Gary Weber (Mugged) is currently a free-lance photographer who resides in Milwaukee. A native of that city, Weber holds a degree in mass communications from the University of Wisconsin-Milwaukee and has formerly worked for *Agence France-Presse*, *The Houston Post* and *United Press International*, where he was a staff photographer and bureau manager. The 28-year-old Weber also has worked part time at the *Milwaukee Journal* and served as a team photographer for the Milwaukee Brewers and Bucks. The 1986 prize-winner for best color photograph in *Best Sports Stories* competition, Weber is making his second appearance in the anthology.